ADAM SMITH

ADAM SMITH

R.H. CAMPBELL AND A.S. SKINNER

ST. MARTIN'S PRESS
New York

Library of Congress Cataloging in Publication Data

Campbell, R.H. (Roy Hutchinson)
    Adam Smith.

    Includes bibliographical references and index.
    1. Smith, Adam, 1723-1790.
    2. Economists —
Great Britain — Biography. I. Skinner, Andrew S.
II. Title.
HB103.S6C35 1982   330.15'3'0924 [B] 82-3308
ISBN 0-312-00423-0   AACR2
ISBN 0-312-00424-9 (Pbk)

New in paperback 1985

CONTENTS

Preface

PREFACE

Adam Smith has the rare distinction of having been cited in his own day and subsequently by fellow-scholars and by those in public life. He has been acclaimed as giving authority to diverse theories, policies and actions. Yet many who claim to have his approval know comparatively little about him. Our biography is aimed at such readers in the first instance. More generally, we have tried to use knowledge, built up through our own earlier work on Smith, to introduce the man and his works to all who wish to understand the nature of Smith's abiding influence in intellectual endeavour and in public policy. Our objective in this biography is to provide an introduction to those who know little about either. We are not trying to provide a detailed and thoroughly documented biography, of the type envisaged by Professor I.S. Ross, who has helped us generously with our work.

The writing of even a brief introduction to Smith encounters two major difficulties. The first is that few records of Smith's personal life have survived. Much of it was spent as a scholarly recluse and so was bound to produce few events which excite posterity in any case, and he was a notoriously bad correspondent. His biographers have therefore had to work from limited and often peripheral material. The second difficulty, though it is also a challenging opportunity, is that Smith's intellectual interests were more widespread than many realise, stretching far beyond his best-known work of the *Wealth of Nations*, and far beyond the economic ideas on which it centred. These two difficulties have determined some of the features of our biography. It has gaps, which we should have liked to fill, but which we could have done only by speculation which would have bordered on imaginative fiction. To compensate, Smith's varied writings enabled us to give them a central place in our study. To emphasise these writings is appropriate in any case. Smith's life provides interesting insights into his times, but studies of some of his contemporaries would do likewise, and his writings are truly unique. Those who think his method or conclusions are relevant to current issues and problems will find them most interesting. For that reason we try to explain their main characteristics, while stressing that it is important to see how they may be linked to the main events of his life as far as they can be determined.

In this biography we have drawn on our earlier work in the field, but have tried to avoid repetition. In one case in Chapter 10 we have made use of passages which occur at pages 112-14 in *A System of Social Science* (Clarendon Press, 1979).

Smith's works are now available in the Glasgow edition of the Works and Correspondence of Adam Smith published by the Clarendon Press. We are grateful for permission to draw on the various volumes in that edition and in other associated volumes. Acknowledgement of other works used are in the chapter notes. We are well aware how much a work of this nature depends on the scholarship of others.

The Glasgow edition consists of the following volumes, with the abbreviations we have used cited where appropriate:

I. *The Theory of Moral Sentiments*
   (eds. D.D. Raphael and A.L. Macfie) *TMS*.
II. *An Inquiry into the Nature and Causes of the Wealth of Nations*
   (eds. R.H. Campbell, A.S. Skinner and W.B. Todd) *WN*.
III. *Essays on Philosophical Subjects EPS*.
   (eds. W.P.D. Wightman, J.C. Bryce and I.S. Ross), including Dugald Stewart, *Account of the Life and Writings of Adam Smith Life of Smith*.
IV. *Lectures on Rhetoric and Belles Lettres*
   (ed. J.C. Bryce) *LRBL*. This edition was published only after the first print of the biography and that used was prepared by J.M. Lothian (1963).
V. *Lectures on Jurisprudence*
   (eds. R.L. Meek, D.D. Raphael and P.G. Stein). Report of 1762-63 *LJ*(A) and of 1763-64 *LJ*(B).
VI. *Correspondence of Adam Smith*
   (eds. E.C. Mossner and I.S. Ross) *Corr*.

The manuscript was typed by Mrs J. Finlayson, Miss M. Hendry and Miss C. MacSwan. Early drafts were read by Dr D.W. Bebbington, Professor D. Stevens and Professor D. Winch. We thank all for their help and co-operation.

R.H.C.
A.S.S.

1 KIRKCALDY

The burgh of Kirkcaldy was well-established by the 1720s. Though alleged to be 'one of the most ancient burghs in Scotland' as early as 1304, the claim may have been exaggerated since the town's evolution was protracted, its final charter as a royal burgh being granted on 5 February 1644.[1] On the Forth, and particularly in south-east Fife, Kirkcaldy's status was by no means unique, being one of a string of nine royal burghs along the coast stretching from Crail to Burntisland. Some were so close to each other, as was Dysart to Kirkcaldy, that they gradually merged. Interspersed between the royal burghs were burghs of barony and of regality – Leven, Methil, Aberdour, Wester Wemyss – many but not all chartered in the seventeenth century and soon to provide a challenge to the ancient established rights and privileges of the royal burghs. A number of geographically separate and distinct non-burghal communities, in many cases with different economic interests and social structure, lay close to Kirkcaldy and were effectively linked to it, though not even in the same ecclesiastical parish: for example Linktown in the parish of Abbotshall to the south-west and Pathhead and Gallatown in the parish of Dysart to the north-east. The parish of Kirkcaldy itself was small, with a population of 2,296 when Alexander Webster carried out his census in 1755, but geographically it was appropriate to designate it the 'lang toon'.

The administration of the burgh lay in the hands of the town council, with responsibilities covering the usual fields of ecclesiastical provision, poor relief and, of particular relevance to Adam Smith, the burgh school. Like many another, the burgh was not always well administered. In the year of Smith's birth, the existing tenants of the burgh lands could not pay their rents and application was made to the Convention of Royal Burghs for help to pay the cess or taxes levied on the burgh. At the same time, the pier, so vital for the local economy, needed repair, so that the renunciation of leases was accepted and the lands feued.[2] In these conditions parsimony was always a continuous and guiding principle of administration. Though the privileges of burghs such as Kirkcaldy were not subjected to major reforms until the nineteenth century, many were whittled away earlier by changing economic conditions. The long-standing reputations of both the Forth and Fife as centres of Scottish trade suffered temporary interruptions in the Civil War and Interregnum (when Kirkcaldy reputedly lost heavily). Then a more serious long-term decline set in, most evidently in the fishing ports of Crail and Pittenweem. From the mid-1680s Kirkcaldy's established position and reputation were also challenged as local landowners exploited the mineral resources of their estates and promoted the coal trade of Leven, Methil, Aberdour and Wester Wemyss. By the later seventeenth century the carrying trade in which Kirkcaldy and Burntisland specialised was suffering and in 1692 the antiquated nature of Kirkcaldy's shipping was cited as an example of the port's decay. In the long run the growing challenge of the ports on the west of Scotland was to prove more important still. While the Forth still led in many ways, the buoyant trade was in the west and with the New World.

In the 1720s, the community was still dominated by old and traditional ways but showed the symptoms of the transformation which eventually engulfed it. The town council carried on in its self-perpetuating, oligarchic ways, little affected even by changes in its parliamentary representation; the chief manufacture in the adjacent villages was nailmaking, still organised on its old domestic basis, and whatever the encouragement and progress of textiles, especially linen, the activity was still trade.

Adam Smith was born in a house in the High Street, though not the one he was later to occupy. The date of his birth is uncertain, although it is known that he was baptised on 5 June 1723. His father, another Adam, was twice married. His first wife was Lilias Drummond, the eldest daughter of Sir George Drummond, of Milnab, Provost of Edinburgh. She died around 1717, leaving one child, Hugh, who was born in 1709 and died unmarried in 1750. Since Hugh made no disposition of his property, his half-brother Adam was served as heir. The second marriage, to Margaret Douglas, was in 1720 but, before their only child was born, the father died on 25 January 1723.

The origins of Adam Smith's paternal family lie deep in Aberdeenshire, in the minor landed but well-established families of the Smiths of Rothiebirsben, Inveramsay and Seaton. His immediate ancestors were in Seaton, held by grandfather John Smith, who had a numerous family, of which Adam Smith, senior, was the youngest. As was common among many of the smaller landed families, its members held a variety of official posts. Smith's uncle, Alexander, a writer in Edinburgh, was General Collector of Taxation in Scotland and Postmaster-General. His cousins included William Walker, an influential burgess in Aberdeen, and William Smith, who among other offices was secretary to the Duke of Argyll, at a time when Argyll was chief dispenser of patronage in Scotland. Kinsmen – of the Inveramsay line – were regents at King's and at Marischal Colleges.

Adam Smith's mother, Margaret Douglas, came of a more easily identified and better-connected landed family from Fife. Her father was the second son of Sir William Douglas of Kirkness, an estate settled on his fourth son – Smith's great-great-grandfather – by Sir William Douglas of Loch Leven, when he succeeded as fifth Earl of Morton. The maternal grandfather married Helen Forrester of Strathenry as her second husband, and after her death he married Susan, daughter of Lord Burleigh, in 1688. Their daughter Margaret was baptised on 17 September 1694.

The ancestry of Adam Smith's parents was not obscure. His mother's fortune was more substantially based on the land, which was then the source of so much power, and her father sat in the Scottish Parliament from 1703 until his death in 1706. But her husband's source of distinction came more from his association with the ranks of minor officialdom. The life of Adam Smith, senior, showed a progression very similar to that of many of his relatives. He was born in 1679. Studies at King's College, Aberdeen, and possibly at Edinburgh, were followed by an adventurous voyage to Bordeaux, which included shipwreck. His appearance as private secretary to Hugh Campbell, Earl of Loudoun, who became Secretary of State for Scotland in 1705, showed that he was bound for higher office, and in March 1707 he was admitted a Writer to the Signet. In the following month a Commission was issued appointing him to the post of Clerk of the Court Martial in Scotland. The Clerk provided a general surveillance of legal procedure and was entitled to refer in his report to any legal matter to which he considered the court had failed to give adequate attention. As the clerkship was only a part-time post, Smith continued to serve as private secretary to Loudoun, until he passed that office to his nephew William Smith early in 1714. The occasion was his appointment as Comptroller of Customs at Kirkcaldy. At the same time his cousin Hercules moved there as Collector from the same office at Montrose. The Collector was the senior officer, with the Comptroller acting as a check on him, though they combined to enforce the legislation.

As both Clerk of the Court Martial and as Comptroller of Customs at Kirkcaldy, Adam Smith was placed in a comfortable position. His income from the former office was £137.5s, but his income from the latter is difficult to determine because the nominal amount was exceeded by various fees, especially the one shilling in each pound of the value of any goods detected being brought in duty free. The cost of paying a clerk had to be deducted, but in aggregate Adam Smith's total emoluments must have been almost £300 sterling a year, giving the family a degree of affluence. Other evidence, which emerged when Adam Smith, senior, died, shows the standing of the family. On his death the father had a small library of less than 100 volumes, of which about one-third were works of theology and devotion, while the remainder covered a wide spread of interests. An elaborate will appointed an impressive range of friends and relations as executors and tutors. The details of the will, dated 13 November 1722, are less important than the evidence it provides of a man of social standing and some substance.

Of Smith's boyhood in Kirkcaldy practically nothing of detail is known from direct evidence. Subsequent commentators indicate that the undoubtedly close and lasting links between Smith and his mother were established in these early years in Kirkcaldy, the intimacy of the links being hardly surprising in the case of an only and posthumous child. Information on his half-brother Hugh is even more sparse. He was at a boarding school in Perth the year after Adam Smith's birth and seems to have suffered from ill health, which led his tutors to hold that Kirkcaldy was not a suitable place for him to live. It is probable, therefore, that there was little contact between the two half-brothers and that the family in Kirkcaldy consisted effectively of the mother and child.

In 1731 or 1732 Smith began his own educational career when he entered the burgh school. Since Kirkcaldy was neither geographically extensive, nor heavily populated, its educational provision was as adequate as in many other parts of Scotland and in 1818, with twelve day schools in addition to the parish school, it was reported that: 'There are ample means of education for all who desire it.'[3] But a major hazard of the path of educational progress in Scotland was the competence of the schoolmaster, always a matter of some doubt when schoolmastering was often a path to better things. But Smith was probably fortunate in his schoolmaster David Miller. Miller was remotely linked to Smith's mother by marriage, and had come from Cupar to Kirkcaldy as part of an attempt by the town council to build up the school. In 1733 the council set out a detailed minute on 'the Method of Teaching and the Regulations to be observed', but it is doubtful how far the schoolmaster and his assistant were able to implement the complicated arrangements set out for the work of six classes, chiefly instructed in Latin, and all in two cramped rooms. Of Smith's efforts under this hardy regime the only surviving evidence is his copy of a

Latin textbook *Eutropius*, dated 1733. Miller and his assistant were sufficiently able to instruct the young Smith, and he to survive their instruction, not only without harm but with sufficient retrospective admiration that he was able to commend the parish schools of Scotland as an example to be followed to offset the harmful effects of the division of labour. However, his virtually uninterrupted drilling in Latin vocables in the parish school may have led him to suggest a minor change in the curriculum.

> In Scotland the establishment of such parish schools has taught almost the whole common people to read, and a very great proportion of them to write and account. . . If in those little schools the books, by which the children are taught to read, were a little more instructive than they commonly are: and if, instead of a little smattering of Latin; which the children of the common people are sometimes taught there, and which can scarce ever be of any use to them: they were instructed in the elementary parts of geometry and mechanicks, the literary education of this rank of people would perhaps be as complete as it can be.[4]

The burgh school of Kirkcaldy set Smith on an educational path which led to international distinction; it also gave him some lasting friendships, some of which were rooted in the attendance of a remarkable group of boys at the burgh school at much the same time. Since no register survives it is not certain how far attendance at the burgh school may have overlapped, especially since some of the friends of Kirkcaldy days were not his exact contemporaries.

Two of these acquaintances who achieved some distinction in public life, but whom Smith esteemed very differently, were sons of Oswald of Dunnikier, who, as the chief local landowner, dominated the life of the community. The links between the Oswald and Smith families were well-established and indicated the acceptance of the Smiths in the society of the lesser landed proprietors of Fife. When Smith's father died, Dunnikier was then held by James Oswald, sometime provost of Kirkcaldy, MP from 1702 to 1707 in the last Parliament before the Union (against which he voted consistently) and subsequently in the Union Parliament from 1710 to 1715. He witnessed the will of Adam Smith senior, became one of the active curators (or trustees) appointed under it, acted as their agent, but did not survive to discharge his duties for long. His son James succeeded to Dunnikier when still a minor. Adam Smith was a near contemporary of James (1715-

1769) and of his brother John (?-1780), whose respective careers took them far from Kirkcaldy but in different directions. James was a member of parliament from 1741 until his death and a privy councillor from 1763, Commissioner of the Navy from 1745 to 1747 and then successively from 1751 until 1767 Lord of Trade, Lord of Treasury and Joint Vice-Treasurer of Ireland. John, the younger brother, was successively Bishop of Clonfert and Kilmacduagh, Dromore and of Raphoe. The link between Smith and James Oswald was obviously close and remained so. He was someone to whom Smith wanted to introduce his acquaintances: be it the Count de Sarsfield,[5] or the young William Johnstone, later to acquire fame and fortune under the name of Pulteney, but whom Smith commended to Oswald in 1752 as someone of many estimable virtues '. . . as much improved as study, and the narrow sphere of acquaintance which this country affords, can improve it. He had, first when I knew him, a good deal of vivacity and humour, but he has studied them away.'[6] The links were not only those of personal respect and esteem. James Oswald was an acute commentator on economic problems. His views were sought by Hume on some of his essays on economic subjects which were published as *Political Discourses* in 1752[7] and, on the authority of Dugald Stewart, Smith himself acknowledged in a manuscript no longer extant that he had derived the division of price into its component parts of rent, wages and profits of stock from him.[8] The links between Smith and James Oswald may perhaps be best illustrated by one of the many witticisms with which Hume greeted the publication of the *Theory of Moral Sentiments*: 'Oswald protests that he does not know whether he has reap'd more Instruction or Entertainment from it: But you may easily judge what Reliance can be put on his Judgement, who has been engaged all his Life in public Business and who never sees any Faults in his Friends.'[9] If the links with James Oswald were close, those with his episcopal brother, and nearer contemporary, were not. 'The Bishop is a brute and a beast and unmerited preferment has rendered him, it seems, still more so.' In the same letter to Hume, he was simply 'this haughty Blockhead'.[10]

Another family of note in the Kirkcaldy of Smith's youth was that of Adam, the architects. The greatness of Robert Adam (1728-92) has tended to overshadow the distinguished contribution of other members of the family. His father William was the King's mason and architect in Scotland, sufficiently well-established that he was able to afford a grand tour for Robert and James after they had served their apprenticeship with him. His four sons all followed in the family profession. Firm evidence of direct links between Smith and the Adam family does not exist as it does in the case of James Oswald, but there are occasional references in the correspondence of the circle of which they were all part, although the links in this case are general and not of the same particular detail as with the Oswalds.

A third family from which contemporaries of Smith made their mark much later, though in a more restricted sphere than the Oswalds or the Adams, was that of John Drysdale, minister of the second charge from 1712 to 1726. His son John became minister of the Tron Church in Edinburgh and Moderator of the General Assembly in 1773 and 1784; a leading moderate, his reputation, unlike the Oswalds and Adams, was built only in Scotland and even there it soon faded. His brother George made a greater contribution to the biographical knowledge of Smith by being the source of the story, handed on through Dugald Stewart, that Smith was stolen by gypsies in 1726 from Strathenry, the home of his mother's family.

Notes

1. G.S. Pryde, *The Burghs of Scotland* (London, 1965), 33, 45.

2. Report on Municipal Corporations, Scotland, 1836, British Parliamentary Papers, 1836 XXIII 157.

3. Digest of Parochial Returns made to the Select Committee . . . on . . . the Education of the Poor (1818). BPP 1819 IX – Part III. 1349.

4. *Wealth of Nations* (1776) eds. R.H. Campbell, A.S. Skinner and W. Todd (Oxford, 1976), V.i.f.55.

5. *The Correspondence of Adam Smith*, eds. E.C. Mossner and I.S. Ross (Oxford, 1977), letter 103, Adam Smith to David Hume, 7 June 1767.

6. *Corr.* letter 11, Adam Smith to James Oswald, 19 January 1752.

7. *The Letters of David Hume*, ed. J.Y.T. Greig (Oxford, 1932), i, 142–3.

8. *The Collected Works of Dugald Stewart*, ed. Sir William Hamilton, IX (Edinburgh, 1856), 6.

9. *Corr.*, letter 31, David Hume to Adam Smith, 12 April 1759.

10. *Corr.*, letter 109, Adam Smith to David Hume, 13 September 1767.

2 SMITH AS A STUDENT

Smith left the burgh school of Kirkcaldy to go to the University of Glasgow when aged fourteen, which was not exceptionally youthful at that time. He matriculated in November 1737. Why Glasgow was chosen has been variously interpreted: perhaps in order to be cared for directly or indirectly by relatives who lived there on this first occasion when the only posthumous child was separated from his mother; perhaps to become eligible for the Snell Exhibition to Balliol College, Oxford, which he was later to hold. As with so many of the biographical details of Smith's life, the answer will never be known, but to Glasgow he went to begin a stay of three years, which was to be renewed later by his thirteen years as a professor, and so to establish a connection which was to be perpetuated further when he was elected Rector in 1787.

The change from Kirkcaldy to Glasgow, a town about ten times as big, must have required a major effort of personal and social adjustment. Though growing, the city was still far from the industrial centre it was to become, but at least the College, with over a century yet to pass in its cramped High Street quarters, half-way between the Cross and the Cathedral, was a small and intimate place. No information survives of how Smith lived in Glasgow, nor can any hints be gleaned even from some of Smith's later letters when he deals with the accommodation of others, and its cost, when he was a professor at Glasgow. Various options were open to students. Very spartan and cheap provision was available, but even the most luxurious was not expensive. The cheapest method was for a student to take lodgings and to feed himself, preferably on bulk supplies of oat- or pease-meal. Board had been discontinued at the College, but rooms were available at around £1 a year. On that basis of minimum subsistence, even by Scottish standards, the cost of maintenance was about £5 a year, to which should be added the payment of fees which, on the assumption the student was attending the maximum number of classes, might be about £3.10s a year, so that, allowing for other expenses, an education at Glasgow was available for cash expenditure of about £10 a year.

Smith's family resources were such that there would be no need for him to live so spartanly, and it is improbable his attentive mother would have countenanced such primitive living. He could choose from the other options, live in a boarding house, kept by such a respectable female as the widow of a professor; live with a family, perhaps one known to the family of the student; or live with a professor, to whom the more affluent students began to provide a very convenient supplementary income, as they did later to Smith himself. Of these three options, probably living with a family was most likely to have been acceptable both to Smith and to his mother. Even the more expensive method of living with a professor was cheap. Smith himself left a record of the cost in a letter written to Lord Shelburne, the father of one of his aristocratic pupils, when he was consulted on the possiblity of recommending Glasgow as a suitable place for the education of two sons of his friend, Sir John Colthurst. Though written some twenty years after Smith's own days as a student at Glasgow, prices did not change significantly in the mid-eighteenth century:

> The expense of board in the common boarding houses is from five to eight Pounds per quarter for each person. The expense of washing is not included in this; the ordinary rate of which is at 1sh. 10D per Dozen. The expence of Masters fees will probably amount to eight or ten Guineas for each Person. There are, besides, some other College dues which, however, will not upon the whole amount to twenty shillings per annum for each Person. Their linnen ought to be sent from Ireland where it is both cheaper and better than here. A suit of plain Cloaths of the finest cloth may be had for about five Pounds. These are all the necessary expences which any Gentlemans son has occasion to be at while he attends upon this University. What the unnecessary expences may be, it is impossible for me to determine. These will depend upon the young gentlemen themselves, upon the habits they have been bred up in and the injunctions that are laid upon them.[1]

Of the classes Smith took, the evidence is circumstantial. It comes from books – inscribed copies in the University Library at Glasgow of the *Encheiridion* of Epictetus and of Grotius' *De Jure Belli ac Pacis* are evidence of work in the Greek and Moral Philosophy Classes; or it comes from the recollections of others. From such diverse and circumstantial sources the curriculum can gradually be built up. It seems to have embraced the six subjects which for so long gave structure to the Scottish M.A. degree: Latin, Greek, logic, moral philosophy, mathematics, natural philosophy. Glasgow students (except those taking occasional classes) proceeding towards their degrees were

examined, orally and publically, on the Black Stone – an ancient seat
of examination – by the professor of the class they were leaving and
by the professor of the class they were entering. While there is no
record of Smith's graduation (as distinct from matriculation) we must
assume that he survived this trying process.

Though the College of Glasgow was to appear to later generations,
and with much justification, as a hotbed of intrigue, of vice rather than
of virtue, it had experienced several major changes before Smith matriculated, changes in both administration and in the academic atmosphere.[2]
A strong Principal of the first quarter of the eighteenth century, John
Stirling, had precipitated disputes, particularly over the right to elect
the Rector, but he also directed the academic reform in ways confirmed
by a Royal Commission which led to an act of 1727, which provided in
turn the basis for the government of the University until 1858. The
administrative problems of the University were to involve Smith
personally when he returned as a professor; as a student he was mainly
concerned with some of the implications of the academic changes. Of
these the most important had been a move to encourage greater special-
isation. Previously instruction had been in the hands of regents, who
had taken students through the entire course for their degrees. The
system was common to all Scottish universities, but was gradually given
up at the beginning of the eighteenth century as appointments were
made to specialist chairs. The final demise of the system at Glasgow
came in 1727 when the three of the original four regents who remained
went to their chosen specialisms. Consequently, when Smith came to
Glasgow in 1737 the Faculty consisted of the Principal, no longer the
masterful and well-connected John Stirling but the much weaker Neil
Campbell, the twelve professors, three of whom (Dunlop of Greek,
Loudon of logic and Dick of natural philosophy) had been among the
last group of regents. Smith therefore encountered a university which,
like so much else in Scottish life at the time, was administratively in
process of transition, with elements of both old and new in it.

Of that earlier generation of the first years of intellectual ferment,
none had more influence, though indirectly, on Smith than Gershom
Carmichael, one of the last group of regents, who had become the
first professor of moral philosophy on the demise of the old system of
instruction. Carmichael was particularly interested in the study of law
and made his main scholarly contribution in his edition of Pufendorf's
De Officio Hominis et Civis, a work which is mainly concerned with
jurisprudence and only incidentally with economics and ethics, though
the balance of Carmichael's notes is more towards ethics. The interest

and the links it provides with wider thought is important. The general link was with European thought on common and civil law, and so to the broad streams of Roman and Stoic philosophy. The emphasis was on jurisprudence, on the doctrine of natural law which was to be developed by Francis Hutcheson in the context of an empirical study of historical and social relations, thus introducing a tradition which was to be continued by Smith himself.

Glasgow was becoming a centre from which new ways of thought, especially more secular and less authoritarian ways, began to disturb many of a more traditional cast of mind in Scotland. To some the developments in Glasgow in the early eighteenth century were signs of disturbing heretical opinion which had to be suppressed as quickly and effectively as possible. To others they were symptomatic of a freer and more enlightened thought, no longer subject to the dogmas of the past. At the centre of this particular movement was John Simson, professor of divinity from 1708 to 1740, but important as Simson's own views were, equally important was the support he received more generally in the University. Twice Simson was accused before the General Assembly of the Church of Scotland of heretical teachings. In 1717 he was acquitted, but ten years later he was suspended for two years and then in 1729 prohibited from exercising all his ecclesiastical functions, even though on the second occasion he suggested that students were unreliable witnesses since they could not fully understand the Latin in which he lectured. Simson was prohibited from teaching by the General Assembly, but still continued to enjoy the emoluments of office and to take part in University business. The new Principal, Neil Campbell, was left to do the teaching of divinity until Simson's death in 1740, for which he was flatly refused any extra remuneration until 1751 when he was given a small sum, ostensibly for other purposes, so that the only person who probably gained from the prohibition was the heretical professor himself.

Smith had, of course, no direct contact with John Simson, but was much influenced by his nephew, Robert, the professor of mathematics at this time. Testimony to Smith's interest in mathematics and science comes from a fellow student, Archibald Maclaine, minister of the Scots kirk at the Hague, who told Dugald Stewart that Smith's

favourite pursuits while at that university were mathematics and natural philosophy; and I remember to have heard my father remind him of a geometrical problem of considerable difficulty, about which he was occupied at the time when their acquaintance commenced, and which had been proposed to him as an exercise by the celebrated Dr. Simson.[3]

Of his particular admiration and respect for Simson there is evidence in Smith's own writings, notably in a passage inserted in the sixth edition of the *Theory of Moral Sentiments*, where Smith cited Simson and Matthew Stewart as 'the two greatest [mathematicians] that have lived in my time', and described the way in which they 'never seemed to feel even the slightest uneasiness from the neglect with which the ignorance of the public received some of their most valuable works', as an example of how mathematicians, 'who may have the most perfect assurance, both of the truth and of the importance of their discoveries, are frequently very indifferent about the reception which they may meet with from the public'.[4]

While Simson was not without his peculiarities, his claim to recognition rests on two characteristics of his work which reveal an obvious attraction to someone of Smith's bent. First, in the description so commonly applied to him, he was the restorer, or rediscoverer, of Greek geometry, and produced a convincing explanation of Euclid's lost porisms. But the second feature of his work showed that he was more than a mathematical antiquarian providing an historical account, even refurbishing, of Greek geometry when it was under attack from the algebraic geometry which followed Descartes. His advocacy of Greek geometry and his relegation of algebraic formulations was part of his interest in the origins of the subject as the means by which the study of mathematics could be seen to merge with the study of philosophy. Simson's interests were shared generally in Scotland. From their stress on Greek geometry the Scots built up a reputation for their philosophical elucidation of Newtonian fluxions, notably in the *Treatise on Fluxions* (1724) by Colin Maclaurin (1698-1746), another pupil of Simson's, who held the chairs of mathematics in Aberdeen and Edinburgh.

Even Simson's influence paled beside that of Francis Hutcheson, professor of moral philosophy at Glasgow from 1729 to 1746. That Smith held him in lasting affection is evident in the letter which he wrote to the Principal of Glasgow University on his election as Rector in 1787, more than forty years after Hutcheson's death and fifty years after Smith first came under his influence. He then wrote of 'the abilities and Virtues of the never to be forgotten Dr. Hutcheson',[5] echoing a phrase — consciously or unconsciously — which he had used eleven years earlier when he had sent John Hume a copy of the addition he proposed making to the account of his own life left by 'your never to be forgotten brother'.[6]

Hutcheson (1694-1746) was Irish by birth, though Scottish by descent, and so, when he came to Glasgow as a student in 1710 was one of a group of Irish students who for long played a distinctive role in the life of the College. He was brought up in the burgeoning philosophical tradition, influenced by John Simson and above all by Carmichael. After teaching in Dublin he was appointed professor of moral philosophy in 1729, and proceeded forthwith to introduce a number of innovations. He lectured in English, rather than Latin, and also brought real discipline to the task of teaching by 'keeping the students to rules, catalogues, exact hours, etc., wherein ther is certainly a very great decay'.[7] He also worked hard, especially by the standards of today, lecturing as he did on ancient ethics three days a week and giving public lectures each Sunday. In addition to tutorial instruction, Hutcheson lectured five days a week on his main course, covering the fields of natural religion, morals, jurisprudence, and government. In this course he seems to have relied initially on Pufendorf and the 'Compend' of his predecessor, Gershom Carmichael, before developing the course which was to be published, posthumously, in 1755 under the title of a *System of Moral Philosophy*.

> A stature above middle size, a gesture and manner negligent and easy, but decent and manly, gave a dignity to his appearance. His complexion was fair and sanguine, and his features regular. His countenance and look bespoke sense, spirit, kindness and joy of heart. His whole person and manner raised a strong prejudice in his favour at first sight.[8]

The impression was evidently sustained on closer acquaintance, since to these qualities Hutcheson added those of a brilliant and persuasive lecturer so that it is hardly surprising to find his biographer suggesting that he loved truth and fought after it with impartiality and courage.[9] Clearly an important figure in the context of the Scottish 'Enlightenment', Hutcheson was to have a profound influence on Smith, especially as a source of interest in classical, and particularly Stoic philosophy. Apart from establishing the subject matter to be taught from the chair of moral philosophy, Hutcheson also had a considerable impact on Smith's work in economics and ethics. In the former case it is a striking fact that the order of subjects chosen by Smith closely follows that of his teacher as contained in the *System*[10] − the important difference being that Smith produced a single coherent argument, as distinct from treating topics such as the division of labour, money and price in isolation from one another. In ethics too there are clear differences and yet a fundamental community of interest in that Hutcheson found moral judgement to be based upon 'immediate sense and feeling' rather than reason. As Smith later remarked:

> In his illustrations upon the moral sense he has explained this so fully, and, in my opinion, so unanswerably, that, if any controversy is still kept up about this subject, I can impute it to nothing, but either to inattention to what that gentleman has written, or to a superstitious attachment to certain forms of expression, a weakness not very uncommon among the learned.[11]

More important than examples of the detailed links between the two is the similarity in some of the fundamental doctrines which led them to adopt similar approaches to their study of society. For example, following the tradition which he himself had inherited from Carmichael and through him from the Dutch jurists, Hutcheson expounded the doctrine of natural law, which led him when dealing with more practical matters of government in his lectures to ensure that

> he took peculiar care ... to inculcate the importance of civil and religious liberty to the happiness of mankind: as a warm love of liberty, and manly zeal for providing it, were ruling principles in his own breast; he always insisted on it at great length, and with the greatest strength of argument and earnestness of persuasion; and he had such success on this important point, that few, if any of his pupils, whatever contrary prejudices they might bring along with them, ever left him without favourable notions of that side of the question which he espoused and defended.

So wrote William Leechman, Hutcheson's colleague at Glasgow in the chair of divinity, and Principal from 1761 to 1785.[12]

The theme of economic and political liberalism expounded by Hutcheson finds its reflection in the work of his pupil, although here too there are interesting differences of emphasis. In economic terms, Hutcheson was more pragmatic than doctrinaire and this led him to espouse general statements which Smith would not have made regarding, for example, the regulation of trade. But perhaps the contrast is most marked in terms of political philosophy at least to the extent that Hutcheson is now seen as one of the leading representatives of the radical whig position with its associated emphasis on the contract theory of government and on the right of resistance – a position which goes far towards explaining Hutcheson's popularity with the political thinkers of the American Revolution.[13]

But whatever the implications of Hutcheson's teaching, ethical, religious, or political, he did not in general advance his own views provocatively. Hutcheson may have been unorthodox by the standards of his predecessors and of many of his contemporaries, but his actions indicate that he realised his position and showed a discretion appropriate for anyone charged with responsibility for the education of the young in a university closely knit to its society. Smith showed a similar discretion, perhaps partly derived from his equable temperament, on the one hand, and from Hutcheson on the other. The subtler influences were probably even more radical and certainly more long-lasting than some of those affecting specific doctrines.

The influence of Glasgow was deep-seated and permanent, but Smith's period there as a student came to an end in 1740 when he was appointed to the Snell Exhibition at Balliol College, Oxford. He rode south to Oxford, probably after having returned briefly to Kirkcaldy, and matriculated on 7 July. John Snell's foundation was an attempt by a one-time Glasgow student to encourage a supply of trained men for the ministry of the Episcopal Church in Scotland, but the terms of his benefaction, which compelled exhibitioners under penalty of £500 to 'enter holy orders and to serve the Church of Scotland' had been nullified by the Presbyterian settlement of the Church of Scotland in 1690. An attempt by Oxford to force entry to orders in the Church of England failed in Chancery in 1744. Restrictions on the exhibitioners were therefore minimal. When Smith was appointed, a Snell Exhibition, of which there were five, was worth £40 annually for eleven years, and to that he added in November 1742 a Warner Exhibition worth £8.5s a year. There was little left to spare, a minimum estimate for an Oxford education being then £30 per annum with most commoners spending over £60 a year. Though more expensive than Glasgow, Smith, with his abstemious habits, was unlikely to call much on family resources, even though he complained shortly after his arrival of 'the extraordinary and most extravagant fees we are obliged to pay the College and University on our admittance'.

If information on Smith's stay in Glasgow is sparse, that on his stay in Oxford is even sparser. In only one respect is it better. The first letters from Smith which have survived date from that period, a mere six, five to his mother and one, the first of 24 August 1740 to his kinsman and guardian who was secretary to the second Duke of Argyll. All are concerned with mundane matters. 'I have not yet received the money' '. . . send me some Stocking's, the sooner you send 'em the better' 'Tar water is a remedy very much in vogue here at present for almost all diseases. It has perfectly cured me of an inveterate scurvy and shaking in the head.'[14] All very brief, though in some cases it is obvious that only fragments have survived, but even then they show signs of the bad correspondent which Smith was, and was to remain.

Such documentary evidence cannot go far in revealing much about Smith's life in Oxford. But the circumstantial evidence, and some of Smith's later comments, enable a picture to be built up, not of his experiences but more of his response to what he found in Oxford. The contrast with Glasgow was marked. Balliol could hardly have been less congenial to someone of Smith's interests and temperament. The University was rent with factions, some of them Jacobite, dissipation was the order of the day and the Scots, including the five Snell Exhibitioners, were always a distinct, and frequently despised group among the total of some one hundred undergraduates in the College, so they tended to keep themselves to themselves.

But the most important contrasts were of an academic kind — for here there were no Simsons and Hutchesons to stimulate the mind. As Smith wrote: 'In the university of Oxford, the greater part of the public professors have, for these many years, given up altogether even the pretence of teaching.'[15] Oxford, in Smith's eyes, had become one of those learned societies which 'have chosen to remain, for a long time, the sanctuaries in which exploded systems and obsolete prejudices found shelter and protection'.[16]

The problem interested Smith to the extent that he later advanced a number of reasons to explain it. His basic belief was that in every profession 'the exertion of the greater part of those who exercise it, is always in proportion to the necessity they are under of making that exertion'.[17] In the context of Oxford he thus drew attention to the endowments of the colleges which secured large incomes irrespective of competence or industry and to the fact that 'the discipline of colleges and universities is in general contrived, not for the benefit of the students, but for the interest, or more properly speaking, for the ease of the masters'.[18] He also drew attention to the fact that the charitable foundations of scholarships and exhibitions 'necessarily attach a certain number of students to certain colleges' independently of the merit of these colleges, and in the same vein, to the point that the privileges of graduation in effect force students to attend universities irrespective of their quality.[19] Edward Gibbon, who entered Magdalen College in 1752 found an atmosphere which Smith would have immediately recognised, commenting as he did that the fellows had absolved themselves from the toil

> of reading, or thinking, or writing . . . . Their conversation stagnated in a round of college business, Tory politics, personal anecdotes, and private scandals; their dull and deep potations excused the brisk intemperance of youth; and their constitutional toasts were not expressive of the most lively loyalty to the House of Hanover.[20]

It is hardly surprising that Gibbon should have declined to express any obligation to the University of Oxford, or to find him quoting Smith with approval by way of explanation of its current state.

By contrast, Smith regarded the Scottish Universities, with 'all their faults' as 'the best seminaries of learning that are to be found any where in Europe',[21] and attributed this fact to the absence of the institutional impediments to professional effort which were to be found in England. Yet two points should be noted by way of qualification. Smith was well aware that the Scottish Universities had faults, pointing out as he later did to Cullen:

> Your examination . . . is as serious, and perhaps more so than that of any other University in Europe. But when a student has resided a few years among you, has behaved dutifully to all his Professors, and has attended regularly all their lectures, when he comes to his examination, I suspect you are disposed to be as good natured as other people.'[22]

In speaking of the experience of Oxford Smith was drawing attention to the way in which all men are likely to behave in a particular kind of situation, and that his strictures were applied to universities in general rather than to Oxford in particular.

Smith was clearly unhappy in Oxford and it is probably significant that he never returned after giving up the Snell Exhibition. Only one contact was to remain from this period, John Douglas, son of a Pittenweem merchant, who was also a Snell Exhibitioner, and ended his days as

Bishop of Salisbury. The situation must also have been aggravated by the fact that Smith was unlikely to have been able to visit his home during the period of his six years' stay, since the cost of posting to Kirkcaldy and back would have absorbed about half his income. Visits to Adderbury, near Oxford, a residence of the Hanoverian Duke of Argyll are the only ones which we know of, and here Smith would live with his kinsman and guardian, secretary to the Duke.

Yet Smith, like Gibbon, benefited greatly from the use of a great library and, unlike Gibbon, was of an age to appreciate the opportunity at the time. It is certainly during this period that Smith laid the foundations of an extensive learning which was to stand him in good stead later in life. It may be in recognition of this that his letter of acceptance of the office of Rector of the University of Glasgow should have included an appreciative reference to his stay in Oxford.[23]

Smith left Oxford in the course of 1746 and formally resigned the Exhibition on 4 April 1749.

Notes

1. *Corr.*, letter 35, Adam Smith to Lord Shelburne, 23 July 1759.
2. See below p. 48.
3. Dugald Stewart, *Account of the Life and Writings of Adam Smith*, in *Essays on Philosophical Subjects*; eds. W.P.D. Wightman, J.C. Bryce and I.S. Ross (Oxford, 1980), I.7.
4. The *Theory of Moral Sentiments*, eds. D.D. Raphael and A.L. Macfie (Oxford, 1976), III.2.20.
5. *Corr.*, letter 274, Adam Smith to Archibald Davidson, 16 November 1787.
6. *Corr.*, letter 175, Adam Smith to John Hume, 7 October 1776.
7. R. Wodrow, *Analecta* (Maitland Club edn.), 1843, IV.191.
8. W. Leechman, 'Some Account of the Life and Writings of the Author', in F. Hutcheson, *A Short System of Moral Philosophy* (London, 1755), xliii.
9. Ibid., xx.
10. W.R. Scott, *Francis Hutcheson: His Life, Teaching and Position in the History of Philosophy* (Cambridge, 1900).
11. *TMS*, VII, iii.2.9.
12. Leechman in Hutcheson, *A Short System of Moral Philosophy*, xxxv-xxxvi.
13. Donald Winch, *Adam Smith's Politics :An Essay in Historiographic Revision* (Cambridge, 1978), Chapter 3.
14. *Corr.*, letter 1, Adam Smith to William Smith, 24 August 1740. See also letters 2, 3, and 6, Adam Smith to his mother, all dated in this period.
15. *WN*, V.i.f.8.
16. Ibid., V.i.f.34.
17. Ibid., V.i.f.4.
18. Ibid., V.i.f.15.

19. Ibid., V.i.f.12.

20. *Autobiography of Edward Gibbon* (World Classics edn., Oxford, 1959), 40.

21. *Corr.*, letter 143, Smith to William Cullen, 20 September 1774. The quotation from this long letter occurs at p. 173.

22. *Corr.*, letter 143, p. 176.

23. *Corr.*, letter 274, Adam Smith to Archibald Davidson, 16 November 1787.

3 EDINBURGH

Nothing is known of Smith for two years after he returned to Kirkcaldy from Oxford. He had to assess ways in which he could earn his living, for the resources of the family, while not demanding immediate action, required him to gain additional income. The options in Scotland were limited. The law had opened up a path to a number of offices to his father, after a period as personal secretary in the Argyll family; and Smith's kinsman, William Smith, continued to serve the family as secretary to the second Duke. Though his later work in the University of Glasgow was to show that he was not without administrative competence, it is doubtful if Smith, with his allegedly unpresentable manner and address, his record as a notoriously bad correspondent, and above all his well-attested absent-mindedness, was someone fitted for such offices. To practise the law, especially as an advocate in Edinburgh, was risky even though for a few it brought comparatively high rewards, social status and political power if linked to a major figure. The other path along which most educated Scots sought to walk was towards the ministry. Whatever Smith may once have thought or planned about seeking ordination in the Church of England when he accepted the Snell Exhibition, he showed little evidence that he had any intention of doing so when he left Oxford in 1746; and there is no evidence that he was any more attracted to the ministry of the Church of Scotland. A private tutorship was always possible, or a university post. Both were to come to Smith, but the first move to the life of a teacher came in 1748 when he gave a course of lectures in Edinburgh. The course was repeated for three winters until he had been appointed to the chair of logic at Glasgow.

The origins of the Edinburgh lectures are wrapped in the obscurity so common to many aspects of Smith's life. One point is clear. The lectures were not commissioned by the University of Edinburgh and do not seem to have had any association with it. There is nothing surprising in this situation. Public teaching in such diverse subjects as mathematics, medicine and navigation was frequently available and taught from the lodgings of the 'masters' of such disciplines. In addition, professors in the University of Edinburgh frequently advertised courses as being available to the public at large, at least on receipt of the appropriate fee.

Support for Smith's lecture course seems to have come from Robert Craigie of Glendoick, Lord Advocate and later Lord President of the Court of Session, and whose daughter married Robert Douglas of Strathenry, a kinsman of Smith's mother, and from Smith's old boyhood friend, James Oswald of Dunnikier, who was a member of a circle centering round Henry Home, Lord Kames. The latter's biographer, A.F. Tytler, was in no doubt that it was due to Kames's efforts that:

Mr Adam Smith, soon after his return from Oxford, and when he had abandoned all views towards the Church, for which he had been originally destined, was induced to turn his early studies to the benefit of the public, by reading a course of Lectures on Rhetoric and *Belle Lettres.*[1]

Unlike many others the lectures were not advertised, which may indicate that they were delivered under the auspices of one of the many clubs which flourished in Edinburgh, the most probable being the Philosophical Society in which Kames took a particular interest. In 1752, when its fortunes were languishing, Kames wrote to Cullen: 'Remember also to contribute to the Philosophical Society, about which I am turned extremely keen, now that I have got in a good measure the control of it.'[2]

It is not surprising that Kames should have supported such literary endeavours; a man of ecletic erudition, unrestrained by formal education, he did not conceive the function narrowly. He questioned if it was not desirable that 'a considerable part of that time [preparatory instruction for a profession] may not be more profitably employed in the acquisition of general knowledge; the elements of the sciences, as Physics or Natural History, the principles of Mechanics and Mathematics and in the elegant studies connected with the Belles Lettres and Criticism'.[3]

Given what is known of Smith's early interests it is not surprising that the subjects of the lectures were of a broadly literary nature. His first appearance in print was in the form of a dedication to the collected poems of William Hamilton of Bangour, an old and valued friend of Lord Kames, a fellow-Jacobite, who was the author of an 'Ode to the Battle of Gladsmuir' and is now perhaps best known for his 'Braes of Yarrow'.[4] The lectures came at a time when literary interests were developing rapidly as evidenced in the introduction and relatively wide circulation of such journals as the *Tatler, Spectator, Guardian* and *Rambler*. In addition, professors in Edinburgh University lectured on related topics, with John Stevenson, Professor of Logic from 1730 to

1775 arguably the most important.[5]

Smith's efforts were applied to a ready soil and apparently delivered to 'a respectable auditory, chiefly composed of students of law and theology',[6] which brought him a respectable income, leading David Hume to remind Smith in later years in the course of an attempt to bring him back to Edinburgh, that 'You made above 100 Pound a Year by your Class when in this Place, tho' you had not the Character of Professor.'[7]

The lectures were so successful that they were taken over by Robert Watson when Smith moved to Glasgow. Subsequently Watson became professor of logic in St Andrews while his successor, Hugh Blair, became the first regius professor of rhetoric in Edinburgh. Both these men also commanded the support of Lord Kames.

The determination of the specific content of the Edinburgh lectures is a task which has long absorbed the attention of those studying the life and work of Smith. A clue to a possible source of information lies in statements by a number of authorities that Smith used some of the Edinburgh material in his earliest lectures at Glasgow. Smith himself is a witness to that effect. According to Dugald Stewart, he presented a paper in 1755 to a society of which he was a member. In this paper, the 'Lecture of 1755' as it has been designated, and from which Stewart quoted only briefly, Smith claimed:

> A great part of the opinions . . . enumerated in this paper, is treated of at length in some lectures which I have still by me and which were written in the hand of a clerk who left my service six years ago. They have all of them been the constant subjects of my lectures since I first taught Mr Craigie's class, the first winter I spent in Glasgow, down to this day, without any considerable variation. They had all of them been the subjects of lectures which I read at Edinburgh the winter before I left it and I can adduce innumerable witnesses, both from that place and from this, who will ascertain them sufficiently to be mine.[8]

Smith's assertion was confirmed by the evidence of others. His pupil, John Millar, later professor of civil law at Glasgow, recounted to Stewart how Smith had changed the traditional substance of the lectures at Glasgow in his year as professor of logic by concentrating on 'studies of a more interesting and useful nature than the logic and metaphysics of the schools'. Most of his time was taken up in the delivery of 'a system of rhetoric and belles lettres'. Though never published, Millar went on, 'From the permission given to students of taking notes, many observations and opinions contained in these lectures have either been detailed in separate dissertations, or engrossed in general collections, which have since been given to the public.'[9] Further evidence of Smith's use of Edinburgh material is in a letter from James Wodrow, Librarian at Glasgow from 1750 to 1755, to the Earl of Buchan[10] in which he commented that 'Smith delivered a set of admirable critical lectures on Language, not as a Grammarian but Rhetorician — on the different kinds or characteristics of style suited to different subjects, *simple*, nervous etc., the structure, the natural order, and proper arrangement of the different members of the sentence, etc. . .' In words very similar to those of Millar, he considered them 'well calculated to be exceedingly useful to young composers'. Though neither Millar nor Wodrow state specifically that Smith used Edinburgh material, it is reasonable to assume that he did. Such material may also have appeared in papers Smith contributed to a Literary Society in Glasgow.

Though there is evidence to justify the view that Smith used Edinburgh material in the Glasgow lectures, for long the only specific citations of the substance were the very brief accounts by Millar and Wodrow. In 1958 part of the problem of the possible content of the Edinburgh lectures was removed with the discovery of a set of lecture notes on rhetoric and belles-lettres, which proved to be an almost complete set of lectures given by Smith in the session 1762-3.

The discovery of the notes of the later lectures on rhetoric shed only some light on accusations that some of Smith's close friends plagiarised his work. Dugald Stewart provided an indication of the intriguing, if ultimately rather insignificant possibility when he recounted that in Smith's lost 'Lecture of 1755'

> a pretty long enumeration is given of certain leading principles, both political and literary, to which he was anxious to establish his exclusive right; in order to prevent the possibility of some rival claims which he thought he had reason to apprehend, and to which his situation as a professor, added to his unreserved communications in private companies rendered him peculiarly liable.[11]

To Smith's own general fear of plagiarism three specific allegations may be added in the order in which the alleged plagiarists published evidence by which the accusations may be tested. First is the accusation by Alexander Carlyle against Adam Ferguson,[12] who published his major work *A History of Civil Society* in 1767. Carlyle commented,

'Smith had been weak enough to accuse him of having borrowed some of his inventions without owning them. This Ferguson denied, but owned that he derived many notions from a French author, and that Smith had been there before him.' There is also evidence that, in spite of many examples of close and friendly links, relations between Ferguson and Smith were not always amicable. In reporting Smith's death to Sir John Macpherson, Ferguson wrote: 'We knew he was dying for some months, and though matters, as you know, were a little awkward when he was in health, upon that appearance I turned my face that way and went to him without further consideration, and continued my attention to the last.'[13] Second is an allegation by John Callander of Craigforth against William Robertson, who published his *History of Charles V* in 1769. Callander reported Smith's opinion of Robertson, 'That his judgement enabled him to form a good Outline, but he wanted industry to fill up his plan', and provided his own comment, 'Dr Robertson had borrowd the first vol. of his history of Cha. 5 from them; as every Student could testify.'[14] Third is the admission of Hugh Blair, that he used material from Smith in his own lectures on rhetoric and belles-lettres, which he published in 1783, but which he had delivered in Edinburgh from 1760 and as Regius Professor of Rhetoric and Belles-Lettres from 1762. Blair's admission was specific:

> . . . of the General Characters of style, particularly, the Plain and the Simple, and the characters of those English authors who are classed under them, in this, and the following Lecture, several ideas have been taken from a manuscript treatise on rhetoric, part of which was shown to me, many years ago by the learned and ingenious Author, Dr Adam Smith.[15]

However critical Smith was of Ferguson and Robertson, he does not seem to have been so concerned over Blair's borrowings. Henry Mackenzie is reported to have told Samuel Rogers that when he told Smith that Blair introduced his ideas into sermons, he replied 'He is very welcome, there is enough left.'[16]

If hard and fast evidence of plagiarism is demanded, then it is easy to dismiss some of Smith's fears. Smith was worried about plagiarism as early as 1755, long before Ferguson, Robertson or Blair had published their material, and even before Blair had started to deliver his lectures. In the case of Adam Ferguson the lack of opportunity to plagiarise may seem even more compelling. He was out of Scotland as an army chaplain until 1754. But the dates of publication are only the occasions when the plagiarism became public. In the intellectual community of eighteenth-century Scotland the knowledge of how someone's thought was developing was often common property even before it was embodied in published form. The absence of material published before 1755 by some of those against whom a specific accusation of plagiarism has been made by others does not prevent the application to them of Smith's general accusation of that year. He may have been suspicious of the way the thoughts of some were developing and was warning them of the prior development of his ideas. He may have been excessively proprietorial in intellectual endeavour, but that is another matter.

The discovery of the notes of the lectures on rhetoric did not help to dispose of all the charges of plagiarism, because the charges centred in the cases of Robertson and Ferguson on methodology which is only marginally the concern of the lectures on rhetoric. Blair's case is different, but use of Smith's material was acknowledged, was based on a manuscript given him by Smith, and did not seem to concern Smith greatly in any case. The probability then is that Smith was not much worried over the use of material in those parts of the Edinburgh lectures which were strictly on rhetoric, and of which a version has survived in the lectures to the private class at Glasgow in 1762/3.

He was probably more worried about the use of those parts delivered probably in the second and/or third winters in Edinburgh and developed subsequently in the lectures to the public class at Glasgow, most notably in its third and fourth sections, which, according to Millar as quoted by Stewart, were in jurisprudence and the history of civil society, and which never appeared in a planned published volume, and in economics, the expanded version of which duly appeared in the *Wealth of Nations*. Even before he moved to Glasgow Smith had clearly earned a reputation that went beyond that of a lecturer on rhetoric. He responded readily to William Cullen's suggestion in 1751 that he should undertake, additionally to his duties as professor of logic and at short notice, 'Natural Jurisprudence and Politics' as his contribution to the substitute course of lectures for the ailing and absent professor of moral philosophy.[17] That Smith should have extended his interests in this way is hardly surprising because some of his miscellaneous writing, while published only posthumously, dates to his days in Glasgow and perhaps even earlier, possibly back even to the time he spent in Kirkcaldy between leaving Oxford and delivering his lectures in Edinburgh. But the most direct evidence of the wider coverage of the lectures is Smith's own claim in the 'Lecture of 1755'. The wider nature of the issues about which Smith was concerned is indicated by the tantalising few extracts which Stewart gave:

> Man is generally considered by statesmen and projectors as the materials of a sort of political mechanics. Projectors disturb nature in the course of her operations in human affairs; and it requires no more than to let her alone, and give her fair play in the pursuit of her ends, that she may establish her own designs.
>
> Little else is requisite to carry a state to the highest degree of opulence from the lowest barbarism, but peace, easy taxes, and a tolerable administration of justice; all the rest being brought about by the natural course of things. All governments which thwart this natural course, which force things into another channel, or which endeavour to arrest the progress of society at a particular point, are unnatural, and to support themselves are obliged to be oppressive and tyrannical.[18]

These extracts indicate that in Edinburgh Smith probably moved from a course on rhetoric in his first year to courses on philosophy later. But to move from a possibility to accepting the full development of many of Smith's ideas is another matter. Time was needed, though the germ of many ideas was obviously in his mind early. Plagiarism, on the other hand, may take place even when the ideas are not fully developed. Smith may have responded differently to Blair's action and those of others because the latter were using the ideas in fields in which he was still working and had yet to publish. The difficulty in tackling the allegations is that they lack specificity. Neither Stewart nor Carlyle who reported them seemed willing to take the allegations further, perhaps because they were friends of all the parties involved and Stewart in particular, in his posthumous memoir of Smith, might have wished to avoid too much attention to a charge which could have cast his own university colleagues in an unfavourable light. Perhaps W.R. Scott was right in thinking that Smith was then giving fair warning to those working in allied fields — Ferguson and Robertson in his own field — that he was already immersed in studies of the philosophy of law, jurisprudence and the history of civil society, and that they should keep out.

When Edinburgh lost its status as a parliamentary capital after 1707 many of those who sought political power moved to London and opened the way for the city's social life to be dominated by professional men, especially lawyers. Smith maintained his personal and intellectual links with Edinburgh even when resident in Glasgow, particularly through his membership of societies which proliferated in the eighteenth century. The one in which Smith played a more important part personally than in any other was the Select Society, founded in 1754 on the initiative of Allan Ramsay, the younger, shortly before he left Scotland, and supported by Smith and Hume. The three convened a meeting attended by fifteen of the intellectual luminaries of the day on 22 May when Smith explained the objectives, which were: 'The pursuit of philosophical inquiry, and the improvement of the members in the art of speaking'. The Select Society had two offshoots. The first was the Edinburgh Society for Encouraging Arts, Sciences, Manufactures, and Agriculture in Scotland or, as Hume put it to Allan Ramsay, 'a project of engrafting on the Society a scheme for the encouragement of arts and sciences and manufactures in Scotland by premiums partly honorary, partly lucrative'.[19] The second offshoot was the Society for Promoting the Reading and Speaking of the English Language in Scotland, a venture which was given a stimulus by the successful visit to Scotland in 1761 of Thomas Sheridan offering courses in elocution and the English tongue. The plan of the Select Society was that the new organisation would import teachers from England – Sheridan promised help in choosing them – 'to instruct gentlemen in the knowledge of the English Tongue, the manner of pronouncing it with purity, and the art of public speaking' and to teach children how to read English.

One club in Edinburgh with which Smith was associated had a special significance. Named by Adam Ferguson the Poker Club, it was formed in 1762 with the prime objective of stirring up opinion – poking it up – to achieve the establishment of a militia for Scotland after one had been granted for England. The Club did not act collectively to promote its objective, leaving the initiative to individual members, but it followed the usual pattern of holding regular dinners. In Alexander Carlyle's account it stands out from other clubs in one way: 'The establishment was frugal and moderate, as that of all clubs for a public purpose ought to be', so that, 'During these seven years, a very constant attendant told me that he never observed even an approach to inebriety in any of the members'.[20] Its public objective seems to have been swamped in more general and vigorous intellectual discussion. Hume compared it favourably with his experience in France. To Adam Ferguson he wrote: 'I really wish often for the plain roughness of the *Poker*, and particularly the sharpness of Dr Jardine, to correct and qualify so much lusciousness',[21] and to Hugh Blair: '[The Dauphin] seems a reasonable Man, but would be the better of being *roasted* sometimes in the *Poker*'. James Boswell saw the same characteristics in the Club, but did not approve: 'They would abolish all respect due to rank and external circumstances, and they would live like a kind of literary barbarians. For my own share, I own I would rather want their instructive conversation than be hurt by their rudeness.'[22] However general the interests of the Poker Club might have been in practice, the unifying interest which brought the literati of Edinburgh and country gentlemen together was, as Carlyle put it, 'resentment on its [the militia] being refused to us, and an invidious line drawn between Scotland and England'.[23] When Smith's two friends James Oswald and Gilbert Elliot introduced a Bill for a Scotch militia in 1760 it was thrown out. The Jacobite rebellion was still too recent in the minds of many English members for them to accede to the request. The resentment of the members of the Poker Club had several causes. In 1759 the appearance of Thourat in Scottish waters had posed a visible real threat to security. To some, military service for civilians was attractive, notably to the moving spirits of the Poker Club. Ferguson, the ex-chaplain to the Black Watch, thought it 'the true principle for which arms should be carried'.[24] And above all, to have the proposal for a Scotch militia rejected on the implied assumption that the Scots were dangerous Jacobites, was a slight and an insult which the literati could not take. To consider them inferior to the English cut them to the quick. The heat did not last, and that may be why the Poker Club's activities were more general. In 1776 another Scotch Militia Bill was rejected, with little indignation being shown, even though the Irish were given a militia on that occasion. The Poker Club ended without a whimper. Carlyle dated the end of its active existence in 1784. An attempted revival of a Younger Poker Club seems to have taken place in 1786 or 1787. The description of its alleged last meeting by Sir Walter Scott came after a lapse of years and it was not a success. Perhaps it was as well the Club had passed away, for when the Scotch Militia actually appeared in 1797 it brought forth resentment and riots. The members of the Poker Club may have been too abstract in their discussion of militias.

Whatever the various causes which fuelled the resentment against the refusal of the militia, one factor was the implication that the Scots were inferior to the English and not worthy to be trusted. The dislike of Scots which they encountered in some quarters in London, especially when they consciously regarded themselves not as Scots but as North Britons, was resented, and was one reason why Hume suggested to Smith that he did not relish settling in London. The inferior feeling which resulted had many manifestations and lay behind the desire of so many to speak and write in standard English. Smith was not so troubled by such matters as some of his contemporaries, but then it seems he had no need to be. He wrote, and apparently spoke, standard English well. The desire to promote English had also a simple and understandable reason behind it. Smith, like his other literary friends, saw the future for their writing as being in English. Their books were published in London, even if by expatriate Scots. If they wished to make their mark on a wider public, as they so apparently did, the medium had to be English. Their concern had a practical objective before it, and was evident in one of Smith's contributions to a surviving piece of evidence of the literary achievements of Edinburgh in mid-century, the first *Edinburgh Review*, which ran for only two issues in 1755 and 1756 and of which Smith was not only one of the founders but its major contributor, writing two articles for it, one in each of its two numbers.

The *Edinburgh Review* was projected by a group who had been active in the affairs of the Select Society, its editor being Alexander Wedderburn, the future Lord Chancellor Loughborough. The objectives, as stated in the preface, are indicative of the desire of the Scots to prove their ability and to display their achievements. After suggesting that the promise of Buchanan was not fulfilled because Scotland fell into civil discord until 'What the Revolution had begun, the Union rendered more complete', the preface continued,'If countries have their ages with respect to improvement, *North Britain* may be considered as in a state of early youth, guided and supported by the more mature strength of her sister kingdom.' In spite of the country's educational opportunitites two obstacles had obstructed the progress of science. The first was the difficulty of proper expression in a country with no standard of language, but there was ground for hope that someone born north of the Tweed may acquire 'a correct and even an elegant stile'. The second obstacle was that a slow progress in printing had impeded the means of communication, but that barrier had been wholly re-moved. The *Review* was projected to show the advance of science, which, it was hoped, would encourage others to a 'more eager pursuit of learning, to distinguish themselves, and to do honour to their country' and that objective was to be realised by giving '*a full account* of all books published in Scotland within the compass of half a year' and to take some notice of important books published elsewhere. The intention was obviously to show how far Scotland had advanced in intellectual endeavour, to dissipate from men's minds — particularly in England — any thought that the Scots were a backward race.

Smith's two contributions to the *Review* both make points which are immediately relevant. In the first of his articles, Smith commended the editors for including Johnson's *Dictionary* in their list, and while by no means uncritical of this work, concluded that: 'In this country, the usefulness of it will be soon felt, as there is no standard of correct language in conversation . . . we would earnestly recommend it to all those who are desirous to improve and correct their language . . .'[25]

Smith's second contribution, 'A Letter to the Authors of the Edinburgh Review' was an attempt to encourage them to avoid any suggestion of parochialism in its coverage. You cannot succeed, he warned the editors, 'while you confine yourselves almost entirely to an account of the books published in Scotland.' He went on:

> This country, which is but just beginning to attempt figuring in the learned world, produces as yet so few works of reputation, that it is scarce possible a paper which criticises upon them chiefly, should interest the public for any considerable time. The singular absurdity of some performances which you have so well represented in your first number, might divert your readers for once: But no eloquence could support a paper which consisted chiefly of accounts of such performances.[26]

Some of the reviews in the first issue amply confirm the grounds for Smith's unease. Even though David Hume was later to declare his intention of devoting his declining years to cookery, the review of Elizabeth Cleland's *A New and Easy Method of Cooking* is an ill-assorted companion for Hutcheson's *System of Moral Philosophy*.

Smith therefore exhorted the editors to notice with 'the same humanity and candour' every Scottish production that was 'tolerably decent' but to treat European publications as those from England were being treated already, examining them if they were felt to have a chance of surviving for thirty or forty years. Since Smith felt that the only Continental nation in which learning had any current reputation was France, his proposal meant in effect that the *Review* should provide comprehensive coverage of those publications of England and France which promised to be of some value. The article which supports these arguments, (and which also marked the end of this series), is remarkable for the width of reading and learning which it shows. No less remarkable is the complete absence of any suggestion of insularity on Smith's part; a fact which is no where more admirably demonstrated than in the pleasure with which he observed:

in the new French Encyclopedia the ideas of Bacon, Boyle, and Newton, explained with that order, perspicuity and good judgement, which distinguish all the eminent writers of that nation. As, since the Union, we are apt to regard ourselves in some measure as the countrymen of those great men, it flattered my vanity, as a Briton, to observe the superiority of the English philosophy thus acknowledged by their rival nation.[27]

Notes

1. A.F. Tytler, *Memoirs of the Life and Writings of Henry Home of Kames* (Edinburgh, 1807), i, 190.

2. Quoted in D.D. McElroy, *Scotland's Age of Improvement* (Washington State University, 1969), 35.

3. Tytler, *Memoirs of the Life and Writings of Henry Home of Kames,* i, 15.

4. *Essays on Philosophical Subjects*, 259-62.

5. Sir Alexander Grant, *Story of the University of Edinburgh* (Edinburgh, 1884), ii, 329.

6. Tytler, *Memoirs of the Life and Writings of Henry Home of Kames,* i, 190.

7. *Corr.*, letter 25, David Hume to Adam Smith, 8 June 1758.

8. Stewart, *Life of Smith*, IV.25.

9. Ibid., I.17.

10. Glasgow University Library. MSS 310/26 (folio 171 [170]).

11. Stewart, *Life of Smith*, IV.25.

12. A. Carlyle, *Autobiography*, ed. J.H. Burton (1910), 299.

13. Letter from Adam Ferguson to Sir James Macpherson, 31 July 1790, Edinburgh University Library, DC. 1.77/20.

14. Notes by George Chalmers on Adam Smith, Edinburgh University Library, Laing MSS. II. 451/2.

15. Hugh Blair, *Lectures on Rhetoric and Belles Lettres* (1783), i,381; John Hill, *An Account of the Life and Writings of Hugh Blair* (Edinburgh, 1807), 54-5, 179-81.

16. P.W. Clayden, *Early Life of Samuel Rogers* (London, 1887), 167.

17. *Corr.*, letter 9, Adam Smith to William Cullen, 3 September, 1751.

18. Stewart, *Life of Smith*, IV.25.

19. *The Letters of David Hume*, ed. J.Y.T. Greig (Oxford, 1932), i, 220.

20. Carlyle, *Autobiography*, 440 and 441.

21. Hume, *Letters*, i, 410-11 and 514.

22. *Boswell's London Journal, 1762-1763*, ed. F.A. Pottle (London, 1950), 300.

23. Carlyle, *Autobiography*, 440.

24. Adam Ferguson to Alexander Carlyle, 29 April 1775, quoted in John Small, 'Biographical Sketch of Adam Ferguson', *Transactions of the Royal Society of Edinburgh*, 23 (1864), 620.

25. *Essays on Philosophical Subjects*, 241.

26. Ibid., 242.

27. Ibid., 245.

4 THE MOVE TO GLASGOW

While Smith was engaged in the third winter of his course of lectures at Edinburgh, the Chair of Logic at Glasgow fell vacant through the death on 1 November 1750 of John Loudon, under whom Smith had studied. Smith, who enjoyed the support of Lord Kames and the Duke of Argyll, was appointed unanimously in an election concluded so expeditiously that it left little evidence on the University records. On 9 January 1751 Robert Simson was instructed to write to Smith. Smith's acceptance is dated the following day, when he assured 'the gentlemen of your Society . . . that it shall be my chief study to render myselfe a useful member of their Society'.[1] Smith was formally admitted to the chair on 16 January when he read the dissertation *De origine idearum*, which served as a formal demonstration of his competence, and duly signed the Westminster Confession of Faith. As he had to return to Edinburgh almost immediately, his duties were discharged by Hercules Lindesay the professor of civil law. Smith's contribution to Glasgow in the session 1750/1 was to attend meetings only.

Smith's tenure of the logic chair was to be short-lived. By the beginning of his first full session Thomas Craigie, the professor of moral philosophy fell ill and Smith was one of four who stood in for him. Smith told William Cullen that 'I shall, with great pleasure, do what I can to relieve him of the burden of his class' and agreed with Cullen's suggestion that the lectures on 'Natural Jurisprudence and Politics', would be 'most agreeable for me to . . . teach'.[2] Craigie died in Lisbon on 27 November 1751 and Smith transferred to the vacant chair on 22 April of the following year.

The reason for this change was probably Smith's preference for the subjects which could be taught from the chair of moral philosophy although financial considerations may have played a part. While Smith's income from teaching probably did not exceed £170 per annum, the logic chair seems to have attracted a lower stipend as may be inferred from the fact that Smith was required, on accepting the new chair, to content himself with his present salary until the opening of the new session.

Smith was a sympathetic teacher who enjoyed great success and acquired a growing reputation. His lecturing commitments followed a form common to many of his colleagues. On Mondays to Fridays he lectured to the public class – the taking of which contributed towards the degree – from 7.30 a.m. to 8.30 a.m., and met it again at noon to examine the students on the topic of the lecture. He lectured in addition to the private – or advanced – class from 11 a.m. to noon on three days a week. His lectures to the public class were heard by more students and on them his reputation was to be based. Like many others Smith modelled his lecturing on his own much-admired teacher. Years later one of his hearers recalled:

> He made a laudable attempt at first to follow Hut[ns]. [Hutcheson] animated manner, lecturing on Ethics without papers, walking up and down his class rooms but not having the same facility in this that Hut[n]. had, either naturaly or acquired by continued practise and habit in teaching his Academy at Dublin; Dr Smith soon relinquished this attempt, and read with propriety, all the rest of his valuable lectures from the desk.[3]

John Millar recalled his technique more fully:

> There was no situation in which the abilities of Mr. Smith appeared to greater advantage than as a professor. In delivering his lectures, he trusted almost entirely to extemporary elocution. His manner, though not graceful, was plain and unaffected; and, as he seemed to be always interested in the subject, he never failed to interest his hearers. Each discourse consisted commonly of several distinct propositions, which he successively endeavoured to prove and illustrate. These propositions, when announced in general terms, had, from their extent, not unfrequently something of the air of a paradox. In his attempts to explain them, he often appeared, at first, not to be sufficiently possessed of the subject, and spoke with some hesitation. As he advanced, however, the matter seemed to crowd upon him, his manner became warm and animated, and his expression easy and fluent. In points susceptible of controversy, you could easily discern, that he secretly conceived an opposition to his opinions, and that he was led upon this account to support them with greater energy and vehemence. By the fulness and variety of his illustrations, the subject gradually swelled in his hands, and acquired a dimension which, without a tedious repetition of the same views, was calculated to seize the attention of the audience, and to afford them pleasure, as well as instruction, in following the same object through all the diversity of shades and aspects in which it was

presented, and afterwards in tracing it backwards to that original proposition or general truth from which this beautiful train of speculation had proceeded.

His reputation as a Professor was accordingly raised very high, and a multitude of students from a great distance resorted to the University, merely upon his account.[4]

But content was obviously important. Smith lectured on an astonishing range of topics which included rhetoric, ethics, jurisprudence and economics. While Smith's work in these fields will be considered in later chapters it is worth observing here that the notes which have survived reveal the high level of finish which the lecturer had attained.

Smith's interest in his pupils also spread beyond their academic welfare. Of his pastoral concern for students committed to his care both the Glasgow period and his later stay in France provide one well-documented case each. The pupils concerned were aristocratic, and it is through the preservation of their family muniments that the evidence has survived.

One case which illustrates Smith's concern is that of Thomas Petty-Fitzmaurice, younger son of the 1st Lord Shelburne who was introduced to Glasgow through Gilbert Elliot of Minto, friend of both Smith and Hume. Gilbert Elliot, MP and at the time (1758) Lord of the Admiralty found in London that 'every thinking man here begins to discover the very absurd constitution of the English Universitys, without knowing what to do better', and so thought 'you might even draw a good many of the youth of this part of the world to pass a winter or two at Glasgow, notwithstanding the distance and disadvantage of the dialect ...'[5] By early 1759 young Fitzmaurice was in Glasgow and the first of several complimentary reports from Smith began to go south. To his elder brother, Lord Fitzmaurice, he reported: he 'attends all his classes with the most exact punctuality and gives more application to his studies than could reasonably be expected. I find him perfectly tractable and docile in every respect...'[6] To his father Lord Shelburne, the report was: '... the fault ought to be laid to my charge if he does not turn out at least an uncommonly good Scholar. There is not a poor boy in the college who is supported by charity and studies for bread that is more punctual in his attendance upon every part of College discipline.'[7] Fitzmaurice was certainly worked hard by Smith, who decided he should miss the logic class which would normally have been his first course of study so that he could enter Smith's own moral philosophy course, but he still attended the lectures of the professor of logic every day, as well as Smith's own lectures to both his public and his private class, and one hour each in mathematics, Greek and Latin. Smith was obviously a hard taskmaster:

> . . . in the evening and the morning [he] goes over very regularly with me the business of those different classes. I chuse rather to oppress him with business for this first winter: It keeps him constantly employed and leaves no time for Idleness. The oppression too is not so great as it may seem. The Study of Greek and latin is not at all new to him: Logic requires little attention so that moral philosophy and mathematicks are the only studies which take up much of his time.[8]

The vacation was to bring no respite:

> During this interval I propose that he should learn french and Dancing and fencing and that besides he should read with me the best greek, latin and french Authors on Moral Philosophy for two or three hours every morning, so that he will not be idle in the vacation. The Proffessor of Mathematics too proposes to teach him Euclid at that time as he was too late to learn it in the class.

Looking ahead to the next winter he was to 'be employed in perfecting himselfe in Philosophy and the Languages, but chiefly and principally in the Study of Law and history'. The attendance at the lectures of the professor of civil law, which Smith proposed, though the civil law had no authority in the English courts, was advocated because of its systematic character. By studying it he would carry 'at least the Idea of a System in his head and knows to what part of it he ought to refer every thing that he reads'.

Fortunately Lord Shelburne approved of the regimen:

> I can point out nothing, I can only approve of what you mean to do. The great fault I find with Oxford and Cambridge, is that Boys sent thither instead of being the Governed, become the Governors of the Colleges, and that Birth and Fortune there are more respected than Literary Merit; I flatter'd myself that it was not so at Glasgow, and your commendation of my Son's conformity to the Discipline of the place he is in, persuades me that you think as I do . . .

Lord Shelburne did go on to make only one point: 'Perhaps it is not yet the Season of procuring him some Instruction to mend his hand-writing, but it is what he will want . . .'[9]

During the next year a series of lengthy letters shows a meticulous attention by Smith in his reports to Lord Shelburne on his son's progress with particular and frequent accounts in every physical and medical detail of symptoms, treatment and progress of two illnesses from which he suffered, and in every financial detail of the expenditure Smith incurred on his behalf. When Smith travelled, Fitzmaurice travelled with him: to Edinburgh, where Smith took special care when he was

> obliged either to sup or dine at places where it was improper to carry him. When this happened to be the case, that I might be sure what company he was in in a very dissolute town, I ordered a small entertainment at our lodgings and invited two or three young lawyers to keep him company in my absence;

to Inverary to visit the Duke of Argyll, where 'we happened to be misinformed with regard to Dukes motions and came there two days before him during which time we stayed at a very expensive Inn'.[10] But in 1760 Smith caught a cold in March which lasted for months, found that it returned in Edinburgh in July 'having lain in a damp bed in a house in that neighbourhood',[11] and was told by Cullen that if he hoped to survive the winter he had to ride 500 miles before September. He therefore planned to go to York and return by the west of England, but this time planned to leave Fitzmaurice behind: 'He has had amusement and Dissipation enough during the ten days he staid with me in Edinburgh.'[12] Apparently Smith went further than planned, for in a letter to Shelburne in November he thanked him for hospitality at High Wycombe,[13] and with all accounts, whether academic, medical or financial went praise for the pupil.

The pupil obviously responded affectionately if one long surviving letter is a guide, written in 1762 when Fitzmaurice had gone to Oxford. It made the remark, not uncommon among Smith's correspondents that his letters 'come but Seldom' and pleads for more 'as soon as may be Convenient, tho' to you I think I may say rather sooner than that', and is a delightful mixture of news and views. 'My Mother has desir'd me to ask you concerning the Epitaph which I told her . . . you were not certain whether you could do it or no.' 'Your young People are in general rather brighter than they were in my time I'm told at present.' 'The Expence of this place is prodigious.' Lord Pembroke '. . . has run away with Miss Hunter a young Lady of equal Beauty and Fashion'.

'I heard lately an objection to an Expression in your Book, which I think has some foundation. It is in the Beginning of the 1st Section upon Custom: the Expression is a *Haunch* Button, which is not, I imagine exactly English.'[14]

It was inevitable that Smith's care for his aristocratic pupils should be recorded with care and detail, even if only for their pecuniary aspects, but there is evidence that his interest and care in his students was general. He took up the case of the Snell Exhibitioners, though acting on behalf of a University meeting, and he also interposed on behalf of two other students, 'very worthy young Men' who were about to suffer through the application of rules for bursaries founded by Anne, Duchess of Hamilton in 1694. Smith suggested the way out to the Hamiltons' law agent: 'The best way to make all easy is to give Mr Bruce Mr Watsons Presentation and to reserve for Mr Watson that which is intended for Mr Bruce. That will be equally for the benefite of both the Young Gentlemen and I am assured is agreeable to both their inclinations.'[15]

But perhaps the most surprising aspect of Smith's career at Glasgow was his continuing involvement in the administration and politics of the University — surprising that is, in view of his well-established reputation for absence of mind. The involvement was extensive and began almost immediately with the attempt to fill the vacant Chair of Logic. Smith had an unusual interest in this case, because David Hume was a possible candidate.

In 1745 David Hume had failed in his candidature for a chair at Edinburgh. His indignation at opposition to this appointment because of his philosophical views was a trifle ingenuous, especially in the light of what happened at Glasgow, where, with the patronage firmly vested in the University, the outside influences of Town Council and Presbytery, which helped determine academic appointments in Edinburgh, was absent. In the heart of the Glasgow academic community itself there was opposition to Hume. Its possible grounds, and an admission of its validity by Hume, even though he was probably unaware of the full significance of what he was writing, may be found in a letter to Francis Hutcheson, acknowledging Hutcheson's comments on the yet unpublished Book III (Of Morals) of Hume's *Treatise on Human Nature*. A difference of approach between the two is evident in the concluding paragraph:

I intend to follow your Advice in altering most of those Passages you have remarkt as defective in Point of Prudence; tho' I must own, I think you are a little too delicate. Except a Man be in Orders, or be immediately concern'd in the Instruction of Youth, I do not think his character depends upon his philosophical Speculations . . .'[16]

Hume's candidatures for chairs were for posts which fell within the second of his exceptions.

Their greater delicacy in points of prudence probably explains why both Hutcheson and Leechman were ranged against Hume when his case was being promoted at Edinburgh. Since Hutcheson refused the Edinburgh chair when it was offered to him, his opposition to Hume was not to ensure the chair for himself. But Hume was surprised 'extremely' by Hutcheson and Leechman 'who, tis said, agreed that I was a very unfit Person for such an Office. This appears to be absolutely incredible, especially with regard to the latter Gentleman. For as to Mr Hutcheson, all my Friends think, that he has been rendering me bad Offices to the utmost of his Power.'[17] Though the opposition to his Edinburgh candidature came from those who were in the van of an enlightened and liberal theology, circumspectly they were concerned about its social consequences in the instruction of youth. The same issues arose over Hume's acceptability at Glasgow. As with so many appointments in Scotland the views of the Duke of Argyll were considered critical, whatever his formal power may have been. Hume realised that Argyll's influence would have overcome the objections of the clergy had he been willing to exercise it, and it was well-known that Smith had family interests and influence in that quarter. But Smith was not happy about the appointment of Hume. An arch-proponent of the appointment was William Cullen. Even before Craigie, the professor of moral philosophy, had died, Cullen tried to enlist the support of Smith, but Smith replied in a vein recalling the opposition of Hutcheson and Leechman a few years earlier: 'I should prefer David Hume to any man for a colleague; but I am afraid the public would not be of my opinion; and the interest of the society will oblige us to have some regard to the opinion of the public.'[18] Hume's candidature failed. But the failure was more complex than the outcome of strong clerical opposition. At Edinburgh the opposition of Leechman and Hutcheson was a formidable hazard to overcome. At Glasgow the odds were greater, even though the formal influence of external forces was reduced. Smith adopted the same approach as his mentor Hutcheson some years earlier. The man appointed at Glasgow, Clow, though to later generations not comparable to Hume, was someone of wide intellectual distinction, linked with the Glasgow academic community in his work on Simson.

Though Smith had reservations about Hume's suitability for appointment to a chair in Glasgow, shortly afterwards Hume wanted Smith in Edinburgh as part of a general deployment of his friends. In 1758 he suggested he buy George Abercromby's chair of the law of nature and nations there and that Smith be replaced at Glasgow by Adam Ferguson. Though Hume had thought the Argyll interest had effectively impeded the earlier plans for his move to Glasgow, he was 'certain, that the Settlement of you here and of Ferguson at Glasgow would be perfectly easy by Lord Milton Interest'. Lord Milton, Argyll's agent, as a postscript to Hume's letter indicated '. . . can with his Finger, stop the foul Mouths of all the Roarers against Heresy'.[19] Fortunately for Glasgow, Smith was not to be persuaded.

Notes

1. *Corr.*, letter 8, Adam Smith to Robert Simson, 10 January 1751.
2. *Corr.*, letter 9, Adam Smith to William Cullen, 3 September 1751.
3. Letter from James Wodrow to the Earl of Buchan, [?] June 1808, Glasgow University Library. MSS 310/26 (Folio 167, 169).
4. Stewart, *Life of Smith*, I, 21, 22.
5. *Corr.*, letter 27, Gilbert Elliot to Adam Smith, 14 November 1758.
6. *Corr.*, letter 28, Adam Smith to Lord Fitzmaurice, 21 February 1759.
7. *Corr.*, letter 29, Adam Smith to Lord Shelburne, 10 March 1759.
8. *Corr.*, letter 30, Adam Smith to Lord Shelburne, 4 April 1759.
9. *Corr.*, letter 32, Lord Shelburne to Adam Smith, 26 April 1759.
10. *Corr.*, letter 42, Adam Smith to Lord Shelburne, 29 October 1759.
11. *Corr.*, letter 51, Adam Smith to Lord Shelburne, 15 July 1760.
12. Ibid.
13. *Corr.*, letter 52, Adam Smith to Lord Shelburne, 11 November 1760.
14. *Corr.*, letter 64, Thomas Fitzmaurice to Adam Smith, 26 February 1762.
15. *Corr.*, copy enclosed with letter 47, 15 March 1760.
16. *The Letters of David Hume*, ed. J.Y.T. Greig (Oxford, 1932) i, 34.
17. Ibid., i, 58.
18. *Corr.*, letter 10, Adam Smith to William Cullen, November 1751.
19. *Corr.*, letter 25, David Hume to Adam Smith, 8 June 1758.

5 UNIVERSITY ADMINISTRATION

The University of Glasgow was rent by major issues of university politics in the eighteenth century. Though the intellectual achievements of the University were then as great as they have ever been, and it had among its members some of the highest academic distinction, it suffered from all the faults of a small, tightly knit group, which possessed considerable power and prestige for the eighteenth century, power which – worse still in later reforming eyes of the nineteenth century – was wielded unchecked. The potential for tension was increased when the small group had among its ranks some seemingly born to dispute, to disrupt and to litigate, especially when they had to handle such major controversial and constitutional issues as the relationship between the powers of the Principal and his colleagues, questions of the respective jurisdictions of the different bodies which governed the University, and the degree of financial control and accountability exercised over the University property. All these issues simmered through the eigheenth century. Smith's involvement in them, especially when acting as Dean of Faculty or Vice-Rector, and the documentation he then produced, show another side of the scholar and teacher on which his wider reputation is based.

The administration of the University of Glasgow throughout most of the eighteenth century was based on the recommendation of a royal visitation of 1727. A fundamental issue which lay behind the visitation was the contentious issue of the powers of the Principal. Before 1727 disputes were acute, partly because the Principal, John Stirling, was an autocrat, who established his power and his ability to use it by maintaining good relations with the Chancellor, the Rector (a position held continuously by Sir John Maxwell of Pollock from 1691 to 1717), the Dean of Faculty (held successively by three ministers of Glasgow from 1701 to 1717) and by a minority within the University of which John Simson, the heretical theologian, whom Stirling defended at the General Assembly, was the most conspicuous. The majority of the Faculty, led usually by the two philosophers Carmichael and Loudon, opposed the Principal, so strongly that in 1704 Stirling had them suspended as regents until they withdrew allegations that Simson was recording some of his private acts as acts of the Faculty as a whole. In the early eighteenth century the issue of powers centred on the procedure for electing the Rector. In this dispute the majority of professors opposing the Principal were joined by the students, leading to a series of cases of tumult and gross indiscipline. Royal Commissions of 1717 and 1718 failed to bring lasting peace, though with the appointment in August 1726 of the important Commission which was to report the following year there were signs of reconciliation. In any case Stirling died at the same time as the Commission reported and was succeeded by the much less autocratic Neil Campbell.

The academic reforms of the Commission of 1727, particularly its recommendation for the abolition of regenting, are better known than its administrative recommendations, but it was the need for the latter which led to its appointment in the first place and they were to be the basis for the government of the University until 1858. In two ways it may have been possible to expect that the proposals would have ensured that some of the disputes which had rent the University during Stirling's principalship would be reduced or removed, apart from through the removal of Stirling himself: first, through recognition of the distinction between different organs of university government, though their recognition did not remove the possibility of demarcation disputes; and, second, through the provision for external supervision of the University's affairs by lay visitation. In the first field, an important distinction was made between the Faculty meeting and the University meeting, or between the Principal's meeting and the Rector's meeting to provide designations from their respective chairmen, or to apply terms from more modern days, partially if not wholly applicable, the Senate and the Court. The Faculty meeting consisted of the Principal and the professors, twelve of them at Glasgow until 1760 when Alexander Wilson, who designed the type for the foundry in the University, was appointed to the new chair of astronomy. The Rector's meeting had the Rector, the Dean of Faculty and the Minister of Glasgow as members with the Principal and the professors in attendance as assessors. The Rector, the Dean of Faculty and the Minister of Glasgow were the Visitors, following the practice of the Nova Erectio of 1577.

The issue of the election of the Rector which had led to such tumult in the first quarter of the eighteenth century was settled by all members of the University having the right of election by a rather complicated and cumbersome procedure, but the fundamental issues of respective powers and jurisdictions, of which it was a symptom, continued. Before Smith returned to Glasgow as a professor the unsolved nature of the problem of jurisdiction had become evident even where the 1727

Commission had made provision for better government. The old question of the respective jurisdictions of the University and Faculty meetings erupted in the appointment of William Leechman as professor of divinity in 1744, an appointment made largely at the instigation and with the encouragement of Hutcheson. Leechman was elected on the casting vote of the Rector at a University or Rector's meeting, at which assessors voted. Unabashed at their own irregularity in voting at a meeting at which they were present only as assessors, the defeated section, which included the Principal, then queried the jurisdiction of the University meeting over the appointment on the grounds that the emoluments for the chair came mainly from funds under the control of the Faculty. In spite of the attempts of the Commission of 1727 to clarify jurisdictions the Faculty objected to any proposal that its powers to dispose of its funds should be impeded. More generally it resented any dilution of its power by the lay element in the University or Rector's meeting, even when the touchy question of finance was not an issue. Yet a number of matters showed the need for some form of external or lay control in the mid-eighteenth century: by William Cross's four years' tenure from 1746 of the chair of law during which he never gave a lecture; by William Rouet, the professor of ecclesiastical history, who was refused leave of absence to go to tutor the son of Lord Hopetoun in 1759 but still did so and drew his salary until he resigned in December 1761; by John Anderson, who was so ready to find every conceivable fault in his colleagues, but who used his own vote when professor of oriental languages to aid his translation to the chair of natural philosophy in 1757. Smith was personally involved in the second and third of these cases. He showed an awareness of some of the wider implications of the actions of his colleagues. In the case of Rouet, Smith was one of a majority who voted in favour of a resolution declaring his office vacant shortly after he left to become the tutor, but since the chair of ecclesiastical history was a Crown appointment, Smith and John Millar were despatched to Edinburgh to seek the legal opinion of James Ferguson of Pitfour and James Burnet of Monboddo. When the opinion was given that the procedure was irregular, a University meeting on 26 November 1761 'being willing to give satisfaction to the most scrupulous' agreed to reverse the Minute. This time Smith's vote was not one of the only two dissents recorded. By contrast, in the case of Anderson, Smith was the leading figure among the dissenters, always supported by Joseph Black, from the first intimation of the vacancy to Anderson's ultimate appointment. When the election was ratified, at a University meeting on 21 October 1757, the minute states

Smith's position clearly. He did not vote, not because he had any objection to Anderson 'in whose Election he would willingly have concurred with the majority of his Colleagues; but only because he regards the method of proceeding as irregular in consequence of yesterday's Protest, [at the precipitate nature of the proceedings and at Anderson's use of his own vote in proceedings where he was a candidate] and as what may establish a proceeding which is liable to the greatest abuse . . .'[1]

Smith's approach to these two problems of possible abuse of power by the Faculty for the benefit of their own members justifies, or at least explains, why the University was subjected to so much venomous criticism from William Thom, the Minister of Govan, and from John Anderson himself, where his own interests were not involved, and so why the protests of later reformers led to the major Royal Commission on the Scottish universities of the 1830s. But Smith was sufficiently of the eighteenth century that, while apparently aware of potential danger in individual cases, he did not move wholly to the position of the Commissioners of 1727 and accept the need for some form of external supervision and check on the activities of the Faculty. The chief forms of that supervision after 1727 were the introduction of the Rector and the Dean of Faculty into the University meeting and the provision for Visitation by the Rector, the Dean of Faculty and the Minister of Glasgow. As the matter of Leechman's election to the chair of divinity had shown, the powers of the University, or more specifically of its non-Faculty members were soon challenged, both by the assessors acting effectively as full members and by attempts being made to have business transferred to the Faculty meeting, where the lay element was absent. The provision for outside intervention had been effectively eroded before Smith returned to Glasgow as a professor, yet he was not merely to condone such action but to be a major participant in the further erosion, leading to the conclusion that his objections in the case of Rouet and Anderson were specific to the procedure being adopted in each case and not part of a general desire to restrict the power of the Faculty. Later actions indicate Smith was probably as much on the side of the advocates of the power of the Faculty as any. External influence was removed, in effect, by the outside offices or their deputyship being held by members of the Faculty, including Smith. From 1732 to 1767, except for 1746 to 1750, the Dean of Faculty was a professor, including Smith from 1760 to 1762; from 1754 the Rector rarely attended meetings and left his duties to be discharged by a Vice-Rector, again a professor, and once more Smith in his last days at Glasgow, from 1762; though it was only from 1803 that the Minister of Glasgow was also the Principal of the University. In these ways, whatever the constitution, the practice of it gave control to the Faculty, and an appeal to the Visitors meant an appeal to its members.

The general irregularities came to a head in a particular case while Smith was at Glasgow and led him to play an important mediating role in trying to unravel the issues. The roots of the trouble in the particular case lay in the incapacity of the Principal Neil Campbell after 1752 and came to a head in consequence of the appointment of Leechman as Principal in 1761. In the incapacity of a Principal the Commissioners of 1727 had held that the Faculty or Principal's meeting should be convened by the Senior Regent. By 1752 the regents had become professors and so the responsibility to act fell on James Moor, the professor of Greek, but Moor ceased to hold meetings after 7 November 1755. No meeting of the Faculty was then held for exactly six years, until 6 November 1761. Moor's failure to act was of little practical consequence because much of the business was being transferred to the Rector's or University meeting, and so the business of the University was being carried on. But in consequence the practice of the government of the University, in which Smith was an active and willing participant, had departed from the constitutional procedure laid down in 1727. One feature of the practice seems certain. The position and power of the Faculty had been established. Its members had been appointed to offices whose incumbents were supposed to exercise some form of external constraint, or were acting as deputies to the holders of such offices; such individuals legally dominated the Rector's or University meeting and, since the other members of the Faculty did not limit their activities at its meetings to their proper role as assessors, the distinction between the Principal's or Faculty meeting and the Rector's or University meeting was unclear. In these circumstances the power of the professors could be exerted against the Principal, particularly when Campbell was not an autocrat of the type of his predecessor, Stirling, or of his successor, Leechman, and partly through the increasing use of the Rector's meeting, which the Principal did not chair, to transact business.

In June 1761 Leechman became Principal and promptly asserted the power of the principal. Smith quickly became a central figure in the subsequent negotiations. Leechman, who had been Vice-Rector, refused to attend the first Rector's meeting after he became Principal and argued that it could not be held in the absence of the Rector, since he

(Leechman) was no longer Vice-Rector. The professoriate met, elected Smith, who was Dean of Faculty, as chairman, and proceeded to transact the business of the day. Though Smith moved backwards and forwards between Leechman and the meeting, the Principal could not be moved. Whatever the merits of Leechman's behaviour, the meeting of professors, all assessors, as the Rector's meeting, when neither Rector or Vice-Rector were present, was palpably irregular. Its transactions were ratified at a meeting at which the Rector was present in the following month. Smith was being propelled into a key role in the constitutional wrangling. Once the immediate matter was over, he was appointed in April 1762 to chair a committee to adjudicate on the thorny question of the respective powers of the Rector and the Principal and reported in August of the same year. The report of the Committee over which Smith presided is long and detailed; it shows a command of University business both in theory and in practice. It stresses how practice had evolved beyond the Charter of 1577, to be reorganised by the Commissioners of 1727, but that much that had taken place since had no formal statutory backing. Yet the report does not reveal Smith as a stickler for constitutional nicety but rather as someone, who, while fully recognising the constitutional requirements, was anxious to show the variety of practice over the years and the need to follow ways of conducting University business which had proved effective in the past. Good working methods rather than exact legal procedure seemed to be his objective. So a role was recognised for almost everyone. 'First to the Rectors meeting fell the Elections of masters, the employment of the Excrepence of the Revenue and the final passing and approving of the annual accounts of the ordinary Revenue.' 'To the Dean of facultys meeting fell the conferring of degrees, the care of the Library, the Election of the Kings bursars 26th of June, and in general every thing relative to Learning.' 'To the Principals meeting fell all the other ordinary affairs of the College.'[2] Smith recognised that the Rector and Dean of Faculty were auditors by the Charter of 1577, and ought to be so for the revenues from the Archbishopric and Sub-Deanery which were given to the Faculty and which some of his colleagues held should not be externally audited. But he did not tackle the anomalous situations which had evolved through provisions for external auditing and more general external supervision, being largely nullified through the appointment of members of faculty to the office of Dean of Faculty, which Smith himself held when he submitted his Committee's report, and to that of Vice-Rector to absentee rectors, as Smith himself was to become later in 1762. While Smith was trying to resolve a difficult constitutional wrangle between the powers of the Principal's and the Rector's meetings, he was doing little to remove the increasing power of the Faculty. Though formally the dispute may seem to be between the respective powers of those inside and those outside the University, it was effectively a dispute on the power of the Principal against those of his colleagues who held the offices of Vice-Rector and Dean of Faculty. It was an internal dispute; nobody wanted outside intervention. Smith left Glasgow with the dispute still rumbling on. In 1771 the Court of Session gave the Principal's meeting the power to appoint the professors and to administer all the funds, so the practice which had grown up may have been considered to be regularised. It certainly concentrated power in the professoriate, especially if the Visitors were ineffective. Smith's activities over this complex issue are therefore interesting, not only in showing a competent university administrator at work, and how as a member of a closed corporation he was guilty of many of the faults which he pointed out in such bodies. He knew the snares and pitfalls from the inside.

The wrangle over the constitutional position of the Rector and Principal was only the major matter of University administration with which Smith had to deal. His appointment as Dean of Faculty and as Vice-Rector showed the general respect and trust he enjoyed both in and out of the University, so his employment in University business is not surprising, and the University records show him tackling various matters. They fall into different categories: the first concern was buildings, repairs to many of the professors' houses and the rebuilding of the Principal's; ensuring adequate academic accommodation — the building of a new laboratory and the conversion of the old into a mathematics classroom 'with all proper frugality' or the provision of a room to hold new apparatus purchased for the natural philosophy class; the provision of a fencing room. Secondly, Smith undertook much responsibility for supervising some of the College's complicated financial transactions, and especially of having the accounts approved wherever necessary; sometimes these related to the administration of various mortifications for bursaries, at other times he was commissioned to gain the requisite approval in Edinburgh and London of the Scottish Barons of Exchequer and of the Treasury for the revenues of the Archbishopric, the Sub-Deanery and other revenues of the University. Thirdly, Smith became involved in external negotiations, notably with the town council — to obtain an assurance from the Provost that students who brought meal into Glasgow were not subjected to the usual exaction on entry; and, with others, 'to confer with the Magistrates concerning the most proper methods of preventing the Establishment of a Playhouse in Glasgow';[3] 'to inspect the Incroachments upon the College lands bordering upon the Molendiner burn, as also the dunghill in the Weavers Vennel laid close to the College houses . . . and to get a visit of the Magistrates, and also of the Dean of Guild, if needful'.[4] It is therefore hardly surprising that Smith was frequently commissioned to undertake specific matters of University business and that he often acted in other University business even when his role in doing so was unclear. The best example is his occupation of the chair of the University meeting after Leechman became Principal, but there are other less dramatic examples. In the running disputes with Balliol College over the Snell Exhibitions, perhaps with his own experiences in mind, he wrote in 1762 after 'several remonstrances from the Exhibitioners . . . complaining that they yet enjoy but a very small part of the Advantages which they expect to derive from the late degree in Chancery . . .' A clue to Smith's influential role in the University comes at the conclusion of the letter, when he informs the recipient, Joshua Sharpe at Lincoln's Inn, who dealt with the University's business in Chancery, that though Joseph Black had succeeded Robert Simson as Clerk 'The University meeting desires . . . that for the future you would correspond either with him or with me as you think proper.'[5] Smith was a leading figure in all affairs of the University. Perhaps, as one issue shows, it was because he had a marked degree of perception of the problems involved, the relevance of which in this case his irascible and litigious colleague John Anderson was to illustrate by litigation after Smith left. It concerned another complicated matter. The University had been granted tacks [leases] on the revenues of the old Archbishopric and Sub-Deanery of Glasgow. In return for collecting all the revenues the University was allowed to retain £300 annually, but accounts had to be submitted for one tack to the Treasury and for the other to the Scottish Barons of Exchequer. Smith became much involved in the accounting procedure, and was the university's main agent in the tedious and protracted negotiations which always ensued. A major difficulty in accounting, which Smith foresaw, was that the accounts of the crop of one year could not be closed until several years had passed, with the danger that the deficiencies of one year could be made good by the surplus of another because of the overlap. After Smith had left, John Anderson — while still a professor — took the University to court on this issue in 1775, an acrimonious dispute from which Smith was probably only too glad to be free.

One of Smith's formal offices, that of Quaestor, deserves special attention, since it provides an insight into some of his intellectual interests. The Library was in a state of transition when Smith was at Glasgow. The new Library had been built and the move of books to it started in 1745, but the proceedings were protracted, particularly because of the new building's dampness. In January 1754 the minute of a Faculty meeting ordered 'the drains about the new Library to be cleared, and the heap of earth on its north end to be removed; both these being absolutely necessary for removing the moisture from the Library'.[6] Progress was sufficient for the practice of levying a stent [tax or imposition] on students for the purchase of books to be revived later that year. Smith was appointed Quaestor temporarily for six months from 26 December 1755 in place of Cullen on the latter's resignation from the University, and became Quaestor permanently from 1758 to 1760. The sums involved were not large. During Smith's two years of office the charge was £98 10s 10d and the discharge £116 1s 8d.[7] The predominating subject matter of the books purchased is not what might be expected, superficially at any rate, from Smith. Though this was a time when he first published the *Theory of Moral Sentiments* and was formulating many of the ideas which were to merge into the *Wealth of Nations*, the works he ordered are not chiefly philosophical or economic. Though his own library was to grow to about one third of the 5,643 books in the University library in 1760, it was not so large in his Glasgow days and so Smith must have been much more dependent on the University Library's resources than he became later, especially during his Kirkcaldy days after the return from France. The dominating classes of the books he bought show his interest in the field which never came to the fruition of major publication, even though it was planned when he was at Glasgow, and — perhaps even more important — show the basis on which so much of his work was based in any case. The two main classes were law and, even more important, contemporary and especially historical studies of foreign countries. This historical and institutional bias dominated his library purchases as well as his work.

Notes

1. Records of the University of Glasgow, 13 February 1755, quoted in *Adam Smith as Student and Professor*, W.R. Scott, (Glasgow, 1937), 190.

2. Records of the University of Glasgow, 13 August 1762, quoted in Scott, *Adam Smith*, 214.

3. Records of the University of Glasgow, 7 December 1762, quoted in Scott, *Adam Smith*, 165.

4. Records of the University of Glasgow, 21 May 1755, quoted in Scott, *Adam Smith*, 145.

5. *Corr.*, letter 67, Adam Smith to Joshua Sharpe, 15 June 1762.

6. Records of the University of Glasgow, 22 January 1754, quoted in Scott, *Adam Smith*, 175.

7. Quaestor Accounts, University of Glasgow, 26 June 1758 to 26 June 1760, quoted in Scott, *Adam Smith*, 178–84.

6 THE CITY OF GLASGOW

The Glasgow of the last two centuries, the Glasgow of the days after Smith, was very different from the one he knew. The city's reputation was well established long before the eighteenth century. Though an episcopal and not a royal burgh, it had rights and privileges which went with royal burghal status, as well as its duties and liabilities. Its status was enhanced further in the fifteenth century. It followed the lead of St Andrews by the foundation of its university in 1450-1 and by the elevation of its diocese to archepiscopal status in 1491-2. But because of its location another event of the century, of uncertain dating but probably in 1410, the replacement of the old wooden bridge across the Clyde by a stone structure of eight arches, was perhaps as important as educational and ecclesiastical change in building up the status of the city. All brought people and trade to Glasgow, and, whatever its burghal status or lack of it, Glasgow was able to maintain its power and position against its royal neighbours of Dumbarton, Renfrew and Rutherglen, though it was only in 1690, after a century of varying administrative practice, that a new royal charter and act of parliament brought Glasgow into line with other burghs. Though Glasgow finally shed much of its ecclesiastical past only a half-century before Smith went there as a student, its growing economic potential was already evident. In the periodic revisions of the burghs' stent-roll Glasgow gradually ascended: eleventh in 1535, ninth in 1557, seventh in 1578, sixth in 1587, fifth in 1591, joint fourth in 1635, fourth in 1649, but only slightly behind Dundee and Aberdeen; then second only to Edinburgh, though still a considerable way behind, in 1670.

The key to the increased status was evident in a number of ways in the seventeenth century, notably in the growth of the city's trade. The portents of the successes of the eighteenth century were evident. In spite of the restrictions of the Navigation Acts which excluded other nationalities, including the Scots, from trading with the English colonies, Glasgow imported its first cargo of tobacco in 1674 and a prosperous illicit trade was already built up before the Treaty of Union finally made it legal. But apart from the difficulties to which the illegality of some of the trade gave rise there were other problems. During the Protectorate, when a common commercial code was applied to both Scotland and England, Thomas Tucker could predict in his official report that there was a future for the trade of Glasgow 'were she not checquered and kept under by the shallowness of her river'. The problem of the poor navigation on the river was not the concern of Glasgow alone. In 1556 Dumbarton, Glasgow and Renfrew – for all their rivalry – co-operated to try to remove some of the sandbanks at Dumbuck. Attempts at improvement were intermittent and relatively unsuccessful until the eighteenth century.

The growth of trade before the parliamentary union of 1707 was accompanied by some specialised industrial development, which, though its importance was to be swamped by developments of different kinds, left a lasting imprint on the city's industrial structure in some branches of mechanical engineering and in the chemical industry. Sugar-boiling was the pathway to fortune in the west of Scotland in the later seventeenth century and the first of several successful concerns, the Wester Sugar House, was founded in 1667. But a range of other industries appeared at the same time, some linked to domestic needs – candle-making, coal-mining, cloth-making – others linked more directly to trade beyond the city, sometimes overseas – soaperies, ropeworks, glassworks.

Though a thriving city and one to which open access to overseas markets, especially in the colonies, was vital, the city of Glasgow did not generally favour the proposed parliamentary union. The experience of the Darien disaster had a souring effect, for Glasgow as for others, but, whatever the reasons, the protests were evident, both before and after 1707. In the closing sessions of the Scottish Parliament the citizens of Glasgow petitioned against the proposed union, and led riots against the Malt Tax of 1725 which was one of the most resented measures of the Union Parliament. But the attitude to the Union was equivocal. Whatever reservations the city may have had about the parliamentary union, it firmly opposed the Jacobites. It played a large part in the Covenanting opposition to the later Stuarts and in no way supported the Jacobite cause in 1715 and 1745. When Charles Edward returned through Glasgow on his retreat from Derby the city fathers' sole objective was to be rid of him and his followers as quickly as possible, even if it did cost them a payment of clothing. The contrast with the attitude of Oxford, which Smith was then leaving, are obvious. By then the parliamentary union was beginning to have advantages for Glasgow, which were sufficient to bring even the waverers and doubters into the ranks of its supporters. Its citizens were ready to judge the Union by its economic opportunities. When they proved to be real, and the results substantial, acceptance followed.

The Glasgow which Smith entered as a student in the late 1730s, and even more so the city to which he returned in the 1750s was then one in which the Union had strong support, a city which was not attracted by any of the supporters of the old social or political order, particularly not by Jacobitism and especially not if tainted by any non-Presbyterian influences which may have emanated from the Highlands. Glasgow was a city where a changing economy was emerging and growing. The restrictions of the shallowness of the Clyde were recognised and in the 1660s the Glasgow magistrates developed Port Glasgow as a trading outpost. Though a quay was built at the Broomielaw in the centre of Glasgow in 1663, serious attempts to improve the river to allow trade to be brought into Glasgow were delayed for almost a century. John Smeaton surveyed the river in 1755. An Act of Parliament authorising improvement was obtained in 1759, but the action taken — of building jetties along the river, so confining it to a narrow channel, which could be deepened by dredging — followed a survey by John Golbourne in 1768. The improvements in the river coincided with the growth of trade, especially the tobacco trade, from about 1740. Scottish imports, then about 20 per cent of British imports, began to rise and Glasgow to assume its supremacy. The Navigation Acts gave the Glasgow merchants an assured position, though their legal privileges had to be supplemented by greater efficiency to gain predominance, particularly through the exploitation of the use of factors or the storage system instead of the old consignment method of trading. The significance of the Navigation Acts in Glasgow's trade is evident in the collapse in 1776: imports of tobacco in 1775 were nearly 46m lbs; in 1776 they were almost 7.5m lbs; in 1777, less than 300,000 lbs. Re-exports fell correspondingly: in 1775 they were over 30m lbs; in 1776 nearly 23m lbs; in 1777, 5.5m lbs; in 1778, about 2.3m lbs. The success thereafter of Glasgow's trade, more diversified in both commodities and direction, confirmed the existence of the indigenous enterprise which also lay behind the city's commercial success. Yet the intriguing aspect of the rising economic success of Glasgow during the period when Smith was living there, and when he was formulating some of the ideas in the lectures which were to be permanently embodied later in the *Wealth of Nations*, was its basis of a carrying trade which in turn owed much to the privileges of the Navigation Acts. The city's later economic success without the protection of the Navigation Acts does not invalidate the view that the tobacco trade relied on them while it dominated the economy of the city in the mid-eighteenth century.

Though the tobacco trade was central to the city's economy it was not the only point of growth. Other areas of growth were linked to it. Its dominating contribution is evident in the industrial ventures which continued to expand in the city, and which perpetuated the structure which had emerged even before 1707. One branch of the industrial structure which held a portent for the future was textile production, not, however, of linen, of which Daniel Defoe, visiting Glasgow, noted even before the Union, that 'they make a very great quantity of it [linen] and send it to the plantations as their principal merchandise'. Muslin also 'they make so good and so fine that great quantities of them are sent into England and to the British Plantations, where they sell at a good price'. The future textile interest of Glasgow and district lay in the production of cotton in the late eighteenth and early nineteenth centuries. If that specialism lay in the future when Smith lived and worked in Glasgow in the 1750s and early 1760s, so too were the heavy industries which later still were to give Glasgow its reputation. Even then the presence of James Watt in the College of Glasgow itself was only a portent of the future. Watt was first employed by the University in October 1756 to clean a legacy of astronomical instruments which it had received. Thereafter he continued to work as a mathematical instrument maker within the University, thereby avoiding the restrictions which the incorporated trades — in his case the hammermen — retained until 1846. He lived in the College until 1763, kept his workshop there till 1773, and in 1765 devised his main invention of the separate condenser in the steam engine. The famous patent was taken out in 1769, but commercial success came only later after Matthew Boulton took a share in the patent in 1773 and Watt moved south into successful partnership with him. Watt's work at Glasgow was carried out in close association with Smith's colleagues: with the irascible John Anderson, the professor of natural philosophy, whose model of a Newcomen engine Watt was repairing when he had the idea of a separate condenser; with John Robison, lecturer in chemistry and later professor of natural philosophy at Edinburgh; and with Joseph Black, lecturer in chemistry and later professor at Edinburgh, who was to be one of Smith's executors, and whose discovery of the principle of latent heat may be held to have been an essential prerequisite to the idea of the separate condenser. Smith was also on intimate terms with the joint-holder of the first patent of 1769, John Roebuck, so intimate indeed that, when Roebuck's bankruptcy in 1773 forced him to surrender his share in the patent, he informed Smith of his financial affairs in a letter which showed the wide-ranging interests and links of the two men, and in which Roebuck — writing in November 1775 — looked forward to the publication of the *Wealth of Nations*. There is no direct evidence of contact between Watt and Smith, but such a deficiency is insufficient grounds for ruling out any link. The periods of their residence in the College overlapped, and it was a small and intimate society, with Watt entering it not as an obscure cleaner of instruments but as a kinsman of the professor of humanity. Even more important are the close mutual friendships, especially with Black and Roebuck. On the grounds of such circumstantial evidence, the usual absence of correspondence or similar corroborating evidence from Smith is no justification for denying that Smith and Watt were close acquaintances during the period of overlap of their stays in Glasgow. Watt's main achievements came after Smith had left Glasgow, but, as the letter from Roebuck to Smith in 1775 shows the extent of the intimacy between the two, it is not unreasonable to infer some knowledge of these latter achievements on the part of Smith, though such a proposition is less certain than that of their acquaintance. Even if the acquaintance is accepted, and even if knowledge of Watt's later achievements is credited, their significance was not — and probably could not — have been fully appreciated by Smith. The success of the Boulton and Watt partnership emerged after Smith had formulated most of his major economic ideas and the diffusion of the new technology was a relatively slow and protracted process. Whatever knowledge Smith may have had was of its potential rather than of its achievement. Matthew Boulton was able to proclaim that he dealt in power, but the significance of that claim is evident only in retrospect.

The presence of Watt in the College of Glasgow was therefore only a portent of the industrial future of Glasgow and the west of Scotland. Smith worked in a city which in the 1750s had shed most of the trappings of its medieval past, though it was administered by an oligarchic town council and had its incorporations of merchants and of a variety of trades, which perpetuated their own forms of privilege and restrictions, but it was not the centre of an industrial complex. Smith's Glasgow was one in which the old order had given way to a new one, but to one based primarily on the ascendancy of the commercial aristocracy, the economic success of which rested largely on the privileges and restrictions of the Navigation Acts.

Three features of the life of Glasgow are relevant, though the form of the connection varies. First, the carrying trade, which according to Smith in the *Wealth of Nations* was the least productive use of stock, following only after agriculture, manufacturing industry and internal trade, was the source of Glasgow's increasing wealth. Smith's priorities in the distribution of stock did not deny that every one of these four outlets which he cited engendered increased wealth; he was merely placing them in order or priorities. But he emerged as someone who evaluated less highly the contribution of the merchant community of the type in which he lived and worked, and with which he had many contacts. On the other hand the activities and structure of the community illustrated well the principles on which he made his judgement. Being an entrepôt trade, carrying especially Europe's tobacco from the plantations to Europe and then often taking back to the colonies goods which were not of British make, and even more often not of Scottish make, in a three-cornered form of trade, Glasgow's foreign trade of the eighteenth century was not a means of encouraging large-scale development of the home economy. It is even possible to suggest, though the matter is one of some difference of opinion, that foreign trade and the growth of much manufacturing industry operated independently of each other. Certainly when the balance of the Glasgow economy began to change towards an increasing emphasis on manufacturing industry – first of cotton and later of the heavy industries – towards the end of Smith's life, the new and larger scale industrial development of those days was largely independent of the older carrying trade.

Secondly, the merchant community demonstrated some of Smith's most penetrating views on human character, both favourable and unfavourable. Smith's hero, the frugal man, who reinvested his profits, was well represented among the Glasgow merchants, as was their desire to use some – but not all – of their surplus profits to invest in land and so to become country gentlemen. Their success was also a superb example of the beneficial effects of mercantilist restrictions, in this case of the Navigation Acts, as the way of building up their trade and profits, but in this case more probably at the expense of those foreigners to whom the trade and the colonies were closed. In the case of Britain – and especially of Glasgow – the compilation of a balance sheet of the gains and losses from the restrictions, if one had been possible, would probably have revealed a positive balance in favour of Glasgow. After 1776 Glasgow showed that it was still possible to retain a large and flourishing overseas trade even when the mercantilist restrictions began to crumble, and the industrial economy which was built up shortly thereafter depended for its success on the buoyancy of free and unhindered foreign trade. But of the restrictive or mercantilist basis on which the trading successes of Smith's day were built there can be no doubt. A fascinating reflection on Smith's relations with the merchant community of Glasgow therefore is that in his days in the city, its success was built not only on the carrying trade, which he deemed the least productive of the various ways of using stock, but on the mercantilist restrictions which he was so anxious to attack and destroy. It may be held that Glasgow's later and more lasting success was to prove the validity of Smith's propositions — both on the contribution of the carrying trade to increasing wealth and of the mercantilist restrictions as the basis of trading success — but it is still something of a paradoxical conclusion that many of Smith's practical conclusions for his day represented in effect criticism of the contemporaries with whom he was often on terms of friendship. Perhaps neither Smith nor his friends were as aware of the significance of some of his criticisms as later generations have become.

Thirdly, the changing economic conditions were linked to the changing administrative and social structure of Glasgow. To Smith and others, changes in the means of subsistence provided a major explanation of the changes in society, a view he worked out at length in his Glasgow lectures. A possible explanation of that emphasis is to be found in the social and economic structure of Glasgow at the time the lectures were being given.

Evidence of the new social order grew after Smith left Glasgow, as in the organisation of the merchants into the Chamber of Commerce in 1783, but their leadership of civic life was established when he was there. It was not a complete exaggeration when Provost Andrew Cochrane attributed the city's rise to 'four young men of talents and spirit who started at one time in business and whose example gave success to the rest', the four being William Cunninghame, Alexander Spiers, John Glassford and James Ritchie.[1] Smith had personal links with such members of the merchant community and through them gained an insight into commercial practice. In Glasgow he participated fully in clubs and less formal associations in which the intellectual intercourse which accompanied dining ensured that news and ideas circulated widely and were readily and openly criticised. In his days as a professor at Glasgow Smith was associated with three such clubs, each of which differed considerably from the others. The most important of the three, in its own right and because of the influence it was able to bring to bear on Smith's own work, was the Political Economy Club, founded by Andrew Cochrane in 1743, but firmly established only after the Jacobite Rebellion. Its members included most of the leading merchants of the city, notably John Glassford and Alexander Spiers, and, as its title suggests, it encouraged the discussion of all matters relating to trade which would be of interest to its members. Smith gave his lost 'Lecture of 1755' to this club. The contribution of the discussions, and of the personal links which Smith was able to cultivate with its members, gave a practical insight into commercial life and practice. According to Alexander Carlyle, the Minister of Inveresk, Smith acknowledged his obligation to Andrew Cochrane's information when he was compiling material for the *Wealth of Nations*. The second club was the Literary Society, which was founded in 1752 and which had a greater range of members than the Political Economy Club, with the merchant community, while still present, less dominant. Though the Literary Society was chiefly concerned with literary, philosophical and political questions, it extended its interests to commercial matters, as on 23 January 1752, when Smith read to the society his account of Hume's Essay on Commerce. The third club was different yet again, a designedly social club, founded by Robert Simson, the mathematician, which met for supper every Saturday in Anderston, then a separate village on the western outskirts of Glasgow. The clubs show Smith's many links, both personal and intellectual, with the merchants who were behind the rise of Glasgow to its commercial eminence in the eighteenth century. To draw Smith's attention to such issues may have been one of the main contributions which the life of Glasgow made to Smith's thought when he lived and worked there.

Notes

1. David Murray, *Early Burgh Organisation in Scotland* (Glasgow, 1924) i, 447–8.

7 LECTURES ON RHETORIC AND THE CONSIDERATIONS CONCERNING THE FIRST FORMATION OF LANGUAGES

John Millar remarked, in a note to Dugald Stewart, that:

> In the Professorship of Logic, to which Mr Smith was appointed on his first introduction into this University, he soon saw the necessity of departing widely from the plan that had been followed by his predecessors . . . Accordingly, after exhibiting a general view of the powers of the mind, and explaining so much of the ancient logic as was requisite to gratify curiosity with respect to an artificial method of reasoning, which had once occupied the universal attention of the learned, he dedicated all the rest of his time to the delivery of a system of rhetoric and belles-lettres. The best method of explaining and illustrating the various powers of the human mind, the most useful part of metaphysics, arises from an examination of the several ways of communicating our thoughts by speech, and from an attention to the principles of those literary compositions which contribute to persuasion or entertainment. By these arts, every thing that we perceive or feel, every operation of our minds, is expressed and delineated in such a manner, that it may be clearly distinguished and remembered. There is, at the same time, no branch of literature more suited to youth at their first entrance upon philosophy than this, which lays hold of their taste and feelings.[1]

The notes discovered by J.M. Lothian in 1958 and dated 1762-63 amply confirm Millar's claim with regard to Smith's originality, and at the same time clearly reflect what must have been the substance of the Edinburgh lectures.

One of the first major problems to which Smith addressed himself in the *Rhetoric* was that of language. The subject was taken up in Lecture 3 in the midst of the related discussion of grammar and subsequently expanded into the printed version, *Considerations concerning the First Formation of Languages*, which appeared in the *Philological Miscellany* in 1761 and in the third edition of the *Theory of Moral Sentiments* in 1767. Dugald Stewart was correct in saying that Smith 'set a high value' on the piece, although many modern commentators would probably agree with Stewart's judgement that 'it deserves our attention less on account of the opinions which it contains, than as a specimen of

66

a particular sort of inquiry, which, so far as I know, is entirely of modern origin, and which seems, in a peculiar degree, to have interested Mr. Smith's curiosity.'[2] The reference is to Smith's interest in *conjectural* history, to that form of historical investigation where in the absence of direct evidence 'we are under a necessity of supplying the place of fact by conjecture; and when we are unable to ascertain how men have actually conducted themselves upon particular occasions, of considering in what manner they are likely to have proceeded, from the principles of their nature, and the circumstances of their external situation'.[3] Smith provided early evidence of the technique, opening his treatment of the development of language by supposing two 'savages, who had never been taught to speak, but had been bred up remote from the societies of men'.[4]

The conjectural technique is useful in some stages of the enquiry into the origin and development of language. A more telling criticism is that Smith's account is based upon insufficient data. He concentrates chiefly on the classical languages, together with French, Italian and English, and his argument rests upon the view that linguistic structure can be discussed basically in terms of parts of speech.

Smith's treatment is 'genetic' thus placing him in the 'organic school';[5] that is, among those who believed that language grew with the development of mankind. His argument is also distinguished by the emphasis given to those psychological characteristics which help to explain the origin and development of languages which, once formed, serve further to enhance our capacity for expression. Smith gave particular emphasis to man's capacity for comparison, systematisation, and a growing capability for acts of abstraction.

The points at issue can be conveyed by taking some examples from the *Considerations*:

Although Smith stated that 'Verbs must necessarily have been coeval with the very first attempts towards the formation of language', he opened the published version of the argument with the suggestion that his hypothetical savages would institute nouns substantive as 'one of the first steps towards the formation of language'.[6] Initially they would ascribe particular names to familiar objects of immediate relevance such as the cave which gave them shelter, or the fountain which provided water, before extending these terms to cover the whole class of things to which these objects were eventually perceived to belong. Once this step had been taken, Smith observed that the savage would face the need to distinguish one particular object from others of the same general species, by reference either to its peculiar *qualities*, or to the specific *relation* which it might bear to other things. Hence the origin of nouns adjective which express a quality, e.g. the *green* tree and of prepositions which express a relation, e.g. the green tree *of* the meadow.

It was Smith's contention that the emergence of both nouns adjective and of prepositions involved a considerable effort of *abstraction* and therefore that they would be *preceded* by simpler responses to the problems raised. For example it was argued that:

> The man who first distinguished a particular object by the epithet of *green*, must have observed other objects that were not *green*, from which he meant to separate it by this appellation . . . The institution of this name, therefore, supposes comparison. It likewise supposes some degree of abstraction. The person who first invented this appellation must have distinguished the quality from the object to which it belonged, and must have conceived the object as capable of subsisting without the quality. The invention, therefore, even of the simplest nouns adjective, must have required more metaphysics than we are apt to be aware of. The different mental operations, of arrangement or classing, of comparison, and of abstraction, must all have been employed, before even the names of the different colours, the least metaphysical of all nouns adjective, could be instituted. From all of which I infer, that when languages were beginning to be formed, nouns adjective would by no means be the words of the earliest invention.[7]

Smith suggested that variation in nouns substantive would probably precede the emergence of nouns adjective, pointing to the fact that 'in many languages, the qualities both of sex and of the want of sex, are expressed by different terminations in the nouns substantive, which denote objects so qualified . . . Julius, Julia; Lucretius, Lucretia' etc.[8] Smith believed that the different formations of nouns substantive might forestall the need for nouns adjective at least for some time, and that:

> When nouns adjective came to be invented, it was natural that they should be formed with some similarity to the substantives, to which they were to serve as epithets or qualifications. Men would naturally give them the same terminations with the substantives to which they were first applied, and from that love of similarity of sound, from that delight in the returns of the same syllables, which is the foundation of analogy in all languages they would be apt to vary the

termination of the same adjective, according as they had occasion to apply it to a masculine, to a feminine, or to a neutral substantive. They would say, *magnus lupus, magna lupa, magnum pratum*, when they meant to express a great *he wolf*, a great *she wolf*, a great *meadow*'.[9]

The preposition suggests the need for an even greater effort of abstraction than that involved in the development of nouns adjective. Smith offered three reasons in support of this contention. First, that 'relation is, in itself, a more metaphysical object than a quality'. Secondly:

> though prepositions always express the relation which they stand for, in concrete with the co-relative object, they could not have originally been formed without a considerable effort of abstraction. A preposition denotes a relation, and nothing but a relation. But before men could institute a word, which signified a relation, and nothing but a relation, they must have been able, in some measure, to consider this relation abstractedly from the related objects: since the idea of those objects does not, in any respect, enter into the signification of the preposition . . .
>
> Thirdly, a preposition is from its nature a general word, which, from its very first institution, must have been considered as equally applicable to denote any other similar relation. The man who first invented the word *above*, must not only have distinguished, in some measure, the relation of *superiority* from the objects which were so related, but he must also have distinguished this relation from other relations, such as, from the relation of *inferiority* denoted by the word *below*, from the relation of *juxta-position*, expressed by the word *beside* and the like.[10]

Smith concluded, as in the case of nouns adjective, that the problem would be temporarily avoided by using apparently simpler devices, such as the invention of *cases*. For example, he suggested that the use of the genitive and dative cases in Greek and Latin in effect supply the place of the preposition, as in the example *fructus arboris* (the fruit of the tree). Therefore the development of language would feature the appearance of nouns substantive, with different terminations, prior to the appearance of nouns adjective and of the preposition; a process which leads to the emergence of a language which employs all these parts of speech.

Smith then took his argument a stage further and suggested that the perception of a complex whole will lead to its simplification. He availed himself of the analogy of the machine in suggesting that initially, languages are 'extremely complex in their principles' until succeeding 'improvers observe, that one principle may be so applied as to produce several' of the 'movements' required:

> In language, in the same manner, every case of every noun, and every tense of every verb, was originally expressed by a particular distinct word, which served for this purpose and for no other. But succeeding observation discovered, that one set of words was capable of supplying the place of all that infinite number, and that four or five prepositions, and half a dozen auxiliary verbs, were capable of answering the end of all the declensions, and of all the conjugations in ancient languages.[11]

But whereas the simplification of machines is of advantage in respect of their efficiency, the same was not true of language in Smith's view. Apart from the fact that the simplification of languages rendered them less agreeable to the ear, the major problem is found in the fact that they become more prolix in the sense that several words become necessary to express what could have been conveyed by a single word before. Or, as Smith put it by way of example, 'What a Roman expressed in the single word *amavissem*, an Englishman is obliged to express by four different words, I should have loved.'[12]

Three points should be noted before going further. First, there is Smith's belief that the parts of speech should be studied in an analytical manner; a perspective which led him to praise Dr. Johnson for the care he had taken to collect examples of particular usages and yet to draw attention to what he took to be a defect in a plan 'which appears to us not to be sufficiently grammatical. The different significations of a word are indeed collected; but they are seldom digested into general classes, or ranged under the meaning which the word principally expresses.'[13] Secondly, we should observe Smith's argument that the development of the means of communication reveals important features of human nature; most notably with regard to the role of analogy, the capacity for classification, abstraction and reflection. It was Smith's contention that the *actual* (as distinct from the conjectural) record of developing linguistic capacity was of great importance from this point of view – a belief which was neatly expressed in a letter to George Baird, dated 7 February 1763, where Smith commented on William

Ward's projected *Essay on Grammar* (1765). Smith wrote:

> I have read over the contents of your friends work with very great pleasure, and heartily wish it was in my power to give or to procure him all the encouragement which his ingenuity and industry deserve. I think myself greatly obliged to him for the very obliging notice he has been pleased to take of me, and should be glad to contribute anything in my power towards completing his design. I approve greatly of his plan for a Rational Grammar and am convinced that a work of this kind executed with his abilities and industry, may prove not only the best System of Grammar, but the best System of Logic in any Language, as well as the best History of the natural progress of the Human mind in forming the most important abstractions upon which all reasoning depends.

The letter is also interesting for the attention given to the articles on grammar in the French *Encyclopedie* and for the fact that Smith drew attention to the Abbé Girard's *Les Vrais principes de la Langue Francaise* (1747) as the work 'which first set me thinking upon these subjects . . . I have received more instruction from it than from any other I have yet seen upon them'.[14]

Thirdly, it will be observed that Smith's interest in language effectively illustrates his own preoccupation with *grammar*. As he remarked in *Rhetoric*: 'After language had made some progress, it was natural to imagine that men would form some rules according to which they should regulate their language. These rules are what we call grammar.'[15] In this connection Smith drew attention not merely to the parts of speech but also to the constituent elements of the sentence. In particular Smith drew attention to the emergence of *figures of speech* which constitute departures from general rules, or usages which cannot be reduced to rule — topics which 'naturally lead to the consideration of what I call style'.

Smith believed that the 'plain style' was the only acceptable modern form for a rhetoric which was committed to communication and he proceeded to advise his students accordingly in Lectures 6, 7, 8 and 11. He warned that words must be 'put in such order that the meaning of the sentence shall be quite plain' and that a 'natural order of expression, free of parentheses and superfluous words, is likewise a great help towards perspicuity'.[16] Short sentences are recommended as 'generally more perspicuous than long ones, as they are most easily comprehended in one view'.[17] Smith's students were also taught that the words used 'should be natives . . . of the language we speak in' and that they should conform 'to the custom of the country' at least as established by 'men of rank and breeding'.[18] Smith also recommended that the writer should seek harmony of sound 'by avoiding harsh clashings of consonants or the hiatus arising from the meeting of many vowels',[19] concluding this section with the confident remark that 'Many other rules for arrangement have been given, but they do not deserve attention.'[20]

But Smith's main point was to instruct his hearers that

> perfection of style consists in expressing in the most concise, proper, and precise manner the thought of the author . . . This, you'll say, is no more than common sense: and indeed it is no more. But if you will attend to it, all the rules of criticism and morality, when traced to their foundation, turn out to be some principles of common sense which every one assents to . . .'[21]

Earlier he had noted that:

> When the sentiment of the speaker is expressed in a neat, clear, plain and clever manner, and the passion or affection he is possessed of and intends, *by sympathy*, to communicate to his hearer, is plainly and cleverly hit off, then and only then the expression has all the force and beauty that language can give it. It matters not the least whether figures of speech are introduced or not.[22]

The reference to figures of speech is particularly important. Smith did recognise that figures of speech could give 'life' to the expression of an idea, but his position is distinctive in that he believed 'that the most beautiful passages are generally the most simple' and that figures of speech 'have no intrinsic worth of their own'. This argument marks Smith's break with at least one rhetorical tradition as evidenced by his remark that: 'It is . . . from the consideration of these figures, and divisions and subdivisions of them, that so many systems of rhetoric, both ancient and modern, have been formed. They are generally a very silly set of books and not at all instructive.'[23] Smith went on to note that three elements are needed in a sound author:

> first that he have a complete knowledge of his subjects; secondly, that he should arrange all the parts of his subject in their proper

order; thirdly, that he paint or describe the ideas he has of them ... in the most proper and expressive manner — this is the art of painting or imitation.[24]

Having disposed of the issue of style, Smith then proceeded to consider the forms of discourse which were employed for the communication of ideas through the medium of the written word. In Smith's view all examples of the written word could be reduced to four broad types: the poetical, where the purpose is to entertain; the historical, which is intended to relate some fact or facts; the didactic, where the purpose is to prove some proposition; and the oratorical. These different types of discourse, in Smith's view, had some common elements although differing in purpose and therefore in organisation. Thus for example he suggested that the rules of narrative (i.e. historical) discourse were the same as for the poetical even though the purpose of poetical discourse was entertainment while historical discourse aimed to instruct. In the same way he suggested that while both didactic (i.e. scientific) and oratorical discourse were intended to prove some proposition they differ in that the former 'proposes to put before us the arguments on both sides of the question in their true light, giving each its proper degree of influence, and has it in view to persuade no further than the arguments themselves appear convincing'. That is, he suggests that didactical discourse seeks to persuade 'only so far as the strength of the argument is convincing'.[25]

It will be useful to say a little about each of these three types of discourse to which Smith devoted the bulk of the lectures, the narrative (historical), didactic, and oratorical (rhetorical) forms.

On Smith's argument, the purpose of *historical* discourse is to 'narrate transactions as they happened, without being inclined to any part'.[26] The author must then be objective so far as possible and also concern himself with matters of fact. The facts in question may be either *internal* (such as the thoughts and sentiments of the actor) or *external*, and may be described either *directly* or *indirectly* (as for example when we describe the effects produced by some event on 'those who behold it', as distinct from simply describing the event itself). Moreover Smith argued that the facts reviewed should be arranged in a particular way, preferably chronologically, in that 'In general the narration is to be carried on in the same order as that in which the events themselves happened.' But where chronology cannot be observed, the best method Smith believed, 'is to observe the connection of place'. In particular the lecturer advised his hearers that the narrative should be continuous and that 'we should never leave any chasm or gap in the thread of the narration, even though there are no remarkable events to fill up that space' — the reason being that the 'very notion of a gap makes us uneasy'.

Yet important as the connections of time and place may be: 'There is another connection still more striking than any of the former: I mean that of cause and effect. There is no connection with which we are so much interested as this of cause and effect.'[27] These causes, in turn, were separated into the remote or immediate and, as Smith went on to argue, could be defined as internal or external — where the former refer to the passions or sentiments of the actor. Smith went on to argue that writers such as Thucydides and Julius Caesar who actually witnessed the events recorded in their histories tended to explain them by reference to their external causes (the terrain for example, or the disposition of troops), in contrast to Tacitus who leads us:

> So far into the sentiments and minds of the actors, that they are some of the most striking and interesting passages to be met with in any history. In describing the more important actions he does not give us an account of their external causes, but only of the internal ones; and though this perhaps will not tend so much to instruct us in the knowledge of the causes of events, yet it will be more interesting and lead us into a science no less useful, to wit, the knowledge of the motives by which men act.[28]

For Smith, historical or narrative writing quite clearly involves discipline and has something of a scientific character in that such writing 'sets before us the more interesting and important events of human life, points out the causes by which these events were brought about, and by this means points out to us by what manner and method we may produce similar good effects or avoid similar bad ones'. Armed with such a definition it comes as no surprise to find Thucydides described as the most successful of the classical writers,[29] while: 'Machiavelli is of all modern historians the only one who has contented himself with that which is the chief purpose of history, to relate events and connect them with their causes, without becoming a party on either side.'[30]

Didactic writing on the other hand must obviously require similar qualities of mind in that the writer should aspire to be objective in the handling of facts and interested in the causal processes involved. Yet for

Smith this form of discourse was more complex than the narrative and the rules of organisation correspondingly more extensive.

Smith addressed himself to the question of didactic writing in a lecture dated 24 January 1763, apparently delivered 'sine libro, except what he read from Livy'. In this lecture he suggested that didactic writing could have one of two aims: either to 'lay down a proposition and prove this, by the different arguments that lead to that conclusion', or to deliver a system in any science.[31] In the first case the writer may seek to prove a single proposition or present a complex proposition which requires proof of several subordinate ones. In this context, Smith recommended that 'these subordinate propositions should not be above five at most. When they exceed this number, the mind cannot easily comprehend them at one view, and the whole runs into confusion. Three, or there-about, is a very proper number.'[32]

The second function of didactic discourse, namely the delivery of a system in any science, also presents the writer with a choice. As Smith put it:

> in Natural Philosophy, or any other science of that sort, we may either, like Aristotle, go over the different branches in the order they happen to be cast up to us, giving a principle, commonly a new one, for every phenomenon; or, in the manner of Sir Isaac Newton, we may lay down certain principles, known or proved, in the beginning, from whence we account for the several phenomena, connecting all together by the same chain. This latter, which we may call the Newtonian method, is undoubtedly the most philosophical, and in every science, whether of Morals or Natural Philosophy, etc., is vastly more ingenious, and for that reason more engaging than the other.[33]

Oratorical discourse, which Smith divided into the demonstrative, the deliberative and the judicial (or forensic) is the subject of the last nine lectures in the series and brought Smith to what had formerly been the sole concern of the rhetorician. In Smith's view this type of discourse was still more complex than either the narrative or the didactic, being further distinguished from the latter by the fact that such discourses were solely designed to persuade. As he put it:

> The rhetorical . . . endeavours by all means to persuade us, and for this purpose it magnifies all the arguments on the one side, and diminishes or conceals those that might be brought on the side

contrary to that which it is designed that we should favour. Persuasion which is the primary design in the rhetorical, is but the secondary design in the didactic. It endeavours to persuade us only so far as the strength of the argument is convincing: instruction is the main end.[34]

The point is repeated in an even clearer form later in the argument where it is noted:

But when we propose to persuade at all events, and for this purpose adduce those arguments that make for the side we have espoused, and magnify those to the utmost of our power, and on the other hand make light of and extenuate all those which may be brought on the other side, then we make use of the rhetorical style.[35]

All three forms of the rhetorical (or oratorical) discourse have the same basic purpose while differing in their objectives and therefore in terms of their organisation.

Demonstrative eloquence was for Smith the simplest of the three types being so-called 'not because it was that sort which is used in mathematical demonstrations' but because:

The subjects of such discourses were . . . the praises or the discommendation of some particular persons, communities or actions, exhorting the people to or deterring them from, some particular conduct. As it was more safe to commend than to discommend men or actions, these discourses generally turned that way.[36]

It is worth noting that such discourses are to be organised in a way which will catch the interest of the reader or auditor, so that the writer needs some knowledge of the psychology of those whom he addresses. Hence for example Smith's concentration on great men, reflecting the judgement, also employed in the *Theory of Moral Sentiments*, that we are more apt to sympathise or be interested in the great than their more obscure counterparts.[37] In the same vein he warned prospective authors of such discourses that 'there is nothing which is more apt to raise our admiration and gain our applause than the hardships one has undergone with firmness and constance'. Similarly, he drew attention to the existence of certain general preferences which must be taken account of when describing actions; that is, to the fact that there are some virtues which 'attract our respect and

and admiration, and others which we love and esteem' — just as there are some vices 'which we condemn and despise, and others which we abominate and detest'.[38]

Deliberative eloquence differs from the demonstrative in that it is designed to be used in councils and assemblies in regard to matters of public consequence, whereas the *judicial* is used in proceedings before a court of justice. But once again, Smith drew attention to the importance of the psychology of the audience while adding a further dimension in emphasising the significance of the broadly cultural and institutional background which happens to prevail. In the case of deliberative eloquence for example, he suggested that the orator faced a choice of two methods:

> The first may be called the Socratic method . . . In this method we keep as far from the main point to be proved as possible, bringing on the audience by slow and imperceptible degrees to the thing to be proved, and by gaining their consent to some things whose tendency they cannot discover, we force them at last either to deny what they had before agreed to, or to grant the validity of the conclusion. This is the smoothest and most engaging manner.
>
> The other is a harsh and unmannerly one, where we affirm the things we are to prove boldly at the beginning, and when any point is controverted, begin by proving that very thing; and so on. This we may call the Aristotelian method, as we know it was that which he used.[39]

Smith went on to note that the choice of method would depend on the orator's judgement of his audience: the Socratic being used where the audience needs to be persuaded, the Aristotelian where it is basically convinced that the case is sound and merely needs confirmation. While such recommendations may also apply to judicial oratory Smith added a different but related point in suggesting that the orator should take particular care with regard to the ordering and structure of the parts of his argument:

> These when placed separately have often no great impression, but if they be placed in a natural order, one leading to the other, their effect is greatly increased . . . By this means, though he can bring proof of very few particulars, yet the connection there is makes them easily comprehended and consequently agreeable, so that when the adversary tries to contradict any of these particulars it is

pulling down a fabric with which we are greatly pleased and are very unwilling to give up.[40]

Yet at the same time it must be said that there is another and equally interesting dimension to Smith's treatment of rhetorical discourse, as evidenced by the attention given to what may be termed the cultural 'environment' of the speaker. In the same vein Smith noted that the deliberative eloquence of Demosthenes and Cicero was affected not merely by the different political climates which prevailed at the time of writing, but also by the fact that the economic circumstances of Greece and Rome were different. In Athens, commerce and luxury gave the lowest an opportunity of raising themselves to an equality with the nobles, and the nobles an easy way of reducing themselves to the state of the meanest citizen while in Rome a considerable degree of inequality prevailed — with consequent effects on style: 'These considerations may serve to explain many of the differences in the manners and style of Demosthenes and Cicero. The latter talks with the dignity and authority of a superior, and the former with the ease of an equal'.[41]

Looking back over the *Lectures on Rhetoric* it is perhaps hardly surprising that they have not so far attracted the attention given to Smith's better known works on ethics and economics. The notes are not perfect, often rambling in appearance, and occasionally repetitive and disjointed (as most notes are when the lecturer is actively thinking through a subject). Indeed it is really only as a result of the invaluable work of W.S. Howell that the non-specialist has been given the opportunity more easily to understand the structure and intention of this aspect of Smith's writing.[42] Howell sought not merely to expound but also to place Smith in the history of rhetorical theory finding in him a writer who was both original and synthetic, in the sense that Smith drew together those strands of theory which he believed to be of continuing relevance, and combined them in a form which was wholly new. Such topics take us well beyond the restricted scope of this chapter but it may be appropriate to observe that while we cannot comment on the history of rhetoric it can be said that the study of Smith's lectures is helpful in respect of our understanding of the man.

For the fact is that Smith himself employs a variety of forms of discourse ranging from the didactic to the deliberative or forensic, seeking as he does in his major works both to expound a system of social science but also, on occasion, persuade the reader of the truth of its *applications*. No doubt Smith's listeners would look on the lectures and the published work with a keener eye for his changing purposes as a result of familiarity with the rhetoric, and so too may the modern reader.

Notes

1. Stewart, *Life of Smith*, I. 16.
2. Ibid., II. 44.
3. Ibid., II. 46.
4. *Considerations*, 1.
5. S.K. Land, 'Adam Smith's Concerning the First Formation of Languages', *Journal of the History of Ideas*, 38 (1977), 677–90.
6. *Considerations*, 1.
7. Ibid., 7.
8. Ibid., 8.
9. Ibid., 10.
10. Ibid., 12.
11. Ibid., 41.
12. Ibid., 43.
13. Review of Johnson's Dictionary in the *Edinburgh Review* (1755).
14. *Corr.*, letter 69.
15. *Lectures on Rhetoric and Belles Lettres*, ed. J.M. Lothian (Edinburgh, 1963), 22.
16. Ibid., 2–4.
17. Ibid., 5.
18. Ibid., 2.
19. Ibid., 19.
20. Ibid., 21.
21. Ibid., 51.
22. Ibid., 22–3.
23. Ibid., 23.
24. Ibid., 38.
25. Ibid., 58.
26. Ibid., 84.
27. Ibid., 93.
28. Ibid., 109.
29. Ibid., 102.
30. Ibid., 110–11.
31. Ibid., 136.
32. Ibid., 137.
33. Ibid., 139–40.
34. Ibid., 58.
35. Ibid., 84.
36. Ibid., 59.
37. Ibid., 120, 128.
38. Ibid., 126.
39. Ibid., 140–41.
40. Ibid., 167.
41. Ibid., 153.
42. W.S. Howell, 'Adam Smith's Lectures on Rhetoric: An Historical Assessment', in A.S. Skinner and T. Wilson (eds.), *Essays on Adam Smith* (Oxford, 1975).

8 EARLY WRITINGS

The Lectures on Rhetoric clearly illustrate the truth of Millar's claim with regard to Smith's interest in the principles of human nature. Even the brief account which is offered in the previous chapter attests to the emphasis which Smith placed upon the faculties of reason and imagination, together with man's propensity to discover patterns of causality or to classify phenomena. While these faculties and propensities are illustrated by reference to a wide range of literary works, they are further illuminated by writings of a more philosophical or scientific kind.

It is probable that Smith's essay on the 'External Senses' dates from the early 1750s and it is known that at least part of his study of the 'Imitative Arts' was read to a Society in Glasgow. As Dugald Stewart was to point out it is possible at least that Smith's interest in these arts was cultivated 'less . . . with a view to the particular enjoyments they convey (though he was by no means without sensibility to their beauties) than on account of their connection with the general principles of the human mind'.[1] But it is interesting to note that Smith had a very wide knowledge of scientific literature. His article in the *Edinburgh Review* for 1756, for example, contains not only a plea for a wide coverage of all branches of literature, but also references to the French *Encyclopedia* as well as to the specific works of Buffon, Daubenton and Reamur. In addition it is known that Smith owned copies of the works of D'Alembert, Diderot and Maupertuis – all writers who made important contributions to early theories of biology. As already noticed, Smith extended this list to include English writers, such as Bacon and Boyle. One of Smith's purposes was to contrast the 'genius' of the two nations by reference to their different preferences. In literary merit, 'Imagination, genius and invention, seem to be the talents of the English; taste, judgement, propriety and order, of the French'[2] while in natural philosophy 'all the great discoveries, which have not come from Italy or Germany, have been made in England. France has scarce produced any thing very considerable in that way.'[3] In a lengthy discussion of the *Encyclopedia* Smith continued to drive home the distinction between the two nations in remarking that

It seems to be the peculiar talent of the French nation, to arrange every subject in that natural and simple order, which carries the attention, without any effort, along with it. The English seem to have employed themselves entirely in inventing, and to have disdained the more inglorious but not less useful labour of arranging and methodizing their discoveries, and of expressing them in the most simple and natural manner.[4]

'The original and inventive genius of the English' was also to be found in 'morals, metaphysics, and part of the abstract sciences.'[5] In one specific illustration, which occupies most of this section of the article, Smith points out as a representative example of the way in which original English ideas have been transported to France, how the principle in the second volume of Mandeville's *Fable of the Bees* 'has given occasion to the system of Mr Rousseau, in whom however the principles of the English author are softened, improved and embellished, and stript of all that tendency to corruption and licentiousness which have disgraced them in their original author'.[6] Or later, '. . . the principles and ideas of the profligate Mandeville seem in him to have all the purity and sublimity of the morals of Plato, and to be only the true spirit of a republican carried a little too far'.[7]

But in many respects the most remarkable of Smith's essays on philosophical subjects are those concerned with the 'Principles which lead and direct Philosophical Enquiries' illustrated by reference to the Histories of Astronomy, Ancient Physics, and Ancient Logics and Metaphysics. The last two pieces are scarcely more than fragments, but the Astronomy is a truly remarkable piece of work which was composed before 1758, thus confirming the quite astonishing range and level of intellectual activity which Smith sustained in this period. Smith himself took the essay seriously, as attested by a letter written to David Hume on the eve of his departure to London in 1773:

As I have left the care of all my literary papers to you, I must tell you that except those which I carry along with me there are none worth the publishing, but a fragment of a great work which contains a history of the Astronomical Systems that were successively in fashion down to the time of Des Cartes. Whether that might not be published as a fragment of an intended juvenile work, I leave entirely to your judgement; tho I begin to suspect myself that there is more refinement than solidity in some parts of it. This little work you will find in a thin folio paper book in my writing desk in my bedroom. All the other loose papers which you will find either in that desk or within the glass folding doors of a bureau which stands in My bedroom together with about eighteen thin paper folio books which you will likewise find within the same glass folding doors I desire may be destroyed without examination. Unless I die very suddenly I shall take care that the Papers I carry with me shall be carefully sent to you.[8]

There are three broad features of the Astronomy in particular which command attention. In the first place Smith was concerned with the 'principles which lead and direct' philosophical (that is scientific) study. In this section Smith addressed himself to the psychological stimuli to study as they affect both the ordinary man and the philosopher or scientist, thus elaborating on one of the problems which had been touched upon in the lectures on didactic discourse as contained in the *Rhetoric*. The second section illustrates these principles by reference to the History of Astronomy and provides us with a further example of philosophical or conjectural history. As Dugald Stewart observed:

> The mathematical sciences, both pure and mixed, afford, in many of their branches, very favourable subjects for theoretical history; and a very competent judge, the late M. D'Alembert, has recommended this arrangement of their elementary principles, which is founded on the natural succession of inventions and discoveries, as the best adapted for interesting the curiosity and exercising the genius of students. The same author points out as a model a passage in Montucla's History of Mathematics, where an attempt is made to exhibit the gradual progress of philosophical speculation, from the first conclusions suggested by a general survey of the heavens, to the doctrines of Copernicus. It is somewhat remarkable, that a theoretical history of this very science (in which we have, perhaps, a better opportunity than in any other instance whatever, of comparing the natural advances of the mind with the actual succession of hypothetical systems) was one of Mr Smith's earliest compositions, and is one of the very small number of his manuscripts which he did not destroy before his death.[9]

While it is important to remember that others were working in the same general field, it seems unlikely that Montucla could have influenced Smith in that his *History* first appeared in 1758. The third and final aspect of the argument which is of interest is the emphasis given to the work of Sir Isaac Newton.

In the first part of the argument Smith assumes that man has certain faculties, such as speech, reason, and imagination; faculties which manifest themselves in a capacity for acts of abstraction, classification, and explanation. Such assumptions will be familiar to readers of the *Rhetoric* and so too will be the additional statement that man seeks pleasure, or ease of mind, and the avoidance of the contrary condition of pain. (It is perhaps appropriate in this connection to recall Smith's reference to the uneasiness with which we confront 'gaps' in narrative and other discourses.) In the present context pleasure relates to a state of the imagination, that of tranquillity and composure. Such a state, he suggested, is often attained when confronted with some familiar succession of events or association of ideas, where:

> There is no break, no stop, no gap, no interval. The ideas excited by so coherent a chain of things seem as it were, to float through the mind of their own accord, without obliging it to exert itself, or to make any effort in order to pass from one of them to another.[10]

So long as an association of ideas is familiar there may be no stimulus actually to *think* about processes which are of themselves quite complex. For example, Smith cited the example of the skilled artisan who handles complex processes and yet cannot conceive 'what occasion there is for any connecting events to unite those appearances, which seem to him to succeed each other very naturally'.[11] Similarly he suggested that men are so familiar with the conversion of food into flesh and bone that they do not typically consider the nature of the processes involved, and noted in the *Imitative Arts* that: 'After a little use and experience . . . looking glasses cease to be wonders altogether; and even the ignorant become so familiar with them, as not to think that their effects require any explication.'[12] It is not then the complexity of the phenomena we confront which stimulates enquiry so much as the lack of familiarity or customary connection: 'We are at first surprised by the unexpectedness of the new appearance, and when that momentary emotion is over, we still wonder how it came to occur in that place.'[13] In other words we feel *surprise* when some object (or number of objects) is drawn to our attention which does not fall into an existing category or expected pattern; a sentiment which is followed by that of *wonder* where the latter is defined in these terms:

> The stop which is thereby given to the career of the imagination, the

the difficulty which it finds in passing along such disjointed objects, and the feeling of something like a gap or interval betwixt them, constitute the whole essence of this emotion.[14]

It then follows that the mind will seek an explanation of the phenomena in question in order to eliminate the sense of wonder, regaining by this means a state of tranquillity. Or, as Smith put it: the imagination 'endeavours to find out something which may fill up the gap, which, like a bridge, may so far at least unite those seemingly distant objects, as to render the passage of the thought betwixt them smooth, and natural, and easy'.[15]

Smith illustrates the point at issue by taking two simple examples: that of the observer who confronts an object for the first time which does not immediately fall within some known classification, and that of the person who confronts the movement of a piece of iron when brought into proximity with a magnet or loadstone (a problem of relation rather than of classification reminiscent of the treatment of nouns, adjectives and prepositions in the *Considerations*):

> when we observe the motion of the iron, in consequence of that of the loadstone, we gaze and hesitate, and feel a want of connection betwixt two events which follow one another in so unusual a train. But when, with Des Cartes, we imagine certain invisible effluvia to circulate round one of them, and by their repeated impulses to impel the other, both to move towards it, and to follow its motion, we fill up the interval betwixt them, we join them together by a sort of bridge, and thus take off that hesitation and difficulty which the imagination felt in passing from the one to the other.[16]

The philosopher too, as the statement just quoted reminds us, is subject to the same basic principles of human nature as any other man. Nature as a whole 'seems to abound with events which appear solitary and incoherent' and which therefore disturb the 'easy movement of the imagination' thus explaining the origin of a wide range of sciences, natural as well as moral, all of which seek to introduce:

> order into this chaos of jarring and discordant appearances, to allay this tumult of the imagination, and to restore it, when it surveys the great revolutions of the universe, to that tone of tranquillity and composure, which is both most agreeable in itself, and most suitable to its nature.[17]

There is one very important difference between the philosopher and the ordinary man to which Smith drew attention; a difference which arises not from any variation in the principles of human nature but from the influence of habit, training and education. For just as the musician differs from his auditor, so the philosopher:

> who has spent his whole life in the study of the connecting principles of nature, will often feel an interval betwixt two objects, which to more careless observers, seem very strictly conjoined. By long attention to all the connections which have ever been presented to his observation, by having often compared them with one another, he has, like the musician, acquired, if one may say so, a nicer ear . . . [18]

On the other hand, the philosopher, like any other man, in search of tranquillity must produce some explanation for the phenomena studied, cast in terms of familiar or plausible principles – a condition which is met by the Cartesian explanation of the relation between the iron and the loadstone above mentioned in that 'Motion after impulse is an order of succession with which of all things we are the most familiar.'[19] Once again we are reminded that an acceptable explanation for a given problem, even when relying on 'familiar' or plausible principles, need not be 'true'.

A second difference between the philosopher and the casual observer stems from the fact that there is a 'pleasing satisfaction' in science both in respect of the exercise of reason and of the very existence of a theoretical explanation for a particular problem; an explanation which may heighten our appreciation of the phenomena to be explained. It is in this way, Smith suggested, that we may learn to understand and hence to appreciate a complex social structure once its laws of operation have been explained. In the same way, the theory of astronomy helps us to comprehend and thus to *admire* the heavens through presenting the theatre of nature as a 'coherent, and therefore a more magnificent spectacle'.[20]

Surprise, Wonder, and *Admiration* are then the three sentiments on which Smith relies for his explanation of the origin of scientific endeavour. He went on to note that 'It is the design of this Essay to consider particularly the nature and causes of each of these sentiments, whose influence is of far wider extent than we should be apt upon a careless view to imagine.'[21]

In the second, and longer, part of the Essay, Smith reviewed four main theoretical 'systems' each one of which had been designed to explain the movements of observable bodies in the Heavens – the classical systems of Concentric and Eccentric Spheres, and the major modern systems of Copernicus and Newton. In each case the purpose was not so much to provide a history of astronomy as a subject (although the detail is often considerable) so much as to illustrate the principles which lead and direct philosophical enquiries by reference to them. As Smith pointed out, the object of the exercise was not to judge 'their absurdity or probability, their agreement or inconsistency with truth and reality' but rather to consider the extent to which each system was in fact fitted to 'sooth the imagination', that 'particular point of view which belongs to our subject'.[22]

On the other hand it is true to say that Smith treats the four astronomical systems in sequence and attempts to show why each one, at least up to the time of Newton, had been fated to give way to its successor. While the argument, especially in its later stages, is often complex, both sides of Smith's treatment can be adequately illustrated in terms of the first and simplest astronomical system, that of Concentric Spheres.

As Smith presents the case, the first astronomers were faced with the need to explain the movements of three different types of object: Sun, Moon and Stars. This was effected, he suggests, in terms of a theory of *Solid Spheres*, each one of which was given a circular but regular motion, for two reasons. First, he suggested that 'A circle, as the degree of its curvature is every where the same, is of all curve lines the simplest and the most easily conceived.'[23] Secondly, Smith considered that:

> The equality of their motions was another fundamental idea, which, in the same manner, and for the same reason, was supposed by all the founders of astronomical systems. For an equal motion can be more easily attended to, than one that is continually either accelerated or retarded.[24]

In the first system, the sky was regarded as the roof of the universe while the stars, being apparently static in respect of their relative positions: 'were naturally thought to have all the marks of being fixed, like so many gems, in the concave side of the firmament, and of being carried round by the diurnal revolutions of that solid body'.[25] Given this explanation, Smith argued, it was equally natural to explain the movements of the Sun and Moon in terms of an hypothesis of the same kind thus rendering the 'theory of the heavens more uniform' than would otherwise be the case. In this instance, since the Sun and Moon change their relative positions, each was given a sphere of its own, one inside the other, (in order to account for the eclipse) and supposed: 'to be attached to the concave side of a solid and transparent body, by whose revolutions they were carried round the earth'.[26] Additional spheres were subsequently added in order to account for the movement of the five planets or 'wandering stars' until a system emerged which represented the earth as:

> self-balanced and suspended in the centre of the universe, surrounded by the elements of Air and Ether, and covered by eight polished and cristalline Spheres, each of which was distinguished by one or more beautiful and luminous bodies, and all of which revolved round their common centre, by varied, but by equable and proportionable motions.[27]

As Smith pointed out, such a system of thought appealed to the imagination by apparently providing a coherent explanation of the 'different movements and effects already in reality performed', and connected by simple and familiar processes, the 'grandest and most seemingly disjointed appearances in the heavens'. He added: 'If it gained the belief of mankind by its plausibility, it attracted their wonder and admiration; sentiments that still more confirmed their belief, by the novelty and beauty of that view of nature which it presented to the imagination.'[28] Indeed even if some contemporaries recognised that such a system did not account for all appearances, the degree of completeness was such that the generality of men would be tempted to 'slur over' such problems. In fact, Smith went on to suggest that this beautiful and appealing construction of the intellect might 'have stood the examination of all ages, and have gone down triumphant to the remotest posterity' had there been 'no other bodies discoverable in the heavens'.[29] But of course such bodies were discovered, and this together with the fact that Eudoxus was not one of the 'generality of men' led to the need to modify the existing system, and to the addition of more spheres, as a means of accounting for changes in the relative positions of the planets. As a result Eudoxus raised the total number of spheres to 27, Callippus to 34, Aristotle 'upon a yet more attentive observation' to 56, until Fracastoro, 'smit with the eloquence of Plato and Aristotle', felt it necessary to raise the number of spheres to 72. In short, the existing, relatively simple system of Eudoxus, was gradually

modified in order to meet the needs of the imagination when faced
with new problems to be explained, until a situation was reached where
the explanation offered actually violated the basic prerequisite of
simplicity. As Smith put it:

> This system had now become as intricate and complex as those
> appearances themselves, which it had been invented to render
> uniform and coherent. The imagination, therefore, found itself
> but little relieved from that embarrassment, into which those appear-
> ances had thrown it, by so perplexed an account of things.[30]

The burden of the argument is perhaps readily apparent. Smith in
effect suggests that this first classical system did succeed in soothing the
imagination at least in the simpler forms given it by Eudoxus in the
sense that it provided a coherent and manageable account of the
phenomena to be explained expressed in terms of plausible principles.
At the same time Smith draws attention to the problem of continuous
development of the system in response to new observations, with the
consequence that it became so complex as to be unable to satisfy the
imagination, thus paving the way for a new account of the same complex phenomena. Hence, Smith suggests, the new system of Eccentric
Spheres and Epicycles as developed by Appollonius (subsequently
refined by Hipparchus and Ptolemy); a system which was to suffer the
same fate as its predecessor and for the same reasons. The modified
system of Eccentric Spheres was ultimately to be replaced by that of
Copernicus, who was motivated as his predecessors had been, by a
desire to explain the movements of the heavens and by dissatisfaction
with current theory. As Smith remarked:

> The confusion, in which the old hypothesis represented the motions
> of the heavenly bodies, was, he tells us, what first suggested to him
> the design of forming a new system, that these, the noblest works
> of nature, might no longer appear devoid of that harmony and
> proportion which discover themselves in her meanest productions.[31]

Yet at the same time, the Copernican system, if complete, was
destined in due time to give way to yet another, capable of accounting
more completely for observed appearances, in terms of a smaller
number of basic principles, and of successfully predicting their future
movement. This was the system of Newton:

a system whose parts are more strictly connected together, than those of any other philosophical hypothesis. Allow his principle, the universality of gravity, and that it decreases as the squares of the distance increase, and all the appearances, which he joins together by it, necessarily follow.[32]

Moreover, the basic principles involved could be regarded as *familiar*, since:

The gravity of matter is, of all its qualities, after its inertness, that which is most familiar to us . . . The law too, by which it is supposed to diminish as it recedes from its centre, is the same which takes place in all other qualities which are propagated in rays from a centre, in light, and in every thing else of the same kind.[33]

While Smith wrote with real enthusiasm about Newton's contribution he added a characteristic warning in stating that:

even we, while we have been endeavouring to represent all philosophical systems as mere inventions of the imagination, to connect together the otherwise disjointed and discordant phaenomena of nature, have insensibly been drawn in, to make use of language expressing the connecting principles of this one, as if they were the real chains which Nature makes use of to bind together her several operations. Can we wonder then, that it should have gained the general and complete approbation of mankind, and that it should now be considered, not as an attempt to connect in the imagination the phaenomena of the Heavens, but as the greatest discovery that ever was made by man, the discovery of an immense chain of the most important and sublime truths, all closely connected together, by one capital fact, of the reality of which we have daily experience.[34]

It will be evident, even from a brief description that the essay on Astronomy is quite as elegant an example of philosophical history as, say, the *Considerations* on Language. We find the same basic ingredients: the same preoccupation with facts and conjectures about 'facts'; the same technique whereby the argument begins with the description of a particular environment (in this case a state of knowledge) before going on to examine the nature of those responses which human nature dictates. The emphasis on the principles of human nature, and on the idea of scientific work as being undertaken in response to psychological need is striking and nowhere more clearly illustrated than in Smith's remark that:

> Wonder, therefore, and not any expectation of advantage from its discoveries, is the first principle which prompts mankind to the study of Philosophy, of that science which pretends to lay open the concealed connections that unite the various appearances of nature.[35]

But if 'philosophy' is the consequence of a desire to soothe the imagination, to relieve it of that anxiety which comes from contemplating the unexplained, it follows that the way in which we express our thoughts may also reflect subjective preferences. This is, perhaps, the true significance of Smith's point made in *Rhetoric* that the Newtonian method in didactic discourse may be preferred because it is 'more ingenious and for that reason more engaging' than the Aristotelian. He continued:

> It gives us a pleasure to see the phenomena which we reckoned the most unaccountable, all deduced from some principle (commonly, a well-known one) and all united in one chain, far superior to what we feel from the unconnected method . . . We need not be surprised, then, that the Cartesian philosophy (for Descartes was in reality the first who attempted this method), though it does not perhaps contain a word of truth — and to us who live in a more enlightened age and have more enquired into these matters, it appears very dubious — should nevertheless have been so universally received by all the learned in Europe at that time.[36]

In the same vein it is interesting that Smith should have referred to a propensity, natural to all men, 'to account for all appearances from as few principles as possible'[37] and that he should have been so conscious of the 'beauty of a systematical arrangement of different observations connected by a few common principles'.[38] Smith also emphasised the role of subjective or psychological preferences as revealed in the history of astronomy in drawing attention to the role of analogy; that is, to the tendency to explain a particular problem in terms of knowledge gained in an unrelated field — such as the Pythagoreans who first studied arithmetic and then explained all things by the properties of number, or the modern physician who produced a system of moral philosophy 'upon the principles of his own art'.[39] The theme is continued in Smith's judgement that the content, reception and succession of astronomical systems often showed how easily 'the learned give up the evidence of their senses to preserve the coherence of the ideas of their imagination',[40] while illustrating the role played by the prejudices of the imagination and of education. In short, Smith draws our attention to the significance of the point that 'all philosophical systems' are 'mere inventions of the imagination'; an argument which helps to explain the note of caution with which he concluded his assessment of Newton.

In view of the above, the attitude to Newton as disclosed in the paragraph quoted above is particularly interesting in that the reader is reminded that in providing an account of the great man's discoveries Smith has been 'insensibly' drawn to write as if the former had attained a true understanding of reality. This could be intended to remind the reader that the whole of the previous argument suggests that this is unlikely. On the other hand, the statement can be read as a reminder that Smith's purpose was not to assess the 'validity' of the theories he reviewed but rather to example the role played by the sentiments of surprise, wonder and admiration; a role which was thought to be 'of far wider extent than we should be apt upon a careless view to imagine'.

This position does not imply that these sentiments are the only ones relevant to philosophical work, nor does it suggest that man can never understand the laws of natural or moral philosophy. Smith's treatment of Newton in the Astronomy does seem to suggest that the latter had 'made the greatest discovery that ever was made by man, the discovery of an immense chain of the most important and sublime truths'. The point finds an echo in the Letter to the Authors of the *Edinburgh Review* (1756) where Smith refers once more to the eclipse of the 'fanciful . . . ingenious and elegant, tho' fallacious, system' of Descartes among contemporary French philosophers while expressing his satisfaction in finding the ideas of Bacon, Boyle and Newton, expounded with such perspicuity.[41]

Smith's admiration for Boyle, Newton, (and Galileo) is reflected in his own use of the 'experimental' technique. For although he argued that scientific thought may be initiated by the sentiments of surprise and wonder, and expounded according to the rules of didactic discourse as stated in *Rhetoric*, he seems to have believed that its true principles could only be *established* by the experimental (empirical) method of Newton. This method was stated in classic form by Colin Maclaurin (1698-1746), who held the chair of Mathematics in Edinburgh in succession to James Gregory. In his *Account of Sir Isaac Newton's Philosophical Discoveries* (1748) it is noted that the scientist:

should begin with phenomena, or effects, and from them investigate the powers or causes that operate in nature; that from particular causes we should proceed to the more general ones, till the argument ends in the most general: this is the method of *analysis*. Being once possessed of these causes, we should then descend in a contrary order, and from them, as established principles, explain all the phenomena that are their consequences, and prove our explications; and this is the *synthesis*. It is evident that, as in mathematics, so in natural philosophy, the investigation of difficult things by the method of *analysis*, ought ever to precede the method of composition, or the synthesis. For in any other way we can never be sure that we assume the principles that really obtain in nature; and that our system, after we have composed it with great labour, is not mere dream and illusion.[42]

If we substitute the terms 'induction' and 'deduction' for 'analysis' and 'synthesis' we have here the kind of statement which is frequently offered to students of those social sciences in which Smith himself was interested even at the present time.

Notes

1. Stewart, *Life of Smith*, III. 13.
2. *Edinburgh Review* (1756), 4.
3. Ibid., 5.
4. Ibid.
5. Ibid., 10.
6. Ibid., 11.
7. Ibid., 12.
8. *Corr.*, letter 137, Adam Smith to David Hume, 16 April 1773. See below p. 150.
9. Stewart, *Life of Smith*, II. 49.
10. *Astronomy*, II. 7.
11. Ibid., II. 11.
12. *Imitative Arts*, I. 17.
13. *Astronomy*, II. 8.
14. Ibid., II. 9.
15. Ibid., II. 8.
16. Ibid.
17. Ibid., II. 12.
18. Ibid., II. 11.
19. Ibid., II. 8.
20. Ibid., II. 12.
21. Ibid., 7.
22. Ibid., II. 12.

23. Ibid., IV. 51.
24. Ibid., IV. 52.
25. Ibid., IV. 1.
26. Ibid., IV. 2.
27. Ibid., IV. 5.
28. Ibid., IV. 5.
29. Ibid., IV. 4.
30. Ibid., IV. 8.
31. Ibid., IV. 28.
32. Ibid., IV. 76.
33. Ibid.
34. Ibid.
35. Ibid., III. 3.
36. *LRBL*, 140.
37. *TMS*, VII.ii.2.14.
38. *WN*, V.i.f.25.
39. *Astronomy*, II. 12.
40. Ibid., IV. 35.
41. *Edinburgh Review* (1756), 5.
42. The quotation is from the third edition (1775), 9.

9 THE THEORY OF MORAL SENTIMENTS

When Adam Smith moved from the chair of logic to that of moral philosophy he continued to give lectures on rhetoric and belles-lettres each day at twelve noon. These were the so-called 'private' lectures and followed the 'public' performances on moral philosophy which were given at 7.30 a.m. As we know from John Millar, the lectures given from the moral philosophy chair were divided into four parts covering theology, ethics, jurisprudence, and economics.

In the first part of the course Smith evidently considered the 'proofs of the being and attributes of God, and those principles of the human mind upon which religion is founded'.[1] Unfortunately, no record of these lectures has so far come to light, although some evidence of Smith's position is preserved in other writings. He frequently refers to God, to the 'Divine Being', and to the Deity as the author of moral laws. But Smith never revealed his own belief in the God of Christian teaching in an unambiguous way, merely remarking that a belief in a God who would punish the wicked and reward the just was firmly rooted in human nature, and that in every religion and in every superstition that the world has known, 'there has been a Tartarus as well as an Elysium; a place provided for the punishment of the wicked, as well as one for the reward of the just'.[2]

One reviewer of the *Theory of Moral Sentiments* noted that the strictest regard was paid throughout 'to the principles of religion, so that the serious reader will find nothing that will give him any just ground of offence'.[3] On the other hand, some of his audience in Glasgow viewed with suspicion the Professor's smiling countenance during Divine Service, and believed that his works and professorial prayers smacked strongly of an unorthodox position of which the Kirk was unlikely to approve.

It seems probable that Smith's own position was influenced by that of Newton. Newton's work, especially on astro-physics was important not only as an example of sound method but also because it provided Smith and many of his contemporaries with a fertile source of analogy. To many, including Smith, it seemed that Newton had presented the great theatre of nature as a coherent system, what Smith himself described as the 'immense machine of the universe'. Elsewhere he extended the analogy to the study of language, and to the plant and animal creation. Indeed for Smith 'Human society, when we contemplate it in a certain abstract and philosophical light, appears like a great, an immense machine, whose regular and harmonious movements produce a thousand agreeable effects.'[4]

Use of this kind of analogy was commonplace, but it does have some important implications. It is evident that a machine may be composed of a number of parts which are used in conjunction to produce a particular result although of course the parts themselves are inanimate. Looked at in this way it seemed to Smith that a great range of social activity had the same characteristic in that men in pursuing their own objectives seemed frequently to contribute to outcomes which they did not intend or foresee. This doctrine is sometimes described as the law of 'unintended social outcomes' but is more usually cited, in Smith's case, as the doctrine of the 'invisible hand' — as in the statement that man is 'led by an invisible hand to promote an end which was no part of his intention'.[5] This in turn was usually associated with the perception that individual activities in the social sphere resulted in something like the order observable in nature; a position which shows some agreement with another aspect of Newton's work in that 'he infers from the structure of the visible world, that it is governed by One *Almighty* and *All Wise Being*'.[6] This view of God as the Great Engineer, Divine Architect, or Superintendent of the Universe, is frequently mentioned by Smith and although his position is not without ambiguity, it is clearly associated with a distinction between what he called efficient and final causes:

> The wheels of the watch are all admirably adjusted to the end for which it was made, the pointing of the hour. All their various motions conspire in the nicest manner to produce this effect. If they were endowed with a desire and intention to produce it, they could not do it better. Yet we never ascribe any such desire or intention to them, but to the watch-maker, and we know that they are put into motion by a spring, which intends the effect it produces as little as they do.[7]

But the second part of Smith's course, namely that on ethics, is well known to us since we have it on John Millar's authority that its content was embodied in the *Theory of Moral Sentiments* (1759). When the volume first appeared, Smith's friends certainly bestirred themselves. Andrew Millar, the publisher, wrote on 26 April 1759 to tell Smith that he had circulated copies to, amongst others: the Earls of

Bute, Hardwicke and Shelburne; Lords Mansfield and Lyttelton; the Duke of Argyll, Edmund Burke, and Charles Townshend. David Hume, Alexander Wedderburn, and Sir John Dalrymple all had a hand in the affair while a Mr Rose of 'Kew' took a further 25 copies for disposal among his friends.[8] William Robertson, the historian and latterly principal of Edinburgh University was thus able to write to Smith on 14 June assuring him that his work:

> is in the hands of all persons of the best fashion; that it meets with great approbation both on account of the matter and stile; and that it is impossible for any book on so serious a subject to be received in a more gracious manner. It comforts the English a good deal to hear that you were bred at Oxford. . . .[9]

Edmund Burke also wrote Smith a warm letter of congratulation in September of the same year,[10] all of which must have confirmed David Hume's earlier warnings of his likely fate. In a letter dated 12 April 1759, filled with the most delightful humour, Hume teased his anxious friend mercilessly, explaining that he had delayed writing so that:

> I cou'd tell you something of the Success of the Book, and coud prognosticate with some probability whether it shoud be finally dammned to Oblivion, or shoud be registered in the Temple of Immortality. Tho' it has been published only a few Weeks. I think there appear already such strong Symptoms, that I can almost venture to fortell its Fate. It is in short this. . .

Then follows a long record of interruptions from acquaintances, leading into a discourse which ranges from political problems in the University of Glasgow, to the works of Helvetius, Voltaire and Lord Kames:

> But what is all this to my Book? say you. – My Dear Mr Smith, have Patience: Compose yourself to tranquillity; Show yourself a Philosopher in Practice as well as Profession: Think of the Emptiness, and Rashness, and Futility of the Common Judgements of Men: How little they are regulated by Reason in any Subject, much more in Philosophical Subjects, which so far exceed the Comprehension of the Vulgar. . . Nothing indeed can be a stronger presumption of falsehood than the approbation of the multitude; and Phocion, you know, always suspected himself of some Blunder, when he was attended with the Applauses of the populace.

Supposing therefore, that you have duely prepared yourself for the worst by all these Reflections; I proceed to tell you the melancholy News, that your Book has been very unfortunate: For the Public seem disposed to applaud it extremely. It was looked for by the foolish people with some impatience; and the Mob of Literati are beginning already to be very loud in its praises. Three Bishops called yesterday at Millar's shop in order to buy copies, and to ask Questions about the Author . . . You may conclude what Opinion true Philosophers will entertain of it, when these Retainers to Superstition praise it so highly. The Duke of Argyle is more decisive than he used to be in its favour: I suppose he either considers it as an Exotic, or thinks the Author will be serviceable to him in the Glasgow elections . . . Millar exults and brags that two thirds of the edition are already sold, and that he is now sure of success. You see what a Son of the Earth that is, to value Books only by the Profit they bring him. In that View, I believe it may prove a very good Book.[11]

The book was to attract no fewer than three French and two German translations before the end of the century, and went through six editions in Smith's lifetime. Substantial changes were made to the second edition (1761) while major revisions and additions were effected in the sixth edition (1790) — ample evidence of Smith's continuing interest in the ethical side of his work following the publication of the *Wealth of Nations*.

The various editions of the book and the care which Smith took over them also show him to have had a pleasant sense of humour, as when requesting his publisher William Strahan to send a note of the corrections proposed:

I know how much I shall be benefitted and I shall at the same time preserve the pretious right of private judgement for the sake of which our forefathers kicked out the Pope and the Pretender. I believe you to be much more infallible than the Pope, but as I am a Protestant my conscience makes me scruple to submit to any unscriptural authority.[12]

Later in the same year he sent Strahan a list of 'the manifold sins and iniquities you have been guilty of in printing my book', some of which could be described as 'sins against the holy Ghost which cannot upon any account be pardoned' while the remainder 'are capable of remission in case of repentance, humiliation and contrition'![13]

The argument of the book is probably best approached through the study of its concluding section where Smith reviewed different ways of looking at the two main questions which, he believed, confronted the philosopher; first wherein does virtue consist, and, secondly, by what means are moral judgements formed? In this context Smith reviewed the works of a wide range of Greek thinkers with the intention of showing the elements of truth which they had illuminated while demonstrating at the same time that each classical system was unable satisfactorily to answer either of the two questions posed.

Smith also considered the contributions of three modern thinkers, namely, Bernard Mandeville, Francis Hutcheson and David Hume. Smith's treatment of these writers may be sufficient to illustrate his own capacity as a synthetic thinker while serving as an introduction to the argument as a whole.

As Professor David Raphael has pointed out, the three thinkers just mentioned can be seen to have been interrelated in Smith's mind. Mandeville, for example, emerges as a proponent of egoistical theory; as a vigorous and amusing writer who infuriated many contemporaries by apparently demonstrating the all pervading force of human vanity and the awesome consequences of austerity. As Smith observed:

> It is the great fallacy of Dr. Mandeville's book to represent every passion as wholly vicious, which is so in any degree and in any direction. It is thus that he treats every thing as vanity which has any reference, either to what are, or to what ought to be the sentiments of others: and it is by means of this sophistry, that he established his favourite conclusion, that private vices are public benefits.[14]

Smith was well aware that the persuasive power of Mandeville's 'coarse and rustic eloquence' had convinced many of the truth of his sophistry, while at the same time containing more than a grain of truth. For the fact is, as Smith recognised, that many of our activities are self interested in character:

> how destructive soever this system may appear, it could never have imposed upon so great a number of persons, nor have occasioned so general an alarm among those who are the friends of better principles, had it not in some respects bordered upon the truth.[15]

Of the modern writers who emerged as the critics of egoistical theory Francis Hutcheson receives most attention from Smith. Hutcheson's basic teaching is available chiefly in his *System of Moral Philosophy* (1755) and is particularly interesting for the attention given to self-regarding propensities, pointing out as he did that a 'penetrating genius, capacity for business, patience of application and labour . . . are naturally admirable and relished by all observers'. Hutcheson also recognised that the 'selfish affections', at least while kept within certain bounds, would contribute to the good of the individual and of society. But while making such points, he insisted that our admiration for certain selfish affections was quite different from the feeling of moral approbation. Virtue, for Hutcheson, was to be found in benevolence and Smith was undoubtedly correct in claiming that for Hutcheson, 'Self-love was a principle which could never be virtuous in any degree or in any direction'. 'Dr Hutcheson was so far from allowing self-love to be in any case a motive for virtuous actions that even a regard to the pleasure of self approbation . . . according to him, diminished the merit of a benevolent action.'[16]

Hutcheson's position was also interesting from another point of view in that he sought to explain the manner in which moral judgements are formed, by reference to a special sense, somewhat analogous to those of sight, sound, or taste. Here he drew attention to a sense of honour and of shame, and also to a moral sense which, he believed, explains our natural and immediate determination to approve certain affections and actions consequent on them. Hutcheson also referred to a sympathetic sense by which, when we apprehend the state of others, our hearts naturally have a fellow feeling with them.

In fact Smith could accept a good deal of Hutcheson's position, noting with approval his argument that moral judgement was to be explained in terms of 'immediate sense and feeling', rather than reason. He also accepted the importance of benevolence as a virtue. On the other hand Smith rejected the argument that our capacity for moral judgement was based on a special (moral) sense, together with Hutcheson's view that self-interested actions could never be virtuous. As he said; 'The condition of human nature were peculiarly hard, if those affections, which, by the very nature of our being, ought frequently to influence our conduct, could upon no occasion appear virtuous, or deserve esteem and commendation from any body'.[17]

With Hume we come a good deal closer to the position which was to be developed by Smith, contending as he did that we can only discover the true origin of moral judgement by beginning with 'the nature and force of sympathy', a 'very powerful principle in human nature'. Hume drew particular attention to those actions or virtues which generate some benefit in arguing that we derive a certain satisfaction from contemplating the pleasure manifested by a third party: for example, by the beneficiary of an action taken by a person other than ourselves. Hence we approve of the natural virtues which frequently generate benefit for others, such as meekness, benificence, generosity and moderation. In the same way we approve of the other virtues, such as justice, as a result of our perception of the point that such virtues tend to the benefit of society at large. Hume in short, had chosen to emphasise the importance of the quality of utility in the discussion of approbation. Smith accepted a great deal in the argument of that 'ingenious and agreeable philosopher, who joins the greatest depth of thought to the greatest elegance of expression', noting in particular that 'utility is one of the principal sources of beauty'. Smith clearly agreed with Hume's suggestion that the utility of an object pleases its owner by 'perpetually suggesting to him the pleasure or conveniency which it is fitted to promote'; and that this reaction also gives pleasure to the spectator by virtue of his sympathetic understanding of the feelings of the person observed. Indeed Smith went rather further than Hume in making the novel point that we derive a particular satisfaction from contemplating not merely the end which some object is designed to serve, but also its very fitness or 'happy contrivance' — in short, its sheer ingenuity. It is for this reason that we place so high a value on 'trinkets of frivolous utility' or lose patience with an elaborate watch which loses two minutes in a day. In Smith's view men are marked by a sheer 'love of art and contrivance' which often outweighs considerations of utility narrowly defined.[18] Smith drew attention to our love of machines, and of ingenious political systems — not to mention of course that appreciation of ingenuity in intellectual argument which we have already noted in the discussion of the *Lectures on Rhetoric*, and the *Astronomy*.

With regard to moral judgement, Smith further agreed with Hume in stating that those qualities of mind which are useful to ourselves or others are approved of as virtuous. But he parted from Hume in arguing that a perception of utility could not be 'the first or principal source of our approbation or disapprobation'. He went on, 'These sentiments are no doubt enhanced and enlivened by the perception of the beauty or deformity which results from this utility or hurtfulness. But still, I say, they are originally and essentially different from this perception.'[19] It seemed to Smith inconceivable 'that we should have no other reason for praising a man than that for which we commend a chest of drawers'.

But the second area of disagreement is the more important, arguing as Smith did that:

the sentiment of approbation always involves in it a sense of propriety quite distinct from the perception of utility. We may observe this with regard to all the qualities which are approved of as virtuous, both those which, according to this system, are originally valued as useful to ourselves, as well as those which are esteemed on account of their usefulness to others.'[20]

Where Smith differs most markedly from both Hutcheson and Hume is in respect of the degree of elaboration which he brought to the question of the means by which moral judgements are formed. It is in this context that the role of the spectator is developed and the concept of sympathy extended to include any shared feeling, not merely those associated with loss or gain. The argument is also notable for the fact that it permitted Smith to make due allowance for both the 'selfish' and the 'social' passions.

Smith's argument, like that of Hume, places a good deal of emphasis on 'sympathy' by which he means 'fellow-feeling', that sentiment which expresses our interest in the situation of other people. For example we may flinch when seeing a blow aimed at another person, or writhe in time with the performer on the wire. But sympathy in Smith's work is chiefly taken to denote our fellow-feeling with any passion or expression of feeling and he went on to note that 'Whatever is the passion which arises from any object in the person principally concerned, an analogous emotion springs up, at the thought of his situation, in the breast of every attentive spectator.'[21] This kind of 'sympathy' can be instantaneous, in effect instinctive, as, for example, when we contemplate an expression of joy or sorrow; a reaction which may later cause the observer to enquire into the circumstances of the person judged with a view to understanding the emotion which he expresses. Thus sympathy arises not 'so much from the view of the passion, as from that of the situation which excites it'. It is this which leads the spectator to form a judgement as to the *propriety* or *impropriety* of an expression of feeling where such qualities are found to consist in the 'suitableness or unsuitableness, in the proportion or disproportion, which the affection seems to bear to the cause or object which excites it'.[22] It followed for Smith that where the spectator of another man's conduct seeks to form an opinion as to its propriety, he must 'bring home to himself' both the circumstances and the 'affections' of the person judged. In short, the spectator must try to visualise how he would feel under the circumstances prevailing; an effort of the imagination which must also be made when we seek to form an opinion as to the propriety or impropriety of our own conduct:

> We can never survey our own sentiments and motives, we can never form any judgement concerning them; unless we remove ourselves, as it were, from our own natural station, and endeavour to view them as at a certain distance from us. But we can do this in no other way than by endeavouring to view them with the eyes of other people, or as other people are likely to view them.[23]

The analysis was extended from this point to take account of situations where the spectator is called upon to form a judgement as to the propriety or impropriety of the actions taken by an agent and the reaction of the subject. Here Smith argued that the merit or demerit of a given action would depend upon a judgement as to the propriety or impropriety of both the action taken and the reaction to it. More specifically, he suggested that our sense of the merit of an action 'seems to be a compounded sentiment, and to be made up of two distinct emotions; a direct sympathy with the sentiments of the agent, and indirect sympathy with the gratitude of those who receive the benefit of his actions'. It follows that:

> In the same manner as our sense of the impropriety of conduct arises from a want of sympathy, or from a direct antipathy to the affections and motives of the agent, so our sense of its demerit arises from what I shall ... call an indirect sympathy with the resentment of the sufferer.[24]

Now it was Smith's contention that any judgement as to the propriety of an action or reaction must involve some effort of the imagination, in that when 'we judge ... of any affection, as proportioned or disproportioned to the cause which excites it, it is scarce possible that we should make use of any other rule or canon but the correspondent affection in ourselves'. At the same time, Smith recognised that we have no 'immediate experience of what other men feel', from which it follows that an action which is considered to be proper by the spectator must involve some restraint in the expression of feeling on the part of the agent. Thus the person whose actions or reactions are judged can only attain the agreement, and thus the approval, of the spectator:

> by lowering his passion to that pitch, in which the spectators are capable of going along with him. He must flatten, if I may be allowed to say so, the sharpness of its natural tone, in order to reduce it to harmony and concord with the emotions of those who are about him.[25]

Smith then suggested that the degree to which the spectator can visualise the feelings of the person judged may involve the virtue of sensibility, while the extent to which the latter is capable of moderating the expression of his feelings may involve that of self-command.

It was Smith's opinion that men would tend to practice both virtues since 'nothing pleases us more than to observe in other men a fellow feeling with all the emotions of our own breast'. In particular it is suggested that we are impelled to self-restraint since:

> Nature, when she formed men for society, endowed him with an original desire to please, and an original aversion to offend his brethren. She taught him to feel pleasure in their favourable, and pain in their unfavourable regard. She rendered their approbation most flattering and most agreeable to him for its own sake; and their disapprobation most mortifying and most offensive.[26]

The capacity to judge the propriety of the actions or affections of others, and our willingness to be the subject of that judgement were also of importance to Smith in that both help to explain the origin and development of general rules of behaviour or morality. Smith suggested in this connection that a capacity to form judgements in particular cases would lead, on reflection, to the appreciation of general rules — thus admitting reason to a formal role in the process of moral judgement:

> It is thus that the general rules of morality are formed. They are ultimately founded upon experience of what, in particular instances, our moral faculties, our natural sense of merit and propriety, approve, or disapprove of. We do not originally approve or condemn particular actions; because, upon examination, they appear to be agreeable or inconsistent with a certain general rule. The general rule, on the contrary, is formed by finding from experience, that all

actions of a certain kind, or circumstanced in a certain manner, are approved or disapproved of.[27]

The statement just considered, while interesting, is not perhaps remarkable when we consider the nature of the argument which preceded it. What is remarkable is Smith's explanation as to why these rules tend to be respected, involving as it does a further elaboration of the spectator concept.

Knowledge is imperfect both in the way in which the actual spectator of another man's conduct forms an opinion as to its propriety, and of the latter's reaction to the knowledge that judgement is being made, even if Smith does suggest that both parties are sufficiently aware of the relevant information as to permit them to adopt an appropriate position. But it is evident that information with regard, for example, to the motives which prompt an action will be needed if the spectator is to decide accurately as to whether or not that action has the qualities of merit or demerit: exactly the kind of knowledge which is most difficult to acquire in reference to another person.

Smith solved this problem by developing the argument that the way in which we judge our own conduct must be similar to that in which we judge others, in that in so doing we 'suppose ourselves the spectators of our own behaviour'.

When I endeavour to examine my own conduct, when I endeavour to pass sentence upon it, and either to approve or condemn it, it is evident that, in all such cases, I divide myself, as it were, into two persons; and that I, the examiner and judge, represent a different character from that other I, the person whose conduct is examined into and judged of. The first is the spectator, whose sentiments with regard to my own conduct I endeavour to enter into, by placing myself in his situation, and by considering how it would appear to me, when seen from that particular point of view. The second is the agent, the person whom I properly call myself, and of whose conduct, under the character of a spectator, I was endeavouring to form some opinion.[28]

In such cases it will be apparent that the imagined spectator of our conduct can be supplied with all the information which would be needed to frame an accurate judgement, and that it must be this spectator whose 'reaction' is of the greatest importance to us. Smith therefore concluded that though man in his capacity of the spectator of the conduct of others may form a judgement of it, an appeal must lie to a still higher tribunal, namely that of 'the supposed impartial and well-informed spectator, the man within the breast, the great judge and arbiter' of our conduct. The jurisdiction of the actual spectator thus emerges as being confined to judgements as to whether or not our actions attract praise or blame, while that of the informed spectator, or the man within the breast extends to an opinion as to whether or not we are deserving of praise or blame, taking everything into consideration. It was Smith's contention that Nature has endowed man:

> not only with a desire of being approved of, but with a desire of being what ought to be approved of; or of being what he himself approves of in other men. The first desire could only have made him wish to appear to be fit for society. The second was necessary in order to render him anxious to be really fit. The first could only have prompted him to the affectation of virtue, and to the concealment of vice. The second was necessary in order to inspire him with the real love of virtue, and with the real abhorrence of vice.[29]

It is, Smith believed, this desire for praiseworthiness which helps to correct the lack of perspective from which we frequently suffer, and which qualifies in particular the importunate claims of self interest. The controlling factor thus emerges as 'reason, principle, conscience, the inhabitant of the breast'; a factor which also helps to explain our respect for those general rules of conduct which were noticed earlier in the argument. Smith added that our respect for general rules is typically enhanced by the belief that:

> the rules which they prescribe are to be regarded as the commands and laws of the Deity, promulgated by those vice-regents which he has thus set up within us. All general rules are commonly denominated laws: thus the general rules which bodies observe in the communication of motion, are called the laws of motion. But those general rules which our moral faculties observe in approving or condemning whatever sentiment or action is subjected to their examination, may much more justly be denominated such. They have a much greater resemblance to what are properly called laws, those general rules which the sovereign lays down to direct the conduct of his subjects. Like them they are rules to direct the free actions of men: they are prescribed most surely by a lawful superior, and are attended too with the sanction of rewards and punishments.

Those vice-regents of God within us, never fail to punish the violation of them, by the torments of inward shame, and self-condemnation; and on the contrary, always reward obedience with tranquillity of mind, with contentment, and self-satisfaction.[30]

It would thus appear that Smith's ethical work is differentiated from those of Hutcheson and Hume on two grounds, rather than one; differentiated not only in respect of the attention given to the way in which the mind forms judgements as to what is fit and proper to be done or to be avoided, but also in respect of the sheer weight of emphasis which is placed on the role of conscience, on the role of the man within the breast.

Two additional features of the argument of the *Theory of Moral Sentiments* may be observed in view of their connection with the parts of Smith's course which were to follow.

The first is the attention given to the role of self-interest in the *Theory of Moral Sentiments*. Perhaps with Hutcheson in mind, Smith positively warmed to his task in stating that man was made for action and in insisting that a person appears 'mean spirited' who does not pursue the extraordinary and important objects of self-interest. Ambition in Smith's eyes was entirely laudable, provided always that it was kept within the bounds of prudence and justice. It is equally striking to find in Smith the argument that many self-regarding actions have a social reference, in that they are designed to attract the attention and hence the approval of our fellows. As he put it:

> it is chiefly from this regard to the sentiments of mankind that we pursue riches and avoid poverty. For to what purpose is all the toil and bustle of this world? What is the end of avarice and ambition, of the pursuit of wealth, of power, and preheminence? . . . From whence, . . . arises that emulation which runs through all the different ranks of men, and what are the advantages which we propose by that great purpose of human life which we call bettering our condition? To be observed, to be attended to, to be taken notice of with sympathy, complacency, and approbation, are all the advantages which we can propose to derive from it. It is the vanity, not the ease, or the pleasure, which interests us.[31]

Elsewhere in the book he was to observe that we cannot live long in the world without being aware that our rank and credit in society very much depends on our real or supposed possession of riches. In the same vein he drew attention to the means of attaining these desired ends, such as probity and prudence on the part of the poor. But it was in Part VI of the *Theory of Moral Sentiments*, which was added to the last edition, that we find the most complete statement of the psychology of the prudent man; that man who lives within his income:

> In the steadiness of his industry and frugality, in his steadily sacrificing the ease and enjoyment of the present moment for the probable expectation of the still greater ease and enjoyment of a more distant but more lasting period of time, the prudent man is always both supported and rewarded by the entire approbation of the impartial spectator, and of the representative of the impartial spectator, the man within the breast.[32]

The second point to be emphasised is not unconnected with Smith's view of man as a being whose activities may, wittingly or unwittingly, affect the wellbeing of his fellows. It was in this respect that Smith emphasised the importance of those rules of behaviour which could be regarded as the rules of justice. For Smith the rules of justice, unlike all the other virtues, could be seen to be somewhat akin to the rules of grammar, in that they were 'precise, accurate, and indispensable'. They were also distinctive, he argued, in that violation of the rules of justice generally leads to the approval of punishment as a result of our feelings of disapprobation for the motives and activities of the offender and sympathy for the resentment of the sufferer. It was very much Smith's view that respect for the rules of justice was the indispensable precondition for social order, leading to his well-known statement that:

> Justice . . . is the main pillar that upholds the whole edifice. If it is removed, the great, the immense fabric of human society, that fabric which to raise and support seems in this world, if I may say so, to have been the peculiar and darling care of Nature, must in a moment crumble into atoms.[33]

To this, Smith added one further requirement in observing that:

> As the violation of justice is what men will never submit to from one another, the public magistrate is under a necessity of employing the power of the commonwealth to enforce the practice of this virtue. Without this precaution, civil society would become a scene

of bloodshed and disorder, every man revenging himself at his own hand whenever he fancied he was injured.[34]

The point is an important one, not merely of itself, but also because it served to introduce the third main part of Smith's lecture course, the treatment of jurisprudence, which includes economics.

Notes

1. Stewart, *Life of Smith*, I. 18.
2. *TMS*, II.ii.3.12.
3. Ibid., *27*.
4. Ibid., VII.iii.1.2.
5. *WN*, IV.ii.9; *TMS*, IV.i.10.
6. Colin MacLaurin, *An Account of Sir Isaac Newton's Philosophical Discoveries* (1775), 396.
7. *TMS*, II.ii.3.5.
8. *Corr.*, letter 33.
9. *Corr.*, letter 34.
10. *Corr.*, letter 38.
11. *Corr.*, letter 31.
12. *Corr.*, letter 50, 4 April 1760.
13. *Corr.*, letter 54, 30 December 1760.
14. *TMS*, VII.ii.4.12.
15. Ibid., VII.ii.4.13.
16. Ibid., VII.ii.4.14.
17. Ibid., VII.ii.3.18.
18. Ibid., IV.i.3.
19. Ibid., IV.2.3.
20. Ibid., IV.2.5.
21. Ibid., I.i.1.4.
22. Ibid., I.i.3.6.
23. Ibid., III.1.2.
24. Ibid., II.i.5.4.
25. Ibid., I.i.4.7.
26. Ibid., III.2.6.
27. Ibid., III.4.8.
28. Ibid., III.1.6.
29. Ibid., III.2.7.
30. Ibid., III.5.6.
31. Ibid., I.iii.2.1.
32. Ibid., VI.i.11.
33. Ibid., II.ii.3.4.
34. Ibid., VII.iv.36.

10 LECTURES ON JURISPRUDENCE

Smith's ethical argument was designed in part to elucidate the way in which men form judgements as to what is fit and proper to be done or to be avoided, drawing particular attention to the capacity for acts of imaginative sympathy. The same argument which illustrates the way in which we judge on particular occasions is also important in the sense that it explains the origin and something of the nature of general rules of conduct, including those of justice. The argument taken as a whole has two features, first, it shows that Smith rejected the rationalist approach to ethical questions, and, secondly, it suggests that general rules of behaviour must be related to the experience of what, on particular occasions, is thought to be appropriate. This in turn raises the possibility that since experience may vary, then so too will the content of general rules – a position which is explored to a limited extent in the *Theory of Moral Sentiments* where Smith considers the influence of custom and fashion on moral judgement.[1] That the point was important can be seen from Smith's citation of the classical (Greek) custom of exposing children – a practice once based on necessity but which remained in force long after the circumstances which had first given rise to it were no more. As Smith noted, custom is obviously 'capable of establishing as lawful and blameless, particular actions, which shock the plainest principles of right and wrong'.[2] Yet even here Smith drew attention to what he called a 'natural propriety of action' and while noting the influence of custom and fashion, expressed the belief that their effects

> upon the moral sentiments of mankind, are inconsiderable, in comparison of those which they give occasion to in some other cases; and it is not concerning the general style of character and behaviour, that those principles produce the greatest perversion of judgement, but concerning the propriety or impropriety of particular usages.[3]

The same perspective led Smith to draw a distinction between natural and positive law, and to suggest that while the latter may vary in different ages and nations, the former may show some degree of uniformity. As Smith noted in the *Theory of Moral Sentiments*:

It might have been expected that the reasonings of lawyers, upon the different imperfections and improvements of the laws of different countries, should have given occasion to an inquiry into what were the natural rules of justice independent of all positive institution. It might have been expected that these reasonings should have led them to aim at establishing a system of what might properly be called natural jurisprudence, or a theory of the general principles which ought to run through and be the foundation of the laws of all nations.[4]

He added:

Grotius seems to have been the first who attempted to give the world any thing like a system of those principles . . . and his treatise of the laws of war and peace, with all its imperfections, is perhaps at this day the most complete work that has yet been given upon this subject. I shall in another discourse endeavour to give an account of the general principles of law and government.[5]

Smith obviously believed that such a 'theory of jurisprudence' was possible, although he did not live to complete it. However we do have two versions of Smith's lecture notes which give some indication of his intentions. The first of these, dated 1766 but referring to the session 1763/4 was accidentally discovered by Edwin Cannan in 1895 and published the following year; the second version was located by J.M. Lothian in 1958, and finally appeared almost twenty years later. While showing important differences in terms of scope and organisation, both amply demonstrate Smith's interest in the influence of environment on law — and hence the impact of Montesquieu's *De l'esprit des lois* (1748). As John Millar recalled when commenting on the third part of Smith's lecture course:

Upon this subject he followed the plan that seems to be suggested by Montesquieu; endeavouring to trace the gradual progress of jurisprudence, both public and private, from the rudest to the most refined ages and to point out the effect of those arts which contribute to subsistence, and to the accumulation of property, in producing correspondent improvements or alterations in law and government.[6]

The association of Montesquieu with economic forces and with the dynamic processes of change through time may be somewhat over-drawn, but is, as Millar suggested, very much a feature of Smith's thought. It was in this connection that he made use of four broad types of economic organisation, or modes of earning subsistence, arguing that social, legal, and political structures would vary accordingly. To some extent Smith had been anticipated by two fellow-countrymen: John Dalrymple of Cranstoun who published *An Essay towards a General Theory of Feudal Property in Great Britain* (1757), and by Lord Kames's *Historical Law Tracts* which came out in the following year. Kames in particular succeeded in illustrating the way in which the different stages of society could affect the laws governing property, promises and covenants, and the criminal code.[7] But Smith put the point with singular clarity, and in a way which illustrates his preoccupation with the dynamics of change:

If we should suppose 10 or 12 persons of different sexes settled in an uninhabited island, the first method they would fall upon for their sustenance would be to support themselves by the wild fruits and wild animals which the country afforded ... This is the age of hunters. In process of time, as their numbers multiplied, they would find the chase too precarious for their support ... The contrivance they would most naturally think of would be to tame some of those wild animals they caught, and by affording them better food than what they could get elsewhere they would induce them to continue about their land themselves and multiply their kind. Hence would arise the age of shepherds. They would more probably begin first by multiplying animals than vegetables, as less skill and observation would be required ... We find accordingly that in almost all countries the age of shepherds preceded that of agriculture ...

But when a society becomes numerous they would find a difficulty in supporting themselves by herds and flocks. Then they would naturally turn themselves to the cultivation of land and the raising of such plants and trees as produced nourishment for them ... And by this means they would gradually advance into the Age of Agriculture. As society was farther improved, the severall arts, which at first would be exercised by each individual as far as was necessary for his welfare, would be separated; some persons would cultivate one and others others, as they severally inclined. They would exchange with one another what they produced more than was necessary for their support and get in exchange for them the commodities they stood in need of and did not produce themselves. This

exchange of commodities extends in time not only betwixt the
individuals of the same society but betwixt those of different
nations . . . Thus at last the Age of Commerce arises.[8]

Smith used these stages much as Kames had done, but much more
extensively in illustrating man's right as a member of a family, as an
individual, and as a citizen. In the second case in particular, Smith
traced changes in the laws governing property to changes in the mode
of subsistence, later extending his coverage to embrace voluntary trans-
ference, servitudes, pledges, contract and delinquency. In choosing to
illustrate the burden of the argument by reference to the discussion
of 'public jurisprudence' it is not intended to imply that the other
areas of discussion are less important.

Three aspects of the discussion are particularly worthy of note: Smith's
treatment of the sources of authority and of the origin of government;
the discussion of the classical civilisations; and, finally, the analysis of
the emergence of the modern socio-economic system which followed
the collapse of the Western Empire.

Perhaps the easiest way to approach the first is to consider Smith's
treatment of 'political' obligation. As already noted, the *Theory of
Moral Sentiments* postulated the need for some kind of government or
system of magistracy, but without explaining how such systems origin-
ated or why men obey them.

Smith found the basis of obedience in the principles of utility and
authority. In practice, he placed most emphasis on the latter and
identified four main sources: personal qualifications, age, fortune and
birth. Taking these four sources in turn, he argued that personal
qualities such as wisdom, strength, or beauty, while important as
sources of individual distinction, were yet of rather limited political
value, since they are all qualities which are open to dispute. As a result,
Smith suggests that age represents a more important source of authority
and of respect, since it is a plain and palpable quality about which there
can be no doubt. The third source of authority, wealth, of all the
sources of power is perhaps the most emphasised by Smith, and here he
reminded his listeners that through an 'irregularity' of our moral
sentiments, men tend to admire and respect the rich (rather than the
poor, who may be morally more worthy) as the possessors of all the
imagined conveniences of riches.

Upon this disposition of mankind to go along with all the passions of the rich and the powerful, is founded the distinction of ranks and the order of society. Our obsequiousness to our superiors more frequently arises from our admiration for the advantages of their situation, than from any private expectations of benefit from their good will . . . Neither is our deference to their inclinations founded chiefly, or altogether, upon a regard to the utility of such submission, and to the order of society, which is best supported by it.[9]

The second principle which explains willingness to obey a superior or magistrate is of course utility: 'Everyone is sensible of the necessity of this principle to preserve justice and peace in the society.' Smith therefore concluded that 'In all governments both these principles take place in some degree, but in monarchy the principle of authority prevails, and in democracy that of utility.'[10] But while emphasising the general relevance of the principle, Smith was at pains to reject the notion that either society or government could be seen to originate in some kind of contract; a doctrine which lacked, in Smith's eyes, any form of historical justification.[11]

Having come this far, Smith proceeded to consider 'the nature of government and its progress in the first ages of society' as a means of illustrating the principles just stated.

The first stage of society was represented as the 'lowest and rudest' state, such 'as we find it among the native tribes of North America'.[12] In this case, life is maintained through gathering the spontaneous fruits of the soil, and the dominant activities are taken to be hunting and fishing — a mode of acquiring subsistence which is antecedent to any social organisation in production. As a result, Smith suggested that such communities would be small in size and characterised by a high degree of personal liberty due to the absence of any form of economic dependence. Smith also observed that in the absence of private property which was also capable of accumulation, disputes between different members of the community would be minor 'so there is seldom any established magistrate or any regular administration of justice' in such states. Here, such authority as exists is vested in those who possess particular personal qualities, such as age, wisdom, or valour: 'But this is no regular government, for though there may be some among them who are much respected, and have great influence in their determinations, yet he can never do anything without the consent of the whole.'[13]

The second stage of society is that of pasture, which Smith represented as a more advanced state of society, currently found among the Tartars and Arabs. Here the use of cattle is the dominant activity and this mode of subsistence meant, as Smith noted, that life would tend to be nomadic and communities larger in size than would be possible in the preceding stage. More dramatically, Smith observed that the appropriation of herds and flocks introduced a form of property which could be accumulated and hence the need for government: 'Till there be property there can be no government, the very end of which is to secure wealth, and to defend the rich from the poor.'[14] It is therefore in this stage that wealth first becomes an important source of authority and of dependence, in that owners of the means of subsistence 'have no possible means of spending their property, having no domestic luxury, but by giving it in presents to the poor, and by this means they attain such influence over them as to make them, in a manner, their slaves.'[15]

Although Smith does refer to a sequence of stages, he was far from suggesting that they would necessarily follow in the order suggested. For example, the North American Indians constitute an 'objection to this rule' in that 'They, tho they have no conception of flocks and herds, have nevertheless some notion of agriculture.' He also pointed out that the process depended on the satisfaction of certain physical pre-conditions, such as fertility of the soil and access to good communications:

> Tartary and Araby labour under both these difficulties. For in the first place their soil is very poor and such as will hardly admit culture of any sort . . . Neither have they any opportunity of commerce, if it should happen that they should make any advances in arts and sciences . . . In these countries therefore little or no advances can be expected, nor have any yet been made. But in Greece all the circumstances necessary for the improvement of the arts concurred. The several parts were separated from each other by mountains and other barriers, no less than Arabia, but is far more adapted to culture. They would therefore have many inducements to cultivate the arts and make improvements in society. The lands would be divided and well improved and the country would acquire considerable wealth.[16]

Smith begins what is only a rudimentary sketch of early history by assuming that the early inhabitants of Attica had passed through the stage of hunting to that of pasture: 'The first inhabitants of Greece, as we find by the accounts of the historians, were very much of the same sort with the Tartars.'[17] The relations of authority and dependence would be those appropriate to the second stage, while in addition the organisation of the 'state' would reflect its component associations.

As Smith argued, in drawing a parallel with the hunting state:

> As the affairs of each family would be determined by the members of it, of a village by the members of it, so would the affairs of the community or association of villages by the members of the whole directed by their president, and the chief president receiving the lead in all these would appear a sort of sovereign.[18]

The first source of change in this system may be represented as attributable to the advent of agriculture; the second, to the need for protection against external threat. In practice the latter was particularly important in that it led to the development of the city as a defensive rather than as a trading institution. As Smith represents the case, Theseus, the chief of the chiefs, encouraged this policy in the case of Athens and by so doing helped to reduce the power of the village heads. This is essentially a move towards kingship; one which did not last due to the fact that the distribution of property in such a relatively small state was unlikely to 'give the king or lord of it very great superiority over the nobles or other great men'.[19] But growth, both in terms of manufacture and trade, became possible in the context of a state thus equipped to survive, and to an extent which presented them with two choices: to be defensive or a 'conquering republic' — a politico-military decision which, Smith believed, confronted all republics at some time.[20] It is a choice which is forced upon the state by the need to protect the fruits of its own expansion but one which once made inevitably leads to failure and decay. As Smith put it, the growth of wealth based on commerce not only alters the balance of power away from the 'aristocratic' groups of the older constitution, it also reduces the number of fighting men and even their martial spirit:

> So that the very duration of the state and the improvements naturally going on at that time, everyone applying himself to some usefull art and commerce, the attendant on all these necessarily undo the strength and cause the power to vanish of such a state till it be swallowed up by some neighbouring state.[21]

Exactly the same problem was to arise, Smith noted, in the case of Rome making it a prey to those savage nations which, at a late stage of development, the state had been obliged to use in its own defence.

The nations which overran the Western Empire were represented by

Smith as having been at exactly the state of development which had been attained by the early inhabitants of Greece. Primitive peoples whose military power was of the awesome proportions appropriate to the second stage are thus shown to have come in contact with a much more sophisticated society, but one whose power was already on the decline. The result, as Smith duly noted, was the destruction of civilisation as then known, but also the creation of an environment from which a higher form of European civilisation was ultimately to emerge.

Smith's explanation of this general trend begins with the fact that the primitive tribes which overran the empire had already attained a relatively advanced form of the pasturage economy, with some idea of agriculture and of property in land. He argued therefore that they would naturally use existing institutions in their new situation and that in particular their first act would be a division of the conquered territories. In this way the argument moves from a developed version of one economic stage to a primitive version of another; from the stage of pasture to that of 'agriculture'. Under the circumstances outlined, property in land becomes the great source of power and distinction, with each estate assuming the form of a separate principality. As a result of this situation, Smith argued, a gradual change took place in the laws governing property, designed to protect estates against division and to preserve a 'certain lineal succession'.

Such institutions as these quite obviously reflect a change in the mode of subsistence and in the form of property, thus presenting some important contrasts with the previous stage. On the other hand the great proprietor has still nothing on which to expend his surpluses other than the maintenance of dependants — and at the same time has a positive incentive to do so since they contribute to his own security and hence military power.

It was the state of conflict inherent in this situation Smith suggests which gave the proprietors some incentive to change its outlines by altering the pattern of landholding in two quite different ways. First, Smith argued that the heavy demands which were inevitably made on their immediate tenants for military service would inevitably change the quit-rent system in terms of which land was normally held. Smith argued in effect that the great lords would naturally begin to grant leases for a term of years, and then in a form which gave security to the tenant's family and ultimately to his posterity.

Secondly, Smith argued that the same need for protection which had altered the relationship between the great lord and his tenants, would also lead to patterns of alliance between members of the former groups and, therefore, to arrangements which gave some guarantee of mutual service and protection. It was for these reasons, Smith argued, that the lesser landowners entered into feudal arrangements with those greater lords who could ensure their survival (thus enhancing their ability to do so), just as the great lords would be led to make similar arrangements amongst themselves and with the king. He held these changes took place from about the ninth to the eleventh centuries, and that by imposing some limitations on the free enterprise of the proprietors contributed thereby to a more orderly form of government. Yet the problem presented by the military capacity of the great proprietors, and the relative weakness of kings, remained and was to lead, according to Smith's account, to a still further development.

The policy in question was the encouragement given by kings to cities as a means of acquiring increased revenues and a countervailing power to that wielded by the proprietors; a policy which featured the grant of significant powers of self-government. It was a political act, but one with economic consequences in that the creation of self-governing units established an essential pre-condition for economic growth, namely justice and personal security. Such cities as were located near the means of transportation were thus in a position to grow rapidly through trade and manufacture, thus increasing in absolute terms at least the financial capacity of the Crown.

But at the same time, Smith drew attention to the fact that wealth based on trade and manufacture would change the balance of political power at least in the long run. In particular he emphasised that the great proprietors, when faced for the first time with a means of spending their surpluses would tend to accelerate their own decline; partly through the dismissal of retainers, and partly through the substitution of a cash for the service relationship, which had prevailed between those who owned the means of subsistence and those who worked the soil. As Smith put it when summarising his most complete statement of the argument:

A revolution of the greatest importance to the public happiness, was in this manner brought about by two different orders of people, who had not the least intention to serve the public. To gratify the most childish vanity was the sole motive of the great proprietors. The merchants and artificers, much less ridiculous, acted merely from a view to their own interest, and in pursuit of their own pedlar principle of turning a penny wherever a penny was to be got. Neither of them had any knowledge or foresight of that great revolution which the folly of the one, and the industry of the other, was gradually bringing about.[22]

The 'great revolution' to which Smith referred had resulted in a situation which had a number of distinctive features. To begin with, Smith attributed 'order and good government, and with them, the liberty and security of individuals' to the forces just considered. He also noted that the same trend had generated a number of constitutional changes which were the reflection of the nature and distribution of new sources of wealth. The trend of events was reflected in the Revolution Settlement, which confirmed a structure which Smith described as 'a happy mixture of all the different forms of government properly restrained, and a perfect security to liberty and property'.[23]

In fact, Smith believed that England was really a special case, and that she alone had escaped from absolutism.[24] To a great extent this was the reflection of her own natural economic advantages, but Smith also emphasised other factors, many of a more 'accidental' nature. For example, he argued that the solution to the Scottish problem (brought about by union) allied to Britain's situation as an island, had obviated the need for a standing army, and thus denied her kings an important instrument of oppression. He added that Elizabeth I had also contributed to weaken the position of her successors by selling off crown lands; a policy which was not unconnected with the fact that she had no direct heir. As Smith presents the case, it was the growing weakness of the Stuart kings (reflecting in part their own peculiarities of character), and the growing significance of the Commons, which had ultimately combined to produce that particular system of liberty which was now found in England.[25]

But if the constitutional outcome of attaining the fourth stage of 'commerce' could not be precisely predicted, Smith was able to state that it must have certain economic features, and thus in the fourth and final section of his course to address himself to other questions of analysis and policy (or 'practice').

The economic analysis which Smith provided in the lectures is concerned with a system which features the activities of agriculture, manufacture, and commerce where these activities are characterised by a division of labour[26] with the patterns of exchange facilitated by the use of money.[27] There are three main features of the central analysis: the treatment of the division of labour, of price and allocation, and the exposure of the mercantile 'fallacy'.

The division of labour is central to the analysis because it is by reference to this institution that Smith explains the growth in opulence which is associated with the development of the arts under the stimulus of the 'natural wants' of man. Smith here rehearses points which have now become familiar, explaining the increase in productivity in terms of improved dexterity, the saving of time otherwise lost in passing from one function to another, and the scope given to the use of machines. But the second aspect of the argument is equally important in the sense that Smith draws attention to the high degree of interdependence which follows from the division of labour in two ways. First, it is pointed out that in the modern state even a relatively simple product such as the labourer's woollen coat is the creation of a large number of different workmen including the wool-gatherer, the spinner, the dyer, weaver, tailor, etc. – not to mention the different processes involved in the manufacture of the tools required. Secondly, it is emphasised that in such a situation every man in effect acquires the goods he needs through exchange – a point which leads directly to the discussion of price and allocation.

As in the case of the *Wealth of Nations*, Smith's handling of price theory is amongst the most successful aspects of the study, featuring as it does a clear distinction between natural and market price together with an examination of their interdependence. *Natural* price is defined in effect as the supply price of a commodity, where the latter refers to labour cost:

> A man then has the natural price of his labour, when it is sufficient to maintain him during the time of labour, to defray the expence of education, and to compensate the risk of not living long enough, and of not succeeding in the business. When a man has this, there is sufficient encouragement to the labourer and the commodity will be cultivated in proportion to the demand.[28]

Market price, on the other hand, is the price which may prevail at any given point in time and will be determined, Smith argues, by the 'demand or need for the commodity'; its abundance or scarcity in relation to the demand (a point which is used to explain the 'paradox' of value) and, finally, the 'riches or poverty of those who demand'.[29] Smith then went on to suggest that although the two prices were logically distinct, they were also 'necessarily connected'. Thus in the event of market price rising above the natural level, the reward of labour in this employment will rise above its natural (long-run equilibrium) rate, leading to an inflow of labour and an expansion in supply (and vice versa). In equilibrium, therefore, the market and natural price will be the same; a point which allowed Smith to go on to argue that 'whatever police' tends to prevent this coincidence will 'diminish public opulence'.[30] The examples which contributed to keep the market above the natural price include taxes on industry, monopolies, and the exclusive privileges of corporations — all of which affect price either through their impact on the supply of the commodity or on the flow of labour to a specific employment. Similarly, Smith criticised policies such as the bounty on corn, which kept market below natural price. Now these examples refer of course to particular cases, but Smith may be said to have added a further dimension to the problem in grasping the fact that the economic system can be seen under a more general aspect. This much is evident in his objection to particular regulations of 'police' on the ground that they distorted the use of resources by breaking 'what may be called the natural balance of industry' and interfering with the 'natural connexion of all trades in the stock'.[31]

The third main aspect of the argument relates to the issue of money — a concept whose relevance is implied in the previous discussion of price, but which was no doubt introduced at this point perhaps because it provided an easy means of transition to the discussion of a particular branch of policy which attracted Smith's attention — the mercantile system. The subject is approached by way of a discussion of the role of money as the instrument of exchange, and enabled Smith to demonstrate that natural opulence does not consist in money and to expose the absurdity of policies which were designed to prohibit the free exportation of specie. The policy was shown not merely to involve an error, but also to have pernicious effects with regard to the use of resources — once again returning to the general theme stated in connection with the theory of allocation. The advantages of free trade are thus suggested to complement those of domestic economic freedom and the argument closes with the claim that all policies in restraint of trade, whether based on misunderstanding or national jealousy (a point more than a little reminiscent of Hume) should be rooted out:

> From the above considerations it appears that Brittain should by all means be made a free port, that there should be no interruptions of any kind made to forreign trade, that if it were possible to defray the expences of government by any other method, all duties, customs,

and excise should be abolished, and that free commerce and liberty of exchange should be allowed with all nations and for all things.[32]

This theme had already been stated by David Hume in his *Political Discourses* (1752) and Dugald Stewart was very probably correct in his judgement that Smith owed much to this source.[33] Yet the plea for liberty and the often strident criticism of the mercantile system are now peculiarly associated with Smith, perhaps because his confidence in economic growth, especially in the context of Great Britain, seems to have been so unbounded. Yet even in the lectures he drew attention to the social costs of the division of labour; to the effect of this institution on the individual whose 'whole attention is bestowed on the seventeenth part of a pin or the eightieth part of a button, so far divided are we in these manufactures'. He also drew attention to the neglect of education, arising from the fact that 'In rich and commercial nations the division of labour, having reduced all trades to very simple operations, affords an opportunity of employing children very young.'[34] Here Smith commented on the employment of children at six or seven years of age, the impact on parental authority, and on the fact that when attaining manhood such people, when not at work, have limited resources:

> Accordingly we find that in the commercial parts of England, the tradesmen are for the most part in this despicable condition; their work through half the week is sufficient to maintain them, and through want of education they have no amusement for the other, but riot and debauchery. So it may very justly be said that the people who clothe the whole world are in rags themselves.[35]

A further bad effect of commerce is one already noted – the decline of martial spirit. As Smith observed with some feeling, no doubt recalling his days in Oxford:

> In the year 1745 four or five thousand naked unarmed Highlanders took possession of the improved parts of this country without any opposition from the unwarlike inhabitants. They penetrated into England, and alarmed the whole nation, and had they not been opposed by a standing army, they would have seized the throne with little difficulty. Two hundred years ago such an attempt would have roused the spirit of the nation.[36]

As he rather drily concluded: 'To remedy these defects would be an object worthy of serious attention'.[37]

Notes

1. *TMS*. Part V.
2. Ibid., V.2.14.
3. Ibid., V.2.12.
4. Ibid., VII.iv.37.
5. Ibid.
6. Stewart, *Life of Smith*, I.19.
7. For comment, see Peter Stein, *Legal Evolution: The Story of an Idea* (Cambridge, 1980).
8. *LJ*(A), i. 27-32. For comment, see R.L. Meek, *Social Science and the Ignoble Savage* (Cambridge, 1976).
9. *TMS*, I.iii.2.3.
10. *LJ*(B), 14.
11. *LJ*(B), 15-18.
12. *WN*, V.i.a.2. The broadly sociological propositions associated with the 'stadial' analysis are developed in the opening sections of Book V in the context of a discussion of defence and justice.
13. *LJ*(B), 19.
14. *LJ*(B), 20.
15. *LJ*(B), 21.
16. *LJ*(A), iv. 62.
17. *LJ*(A), iv. 56.
18. *LJ*(A), iv. 37.
19. *LJ*(A), iv. 66.
20. *LJ*(A), iv. 75.
21. *LJ*(A), iv. 81.
22. *WN*, III.iv.17. The argument is developed in Book III and again in *LJ*(A) volume iv and *LJ*(B), 1-99.
23. *LJ*(B), 63.
24. *LJ*(A), iv. 168.
25. These arguments are reviewed in the opening lectures of *LJ*(A), volume iv and *LJ*(B), 61-4.
26. *LJ*(B), 160-72.
27. *LJ*(B), 182-90.
28. *LJ*(B), 227.
29. *LJ*(B), 228.
30. *LJ*(B), 230. The term 'police' is used in the sense of civil administration or the system of public order.
31. *LJ*(B), 233-4.
32. *LJ*(B), 269.
33. Stewart, *Life of Smith*, IV.24.
34. *LJ*(B), 329.
35. *LJ*(B), 330.
36. *LJ*(B), 331-2.
37. *LJ*(B), 333.

11 TUTOR TO THE DUKE OF BUCCLEUCH

One of the people to whom David Hume sent copies of the *Theory of Moral Sentiments* was Charles Townshend. A statesman of considerable distinction now best remembered for his disastrous policies regarding the American colonies, Townshend had married the widowed Countess of Dalkeith, mother of the 3rd Duke of Buccleuch, in 1755, and, according to Hume, was so taken with Smith's book:

> that he said to Oswald he wou'd put the Duke of Buccleugh under the Authors Care, and would endeavour to make it worth his while to accept of that Charge. As soon as I heard this, I calld on him twice with a View of talking with him about the Matter, and of convincing him of the Propriety of sending that young Nobleman to Glasgow: For I coud not hope, that he coud offer you any Terms, which woud tempt you to renounce your Professorship: But I missd him. Mr Townsend passes for being a little uncertain in his Resolutions; so perhaps you need not build much on this Sally.[1]

Hume's estimate of Townshend's character was widely accepted, but in this case at least, Hume's fears were not to be realised. Townshend visited Glasgow in the course of 1759 and then in 1763 he wrote to Smith:

> The time now drawing near when the Duke of Buccleugh intends to go abroad, I take the liberty of renewing the subject to you: that if you should still have the same disposition to travel with him I may have the satisfaction of informing Lady Dalkeith and His Grace of it, and of congratulating them upon an event which I know that they, as well as myself, have so much at heart. The Duke is now at Eton: he will remain there until Christmas. He will then spend some short time in London, that he may be presented at Court, and not pass instantaneously from school to a foreign country; but it were to be wished He should not be long in Town, exposed to the habits and companions of London, before his mind has been more formed and better guarded by education and experience.[2]

Smith accepted this proposal while explaining that he would have

123

difficulty in leaving his post in Glasgow before the beginning of April.
He also expressed doubts and uncertainties in a letter to Hume and on
account of them did not immediately resign his Chair but sought leave
of absence.[3] He arranged that the remainder of his course be taken by
a person appointed by the University but paid by himself. The lectures
were given by Thomas Young, although he failed to secure the Chair,
despite support from John Millar and Joseph Black who regarded him
as a better candidate than Smith's eventual successor, Thomas Reid, of
King's College, Aberdeen.[4]

A second condition, which was also accepted, was that Smith should
return the fees already paid by the students in respect of the full
course, but here he met with more difficulty. The circumstances are
described by A.F. Tytler in his *Life of Lord Kames*:

After concluding his last lecture, and publicly announcing from the
Chair, that he was now taking a final leave of his auditors; acquaint-
ing them at the same time with the arrangement he had made to
the best of his power for their benefit; he drew from his pocket the
several fees of students, wrapped up in seperate paper parcels, and
calling up each man by his name, he delivered to the first who was
called, the money into his hand. The young man peremptorily
refused to accept it, declaring that the instruction and pleasure he
had already received was much more than he either had repaid or
ever could compensate; and a general cry was heard from every one
in the room, to the same effect. But Mr Smith was not to be bent
from his purpose. After warmly expressing his feelings of gratitude
and the strong sense he had of the regard shewn to him by his young
friends, he told them this was a matter betwixt him and his own
mind, and that he could not rest satisfied unless he performed what
he deemed right and proper — 'You must not refuse me this satisfaction — Nay, by heavens, gentleman, you shall not,' — and seizing
by the coat the young man who stood next to him, he thrust the
money into his pocket, and then pushed him from him. The rest
saw it was in vain to contest the matter, and were obliged to let
him have his own way.[5]

On 1 March 1764 the University received Smith's formal letter of
resignation which was dated Paris, 14 February 1764. They parted on
the best of terms. Smith wrote: 'I never was more anxious for the Good
of the College than at this moment and I sincerely wish that whoever
is my Successor may not only do Credit to the Office by his Abilities

but be a comfort to the very excellent Men with whom he is likely to spend his life . . .'[6] The University minutes, in noting his resignation, records the sincere regret of its members:

> at the Removal of Dr Smith, whose distinguished Probity and amiable qualities procured him the esteem and affection of his Colleagues; whose uncommon Genius, great Abilities and extensive Learning did so much Honours to this Society; his elegant and ingenious Theory of Moral Sentiments having recommended him to the Esteem of Men of Taste and Literature thro'out Europe; his happy Talents in illustrating abstracted Subjects and faithfull assiduity in communicating usefull knowledge distinguished him as a Professor and at once afforded the greatest pleasure and the most important instruction to the Youth under his Care.

To break with Glasgow was the more difficult because it involved a break with his mother. Immediately after Smith left Glasgow Joseph Black reported that she was 'very happy' with a letter from her son. 'She was particularly overjoyed at the hint that your stay abroad was not to be so long as you expected.'[7] Whatever its defects the move had financial advantages. Smith's income at Glasgow is difficult to assess but from all University sources his total emoluments may have been about £150 to £300 during his stay there. The tutorship gave him the prospect of such a sum for life and the immediate prospect of foreign travel.

The main outline of Smith's continental tour can be reconstructed. It was almost entirely in France and based on Toulouse and Paris. Smith left Glasgow in January 1764 and reached Paris on 13 February. The stay there was brief because by 4 March he had arrived in Toulouse.[8]

Toulouse had a number of attractions as a place of residence for Smith and his pupil. Many British tourists went there and, as the second city of France, it had many of the trappings of an ancient capital. Perhaps even more immediately relevant, Hume was able to provide an introduction to the local society, through one of the many abbés with whom he had close links, but who in this case claimed kinship with him. He was the Abbé Seignelay Colbert, of the family of Cuthbert of Castlehill in Inverness-shire and claimed to be a 'cousin' of Hume's. Whatever the family link, the introduction was valuable. Colbert's letters to Hume show a desire to encourage the traffic of English and Scottish people to Toulouse and a special willingness to help Smith and the Duke of Buccleuch. But there were problems in Toulouse. Smith's French was not good[9] and many of those they had hoped to meet in Toulouse, from the Archbishop downwards, were not in residence. By 5 July Smith was writing rather forlornly to Hume:

> Mr Townshend assured me that the Duke of Choiseul was to recommend us to all the people of fashion here and everywhere else in France. We have heard nothing, however, of these recommendations and have had our way to make as well as we could by the help of the Abbé who is a Stranger here almost as much as we. The Progress, indeed, we have made is not very great. The Duke is acquainted with no french man whatever. I cannot cultivate the acquaintance of the few with whom I am acquainted, as I cannot bring them to our house and am not always at liberty to go to theirs. The Life which I led at Glasgow was a pleasurable, dissipated life in comparison of that which I lead here at Present.

Then comes the interesting announcement of how Smith was passing his time. 'I have begun to write a book in order to pass away the time. You may believe I have very little to do.'[10] This was undoubtedly the *Wealth of Nations*, but a letter from John Glassford, the Glasgow merchant, written on 5 November 1764, shows that the work had its roots in the Glasgow years and was not the outcome of idle days in Toulouse: 'I hope your Time passes agreeably and that you are bringing forward at your Leisure Hours the usefull work that was so well advanced here. It would be a Pity to want it longer than you find necessary to finish it to your own liking, as it may then very safely make its appearance.'[11] As the stay in Toulouse did not work out as planned, time was probably hanging on their hands, and perhaps Smith was seriously worried about the effect on the Duke. The last worry was probably why Smith expressed a hope for a visit from Sir James Macdonald of Sleat, then making a great impression in Paris, and of whom Hume wrote on his early death in Rome in 1766 'Were you and I together Dear Smith we shoud shed Tears at present for the Death of poor Sir James Macdonald. We could not possibly have suffrd a greater Loss than in that valuable young Man.'[12] Hardly surprisingly then in July 1764 Smith felt that 'If Sir James would come and spend a month with us in his travels it would not only be a great Satisfaction to me but he might by his influence and example be of great service to the Duke. Mention these matters, however, to nobody but to him'.[13] It is doubtful if Macdonald went to Toulouse. In October he was still in Paris and

Hume was asked to ensure that Macdonald would conduct Buccleuch's younger brother, who was then arriving in France, 'to any other Place where he would chuse to go'.[14]

At the same time Smith was planning other diversions, which were to develop into a series of expeditions. On 5 July 1764 he told Hume they proposed setting out 'soon' for Bordeaux where they intended 'to stay a fortnight or more'. That they went is attested by a letter from Isaac Barré to Hume written on 4 September, the party having all returned to Toulouse.[15] Before late October, Smith and his charge were back again in Toulouse, having made another 'expedition', this time to Bagnères-de-Bigorre in the Pyrenees, then a fashionable resort. Smith was much pleased with the outcome of these visits, which had made 'a great change upon the Duke. He begins now to familiarize himself to French company and I flatter myself I shall spend the rest of the Time we are to live together, not only in Peace and content-ment but in gayety and amusement.'[16]

The improvement in the circumstances of both men was clearly marked, so that we find Smith writing to Hume in the same letter, thanking him for an introduction to the old Duke of Richelieu, and telling him of further plans:

I take this opportunity of Mr Cooks going to Paris to return to you, and thro you, to the Ambassador, my very sincere and hearty thanks for the very honourable manner in which he was so good as to men-tion me to the Duke of Richelieu, in the letter of recommendation which you sent us. There was indeed one small mistake in it. He called me Robinson instead of Smith. I took upon me to correct this mistake myself before the Duke delivered the letter. We were all treated by the Marechal with the utmost Politeness and attention, particularly the Duke, whom he distinguished in a very proper manner. The intendant was not at Bordeaux, but we shall soon have an opportunity of delivering his letter as we propose to return to that Place in order to meet my Lords Brother.

Smith went on:

When Mr Scot joins us we propose to go to see the meeting of the States of Languedoc, at Montpelier. Could you procure us recom-mendations to the Comte d'Eu to the Archbishop of Narbonne and to the Intendant? These expeditions, I find, are of the greatest service to My Lord.[17]

They were also of great benefit to Smith as the references in the *Wealth of Nations* testify. But the expeditions and the openings offered by Toulouse were still not adequate to satisfy the Duke and his brother. Future plans were discussed in correspondence between Charles Townshend and his stepson. Unfortunately only Charles Townshend's letters have survived, but they indicate that Buccleuch was seeking permission to move to Paris by the spring of 1765. Permission was granted, but in a letter which was full of advice:

> With respect to Thoulouse, I consent to your leaving it when you please & for the very reasons which you alledge, but when you settle at Paris, I must intreat you will still think the place of residence only changed, & not your age nor your Plan of improvement, nor the propriety of continuing the same Study and the same exercises . . .
>
> I have already descried Mr ? to signify to the Ministry of France that you are removing to Paris; I have wrote to Lord Hertford; & I will write to Mr Hume. I wish you to fix upon a residence as near to the best Academy as you can, and at the same time as near to Lord Hertford, that you may take your exercises early, without loss of time, & be as frequently with Lord Hertford as His businesss & your ages admit, by Mr Hume's acquaintance, you will have an easy access to men of letters, who, in France, are men of the world, and are therefore the most useful society to you, who must be one, & ought to be the other, of these characters. The conversation of such men will familiarise subjects to you otherwise abstruse; it will give you the ? without the labor of application, & it will do more, it will lead you to further application & insensibly form your mind to a preference of liberal men & a taste for elegant amusements. This habit once obtained, it is, believe me, my Dear Lord, it is a security against every folly, every meanness, nay and every enemy in life.
>
> In your course of study, I shall leave you to Mr Smith, nor interpose further than to desire, you will anatomise, the Monarchy of France . . .

Finally, Townshend warned in the same spirit of anxiety which typifies his original letter to Smith: 'If you go much into mixed company, as I suppose you will, let me warn you against any female attachment. Your rank & fortune will put women of subtle character upon projects which you should not be the dupe of . . .'[18]

The return to Paris was not immediate however, and was in fact preceded by other visits, including one to Geneva. Geneva offered

Smith the chance to examine the affairs of a small republic at a time when claims for wider participation in government were rife. An even greater attraction to Smith must have been the presence nearby of Voltaire, the great philosopher and historian whom he regarded as 'the most universal genius perhaps which France has ever produced'.[19]

Smith had an immediate entry to Genevan society through the physician Theodore Tronchin, who had sent his son to study under Smith in Glasgow in 1761. Yet evidence of the visits which Smith must have made remains sparse as does his contact with Voltaire. The most direct account is provided by Samuel Rogers, who was told by Smith late in life that he had been in Voltaire's company five or six times, although the only point of substance actually mentioned was that the great man 'has a great aversion to the States [General] and was rather attached to the King'.[20]

The account of Faujas de St. Fond, professor of geology in the Museum of Natural History in Paris and who visited Smith in Edinburgh in 1784 records a fuller comment by Smith on Voltaire:

'Reason', said he, one day, as he showed me a very fine bust of this author, 'owes him incalculable obligations; the ridicule and the sarcasms which he plentifully poured out upon fanatics and hypocrites of all sects, have prepared men's minds for the light of truth, to the search for which every intelligent mind ought to aspire. He has done more in this matter than the books of the gravest philosophers, which everybody does not read; while the writings of Voltaire are in general made for all and read by all' . . .

Another time, when I was taking tea with him, he spoke to me of Rousseau with a kind of religious respect, 'Voltaire', said he, 'sought to correct the vices and the follies of mankind by laughing at them, and sometimes even getting angry with them; Rousseau, by the attraction of sentiment, and the force of conviction, drew the reader into the heart of reason. His *Contrat Social* will in time avenge him for all the persecutions he suffered'.[21]

Though any accounts of Smith's stay in Geneva are extremely sparse, his visit was remembered by those he then met. Immediately after he left, Madame Denis at Ferney submitted to Smith a series of statements on what was apparently a squabble over sporting rights, doing so on the ground that she respected Smith's ethics and the judgement of the English community in Geneva.[22] Further evidence came in 1767 from a continental correspondant, who finding Smith was not in

London, planned to visit him in Kirkcaldy 'Et faire quelques promenades avec vous Sur le bord de la Mer'.[23] The links with Geneva remained as time passed. In 1775 Patrick Clason, who graduated from Glasgow in 1758 when Smith was there and who became a private tutor and schoolmaster at Logie, wrote enclosing a letter from Charles Bonnet[24] to Hume, through whom he sent greetings to Smith, 'the Sage of Glasgow', whose visit was always remembered with great pleasure. Clason himself sent greetings directly from Le Sage and from Tronchin.

While it has usually been assumed that Smith and his party arrived in Paris in mid-December 1765 it is safer to suggest that he reached the city later. David Hume, his old and particular friend, left Paris at the beginning of January without seeing him; an unlikely occurrence if Smith was in the city or even its vicinity, and Horace Walpole, who had been expecting Smith in December, does not record their arrival until mid-February.

The move to Paris changed Smith's activities and his life-style. The Duke of Buccleuch's rank, together with Townshend's introductions, ensured an immediate entry into the highest reaches of English society, then in Paris in large numbers, and through them, to the whole range of their Paris associates. Smith had his own source of introductions in Hume, who had been lionised by Parisian society when he first went there as private secretary to Lord Hertford, the ambassador, in 1763, and who continued to play a leading role to the end as Embassy Secretary and then as Chargé d'Affaires until he left France early in 1766. When Smith learned of Hume's impending departure, and of the 'greatest disappointment to the Duke of Buccleugh not to find you there [Paris]',[25] he wrote: 'Before you set out from Paris I would beg of you to leave me some letters to honest men and women.'[26] Whether some of Smith's old friends and colleagues in Glasgow or Kirkcaldy would have recognised those with whom Hume had been consorting as 'honest men and women' may be open to doubt, but to be a friend of Hume was in itself a passport to some of the most exclusive circles in Paris. The Countess de Boufflers told Hume '. . . I have made the acquaintance of Mr Smith, and . . . for the love of you I have given him a very hearty welcome'.[27] But Smith's own reputation had gone before him, though not so dramatically as Hume's. The first translation of the *Theory of Moral Sentiments* by Marc-Antoine Eidous was published in Paris in 1764, and the book itself attracted a good deal of attention.

The life of Paris led Smith into new relations with his two charges. At Toulouse the letters which survive denote few distractions, so few indeed that diversions had to be arranged, and the time of all was spent in close study. Smith was working on his book, while of the Duke of Buccleuch Smith was able to tell Hume by August 1765, 'He has read almost all your works several times over, and was it not for the more wholesome doctrine which I take care to instill into him, I am afraid he might be in danger of adopting some of your wicked Principles. You will find him very much improved.'[28] But with the Duke of Buccleuch and his younger brother able to lead a more independent life in Paris than at Toulouse, Smith was able to exploit the varied intellectual offerings of the city. The result was that during Smith's stay in Paris, probably more than in any other period, he was absorbed in a personal round of social and intellectual engagements, although as his later life was to show, it was not a period which left him with any permanent desire for such a life. Salons and dinner parties provided him with contrasting intellectual stimuli. Smith attended many, though the evidence has to be culled yet again from isolated remarks and clues in the memoirs and letters of others. Among the salons presided over by the formidable females around whom much of Parisian literary society centred, and to which immediate entry was assured, was that of Madame de Boufflers, mistress of the Prince de Conti, and with whom Hume had been a close and intimate friend. In July 1766 Hume told her 'I am glad you have taken my friend Smith under your protection. You will find him a man of true merit, though perhaps his sedentary recluse life may have hurt his air and appearance as a man of the world.'[29] Mme de Boufflers was clearly much attracted by Smith. She promptly began to read the *Theory of Moral Sentiments*,[30] and the respect lasted. In 1772, long after he had left Paris and was living in the vastly different surroundings of Kirkcaldy, she told Smith of translations which were then being undertaken[31] and in 1777 was speaking much of Smith to Gibbon when he visited Paris.[32] Another salon which he frequented was that of Mademoiselle de l'Espinasse, who had been assistant to Madame du Deffand until 1764 when a breach led to the setting up of a separate salon. A choice had to be made, even by Hume, who was not permitted by Madame du Deffand to remain on good terms with both. The rupture had occurred before Smith reached Paris, but by the time he arrived D'Alembert had taken up residence in the house and the salon of Mademoiselle de L'Espinasse was the most intellectual in the city.

But there were other important contacts to be made, among them the members of the French 'school' of economists which centred round the person and works of Francois Quesnay, the King's physician. Quesnay has the distinction of producing a theory or model of the whole economic process which is usually known as the *Tableau Economique* (1758). The work and its policy implications attracted the attention of the Marquis de Mirabeau, Dupont de Nemours, and, amongst others, Mercier de la Riviere whose book *L'Ordre naturel et essentiel des sociétés politiques* (1767) was considered by Smith to be 'the most distinct and best connected account' of the doctrine.[33] At the time Smith arrived in Paris the school was at the very zenith of its powers. Two journals, the *Journal D'Agriculture* and the *Éphémérides de Citoyen* carried articles of a professional nature while in addition the central texts were already published: most notably Mirabeau's *Friend of Man* (1760) and the *Philosophie Rurale* (1763), written jointly by Quesnay and Mirabeau after the latter had been released from prison.[34] Indeed in the very year that Smith found himself in Paris, Quesnay was working on further versions of the basic model while Dupont de Nemours was writing his account of the *Origin and Progress of a New Science* – that of political economy.

There was a great deal in physiocratic writing which was to prove unattractive to outsiders – most obviously perhaps, the doctrine of legal despotism and a political philosophy which envisaged a constitutional monarch modelled on the Emperor of China. Attitudes too were a source of aggravation, moving Hume to write to Morellet concerning the publication of his *Dictionnaire du Commerce*:

> I see that, in your prospectus, you take care not to disoblige your economists . . . But I hope that in your work you will thunder them, and crush them, and pound them, and reduce them to dust and ashes! They are, indeed, the set of men the most arrogant that now exist . . . [35]

Smith too found the disciples' apparently slavish acceptance of the doctrines rather trying even if he did recognise that this system:

> with all its imperfections, is, perhaps, the nearest approximation to the truth that has yet been published upon the subject of political economy, and is upon that account well worth the consideration of every man who wishes to examine with attention the principles of that very important science.[36]

Smith also had a profound regard for Quesnay whom he once described as:

> one of the worthiest men in France and one of the best Physicians

that is to be met with in any country. He was not only the Physician but the friend and confident of Madame Pompadour a woman who was no contemptible judge of merit.[37]

Such contacts were complemented by a series of dinners, affairs held by a number of the literati, at which Smith was a regular attender. As at the salons, so at the dinners, his circle of acquaintances spread rapidly, though with a considerable degree of overlap. Baron d'Holbach held some of the best known, at one of which Hume is reported to have told his host that he had never seen an atheist, to be informed that fifteen of the eighteen sitting at table with him were, and that the three others had not yet made up their minds.[38] Smith's links with d'Holbach were long and affectionate. When Smith was in Glasgow, d'Holbach was supervising the translation of the *Theory of Moral Sentiments*[39] and years later, in 1786, Smith asked the Abbé Morellet 'to assure him of my most affectionate and respectful remembrance, and that I never shall forget the very great kindness he did me the honour to shew me during my residence at Paris'.[40] Morellet, an ex-farmer-general of the French customs, with whom Smith became a close friend and with whom he continued to correspond, first met him at a dinner given by Helvetius. According to Morellet in his *Mémoires*, they engaged chiefly in direct discussion of economic issues, including the theory of commerce, banking, public credit 'and various points in the great work which Smith was then meditating'.[41] Morellet had a high regard for Smith and was later to translate the *Wealth of Nations*. But perhaps the most important figure that Smith met through both Mlle de L'Espinasse and Helvetius was A-R-J Turgot, later to become Minister of Finance under Louis XVI. Turgot had already addressed himself to issues which were known to be of interest to Smith in his historical treatises 'On Universal History' and on the 'Successive Advances of the Human Mind'; treatises which date from the early 1750s although unpublished at the time. In 1766 Turgot was working on perhaps the most important economic treatise to emerge at this period, the *Reflections on the Formation and Distribution of Riches*, which was published in the *Éphémérides* and is now known to have been in Smith's possession.[42] Smith could hardly fail to have been attracted by the analyses of this eminently liberal thinker and the two men evidently remained on good terms. It was through Turgot that Smith obtained a copy of the rare *Mémoires concernant les impositions et droits en Europe* by J.L. Moreau de Beaumont. This work was first published in Paris in 1768-69; and was so valuable that Smith refused to send it to

John Sinclair in 1778 on the ground that 'If any accident should happen to my book, the loss is perfectly irreparable.'[43]

But two events were to occur during Smith's visit which were much less pleasant in character. The first of these was the famous quarrel between Hume and Jean-Jacques Rousseau, author of the *Social Contract* and of the *Discourse on Inequality* which Smith had mentioned in the *Edinburgh Review*. The key issue was that Hume had taken Rousseau to England, had arranged for him to stay in Derbyshire, and negotiated a pension for him, but, in spite of such aid, Rousseau became more and more suspicious until on 23 June 1766 he wrote Hume with the basic accusation: 'You brought me to England, ostensibly to procure a haven for me, but actually to dishonour me.'[44] Hume wrote to Hugh Blair on 1 July: 'He [Rousseau] is surely the blackest and most atrocious Villain, beyond comparison, that now exists in the World; and I am heartily asham'd of any thing I ever wrote in his Favour.'[45]

The Parisian acquaintances were obviously intensely interested in the quarrel. Smith, as an old friend, and as someone strategically placed to inform others, must have been consulted quickly, though there is no record of any communication from Hume to him. But he replied on 6 July in a letter which, while admitting the injury done to Hume, contrasts sharply with the choleric letters which Hume was then sending to his friends, and which demonstrates well some aspects of Smith's character:

> I am thoroughly convinced that Rousseau is as great a Rascal as you, and as every man here believes him to be; yet let me beg of you not to think of publishing anything to the world upon the very great impertinence which he has been guilty of to you. By refusing the Pension which you had the goodness to sollicit for him with his own consent, he may have thrown, by the baseness of his Proceeding some little ridicule upon you in the eyes of the Court and the ministry. Stand this ridicule, expose his brutal letter, but without giving it out of your own hand so that it may never be printed, and if you can, laugh at yourself, and I shall pawn my life that before three weeks are at an end, this little affair, which at present gives you so much uneasiness, shall be understood to do you as much honor as any thing that has ever happened to you. By endeavouring to unmask before the Public this hypocritical Pedant, you run the risk, of disturbing the tranquillity of your whole life. By letting him alone he cannot give you a fortnights uneasiness. To write against

him is, you may depend upon it, the very thing he wishes you to do. He is in danger of falling into obscurity in England and he hopes to make himself considerable by provoking an illustrious adversary. He will have a great party. The church, the Whigs, the Jacobites, the whole wise English nation, who will love to mortify a Scotchman, and to applaud a man who has refused a Pension from the King.

Smith went on to observe that all Hume's friends in Paris were of a like opinion: Holbach, D'Alembert, Mme Riccoboni etc., adding that 'Mr Turgot, a friend everyway worthy of you, desired me to recommend this advice to you in a particular manner, as his most earnest entreaty and opinion.'[46] The letter is an interesting one, indicating as it does that Smith was a respected and accepted member of the intellectual circle in which he moved. So too is the reaction of one who recognised so clearly the distinction between the desire of praise and that of praise-worthiness.

The second difficulty arose from the illnesses of Smith's young charges. The Duke of Buccleuch suffered from a fever in the summer of 1766 leading Smith to write an anxious letter to Townshend giving details of the disorder and of his difficulties in procuring medical advice:

I sent for Quenay. first ordinary physican to the King. He sent me word he was ill. I then sent for Senac; he was ill likewise. I went to Quenay myself to beg that, notwithstanding his illness, which was not dangerous, he would come to see the Duke. He told me he was an old infirm man, whose attendance could not be depended upon, and advised me, as his friend, to depend upon De la Saone, first physician to the Queen. I went to De la Saone, who was gone out and not expected home until late that night. I returned to Quenay, who followed me immediately to the Duke.[47]

The Duke recovered, but in October his younger brother fell ill. Once again Quesnay was in attendance, as was Richard Gem, the physician to the British Embassy and an intimate of the French intellectuals. But Hew Scott's illness was much more serious and a letter to Lady Frances Scott, the brothers' sister, showed that Smith was obviously very worried indeed. The doctors had little idea of what was wrong or what to do. Smith did not leave the patient for eight days, but then, on being assured by Quesnay that the matter was in hand, he went to his bankers. On his return after one hour he found Scott delirious. Then, in spite of the distinguished medical aid of Quesnay and Gem, Smith summoned the father of his old pupil of Glasgow days, the Genevan physician, Theodore Tronchin:

> Tho' I have entire confidence in the skill of the Physicians that have hitherto attended him, notwithstanding they have been mistaken in their predictions, I have thought proper to call in Tronchin, who will attend him for the future along with them. He is my particular and intimate friend . . . Gem is a man of the most perfect probity and friendship. Since the beginning of Mr Scotts illness he has seldom been less than twelve hours a day by his bedside and has all along acted the part of a Nurse as well as of a Physician. Tho' the event has not hitherto answered their expectations I am convinced, they have both acted a very prudent and proper part. They both have still good hopes.[48]

But the hopes were ill-founded. Hew Scott died on 19 October. There is pathos and humanity in Smith's letter to Lady Frances Scott:

> It is my misfortune to be under the necessity of acquainting you of the most terrible calamity that has befallen us. Mr Scott dyed this Evening at seven o'clock. I had gone to the Duke of Richmonds in order to acquaint the Duke of Buccleugh that all hope was over and that his Brother could not outlive tomorrow morning: I returned in less than half an hour to do the last duty to my best friend. He had expired about five minutes before I could get back and I had not the satisfaction of closing his eyes with my own hands. I have no force to continue this letter; The Duke, tho' in very great affliction, is otherwise in perfect health.[49]

The visit to France was over. Smith and his party returned with the body and reached London on 1 November 1766. He never left Britain again.

Notes

1. *Corr.*, letter 31, David Hume to Adam Smith, 12 April 1759.
2. *Corr.*, letter 76, Charles Townshend to Adam Smith, 25 October 1763.
3. *Corr.*, letter 78, Adam Smith to David Hume, 12 December 1763.
4. *Corr.*, letter 80, John Millar to Adam Smith, 2 February 1764.
5. A.F. Tytler, *Memoirs of the Life and Writings of Henry Home of Kames*, i, 195.

6. *Corr.*, letter 81, Adam Smith to Thomas Miller, 14 February 1764.

7. *Corr.*, letter 79, Joseph Black to Adam Smith, 23 January, 1764.

8. According to John Rae, *Life of Adam Smith* (London, 1895), 175.

9. *Corr.*, letter 142, Adam Ferguson to Adam Smith, 1 June 1774.

10. *Corr.*, letter 82, Adam Smith to David Hume, 5 July 1764.

11. *Corr.*, letter 85, John Glassford to Adam Smith, 5 November 1764.

12. *Corr.*, letter 96, David Hume to Adam Smith, August 1766.

13. *Corr.*, letter 82, Adam Smith to David Hume, 5 July 1764.

14. *Corr.*, letter 83, Adam Smith to David Hume, 21 October 1764.

15. J. Hill Burton, *Letters of Eminent Persons addressed to David Hume* (Edinburgh, 1849), 36.

16. *Corr.*, letter 83, Adam Smith to David Hume, 21 October 1764.

17. Ibid.

18. Letter dated 22 April 1765 in Scottish Record Office (SRO) GD 224/296/6 in RH4/98/Reel 1.

19. *Edinburgh Review*, in *Essays in Philosophical Subjects*, 254.

20. P.W. Clayden, *Early Life of Samuel Rogers*, 95.

21. B. Faujas de Saint Fond, *A Journey through England and Scotland to the Hebrides in 1784* (Glasgow, 1907), ii, 245–6.

22. *Corr.*, Letter 89, Marie Louise Denis to Adam Smith, 10–11 December 1765.

23. *Corr.*, letter 105, George Louis Le Sage (?) to Adam Smith, 23 June 1767.

24. *Corr.*, letter 144, Patrick Clason to Adam Smith, 25 February 1775.

25. *Corr.*, letter 86, Adam Smith to David Hume, August 1765.

26. *Corr.*, letter 88, Adam Smith to David Hume, September 1765.

27. Burton, *Letters of Eminent Persons to David Hume*, 237.

28. *Corr.*, letter 86, Adam Smith to David Hume, August 1765.

29. *The Letters of David Hume*, ed. J.Y.T. Greig (Oxford, 1932), ii, 59.

30. Burton, *Letters of Eminent Persons to David Hume*, 237–8.

31. *Corr.*, letter 130, Adam Smith to Mme de Boufflers, February 1772.

32. *Corr.*, letter 187, Edward Gibbon to Adam Smith, 26 November 1777.

33. *WN*, IV. ix. 38.

34. For comment on the school see the eminently readable account provided by Henry Higgs, *The Physiocrats* (London, 1898) and R.L. Meek, *Economics of Physiocracy* (London, 1962).

35. Hume, *Letters*, ii, 205.

36. *WN*, IV. ix. 38.

37. *Corr.*, letter 97, Smith to Lady Frances Scott, 15 October 1766.

38. E.C. Mossner, *The Life of David Hume* (Oxford, 1954), 483.

39. *Corr.*, letter 77, David Hume to Adam Smith, 28 October 1763.

40. *Corr.*, letter 259, Adam Smith to Abbé Morellet, 1 May 1786.

41. Morellet, *Mémoires*, ed. Lémontey (Paris, 1825), i, 244.

42. Turgot's main works are conveniently collected in R.L. Meek, *Turgot on Progress, Sociology, and Economics* (London, 1973).

43. *Corr.*, letter 196, Smith to Sir John Sinclair, 24 November 1778.

44. Mossner, *Life of Hume*, 526.

45. Hume, *Letters*, ii, 57.

46. *Corr.*, letter 93, Smith to Hume, 6 July 1766.

47. *Corr.*, letter 94, Smith to Townshend, 26 August 1766.

48. *Corr.*, letter 97, Smith to Lady Frances Scott, 15 October 1766.

49. *Corr.*, letter 98, Smith to Lady Frances Scott, 19 October 1766.

12 LONDON AND KIRKCALDY

Although Smith arrived in London in November 1766, he did not reach Kirkcaldy until the following Spring. The affairs of his pupil are unlikely to have detained him. Judging by Lady Mary Coke's *Journal*, the chief activity and interest of the young Duke seems to have been his search for a wife; a matter in which it may safely be assumed Smith would play no part.[1] Nor could an invitation to the wedding on 2 May 1767 have detained Smith in London, since it seems to have been extremely quiet — much to the annoyance of Lady Mary Coke, whose opinion of her nephew as 'very genteel' and 'sensible' was rapidly declining. As she told the Duke's sister, Lady Frances Scott: 'it was a sensible mortification to me the not being permitted to be at the wedding, but that his never so much as made me a visit hurt me still more . . .'[2]

The months in London were not inactive. Smith's business took two forms. First, he was at work correcting the sheets of a new edition of the *Theory of Moral Sentiments*.[3] The second activity, that of giving advice to politicians, was probably more arduous than correcting proofs. Lord Shelburne was given advice on two matters, the first of which was on the geography of the South Seas. Smith sent Shelburne a translation of one of the many memorials of the Portuguese sailor, Pedro Fernandez de Quiros, and used the occasion to introduce Alexander Dalrymple, a younger brother of Lord Hailes and a distinguished Admiralty hydrographer. Shelburne was warned that Quiros' voyage 'is long, obscure, and difficult to be understood except by those who are particular acquainted with the geography and navigation of those countries',[4] and Dalrymple was introduced to provide the exposition Shelburne needed. But Dalrymple had a greater claim to attention, in that he believed there was an undiscovered continent in the South Seas, and although unwilling to take sides in the debate, Smith suggested to Shelburne that Dalrymple was the man to test the proposition. The proposition was not visionary, because in 1768 the expedition sent to chart the transit of Venus, under Captain Cook, explored parts of Australia and New Zealand. Cook's later voyage of 1772-5 was to disprove the theory of a southern continent.

The second piece of advice to Shelburne concerned colonial administration. Smith had been asked to find out what he could about the administration of the Roman colonies. He found little and probably did not try hard, with only days at his disposal.[5] What followed was certainly not very informative, nor always entirely accurate, but it contained enough to give a salutary warning to Shelburne on how to deal with the American colonists:

> They [Roman colonies] seem to have been very independent. Of thirty colonies of whom the Romans demanded troops in the second carthagenian war, twelve refused to obey. They frequently rebelled and joined the enemies of the Republic. Being in some measure little independent republics, they naturally followed the interests which their peculiar Situation pointed out to them.[6]

Smith's work with Charles Townshend was probably rather different. Shelburne was only Secretary of State for the Southern Department, while Townshend was Chancellor of the Exchequer from 2 August 1766 until his death 13 months later. The evidence is contained in a document on the History of the Sinking Fund. This document had been perused by Smith, who had then inserted in the margin a number of figures at points where a blank space had been left in the manuscript. It would seem that Townshend had written the manuscript but left it in an unfinished state, leaving Smith to fill in some of the statistical gaps and to make a number of corrections. To that extent it is quite possible to accept the view of W.R. Scott, who discovered the manuscript among the Buccleuch papers at Dalkeith, 'that Adam Smith supplied a few numerical totals, made some corrections and a few excisions'.[7] W.R. Scott went on to suggest that he also 'supplied a number of ideas as to general principles, and many calculations'.[8] Detailed textual analysis casts some doubt on Scott's suggestion. In any case it seems unlikely that Smith would have a strong influence on the Chancellor at this time. Townshend's last year of life as Chancellor of the Exchequer was one of the more mercurial in his erratic career, with so many problems and so much political intrigue on his hands that it is doubtful if he would have had much time for the thought of a scholarly recluse, however much he may have admired him. He held office under a Prime Minister, Chatham, who was becoming increasingly erratic, even inaccessible; he was plotting in various ways with Rockingham; he disputed with Chatham over the privileges of the East India Company, and when the land tax was reduced from 4s to 3s in the pound by the vote of the House of Commons in February, he raised the revenue by means of the ill-fated American taxes. In short, the high and tempestuous politics in which Townshend was engaged during the winter of 1766/7 probably left little room for an extensive collaboration with Smith.

The nature of Townshend's life, and the improbability of Smith fitting into it comes out with great clarity in the pages of the *Journal* kept by Lady Mary Coke. Townshend's erratic behaviour is fully documented. Smith's old friend, Sir Gilbert Elliot, visited her on 5 March and held that the disagreements of Chatham and Townshend 'will never do'[9] and on 15 March he agreed with her that Townshend 'had been detrimental to the publick affairs'.[10] Later in the month Lady Dalkeith summed up the position neatly to her sister:

> She told me the Ministers were again all quarrelling, that for her part She was sick of politicks, & that tho' She had made Mr. Townshend promise not to resign, yet, if She was sure he wou'd never come in again, She shou'd not be sorry they turned him out.[11]

Lady Mary Coke had her ears open for all the gossip, yet the only reference to Smith is in February 1767, when Sir Gilbert Elliot and Lady George Lennox 'talk'd of Mr. Smith, The Gentleman that went abroad with the Duke of Buccleugh, and said many things in his praise, but added that he was the most Absent Man that ever was',[12] which led Lady George Lennox to retell the story of Smith making tea with bread and butter as an example of his absent-mindedness. This is not the person for whom Townshend would be able to spare much time in his tumultuous last winter of political life.

Smith's winter in London was therefore probably spent more in preparing his own works for publication than in providing advice. If that is a valid interpretation, then the winter in London could be regarded as a period which cleared up a number of issues, before leaving for Kirkcaldy at the end of March or early in April. Before he left London, Smith arranged for his publisher to send boxes of books to Edinburgh, and thanked him for two books which he had recently procured for him and which were to figure extensively in the *Wealth of Nations.*[13]

Smith obviously wished to visit his mother in Kirkcaldy, but earlier correspondence with Hume did not mention it as a place where he thought he might settle. The issue became a live one in the autumn of 1765 when Hume's term of office in the Embassy in Paris was coming to an end and when both Hume and Smith could look forward to a degree of financial independence which gave them freedom to choose where to live. Hume started the correspondence-

> Paris is the most agreeable Town in Europe, and suits me best; but
> it is a foreign Country. London is the Capital of my own Country;
> but it never pleased me much. Letters are there held in no honour:
> Scotsmen are hated: Superstition and Ignorance gain Ground daily.
> Edinburgh has many Objections and many Allurements. My present
> Mind, this Forenoon the fifth of September is to return to France
> ... Pray give me your Judgement.[14]

Smith's judgement was clear, favouring London and showing his sceptical, almost cynical assessment of French society:

> you are wrong in thinking of settling at Paris. A man is always
> displaced in a forreign Country, and notwithstanding the boasted
> humanity and politeness of this Nation, they appear to me to be, in
> general, more meanly interested, and that the cordiality of their
> friendship is much less to be depended on than that of our own
> countrymen. They live in such large societies and their affections
> are dissipated among so great a variety of objects, that they can
> bestow but a very small share of them upon any individual. Do
> not imagine that the great Princes and Ladies who want you to live
> with them make this proposal from real and sincere affection to you.
> They mean nothing but to gratify their own vanity by having an
> illustrious man in their house, and you would soon feel the want
> of that cordial and trusty affection which you enjoyed in the family
> of Lord and Lady Hertford, to whom I must beg to be remembered
> in the most dutiful and respectful manner. Your objections to
> London appear to me to be without foundation. The hatred of
> Scotch men can subsist, even at present, among nobody but the
> stupidest of the People, and is such a piece of nonsense that it must
> fall even among them in a twelvemonth. The Clamour against you
> on account of Deism is stronger, no doubt, at London where you are
> a Native and consequently may be a candidate for everything, than
> at Paris where as a forreigner, you possibly can be a candidate for
> nothing. Your Presence dissipated in six months time much stronger
> prejudices in Edinburgh, and when you appear at Court, in open
> day light, as you must do upon your return, and not live obscurely
> at Miss Elliots with six or seven scotchmen as before, the same
> irresistible good temper will in a very few weeks dissipate much
> weaker prejudices at London ... to hold their tongues. In short I

have a very great interest in your settling at London, where, after many firm resolutions to return to Scotland, I think it is most likely I shall settle myself. Let us make short excursions together sometimes to see our friends in France and sometimes to see our friends in Scotland, but let London be the place of our ordinary residence.[15]

Such discussion was perhaps only the vague talk which can be undertaken when the issue is not a live one. Though Kirkcaldy was not mentioned, it had attractions for someone of Smith's temperament, which the salons of Paris or London could not match.

In the event, Smith rarely moved from Kirkcaldy in the six years following his return, although he was a major, if somewhat ineffective figure in introducing the Duke and Duchess of Buccleuch to their Scottish tenantry in the autumn of 1767. The plans for the introductions were disrupted by a number of causes. The intention was to mark the Duke's 21st birthday on 13 September 1767 by a major celebration, which would have introduced him to both his tenantry and to many connections in the South of Scotland. In spite of the vast possessions of the Buccleuchs, the Duke, who had succeeded his grandfather in 1752, had never visited Dalkeith. The Buccleuchs and Lady Frances Scott arrived at the beginning of September, but Charles Townshend died before the celebrations were held. The immediate effect was a slight delay in implementing their plans; more important, Townshend's death on 4 September 1767 ensured, indeed perhaps made possible, Buccleuch's subsequent life-style, devoted as it was to the affairs of his estates rather than to the public and political life for which Townshend had so obviously and so understandably groomed him. The plan, and Smith's part in it, are evident in a letter Townshend wrote to Buccleuch in Toulouse:

Mr. Smith, among many other advantages, possesses that of being deeply read in the constitution and laws of your own Country. He is ingenious [sic], without being [?]; He is general, without being superficial, and He is learned without being too systematical or singular in his notion of our Government, and from Him you will grow to be a grounded [?] Politician in a short course of study. When I say a Politician, I do not use the Word in the common acceptation, but rather as a phrase less severe, and for that reason more proper to your age, than statesman, tho' the one is the beginning of the other, and they differ chiefly in *this* is the work of study, and *that* the same work finished by experience and a course of office. Mr. Smith will make you a politician, and time will after-wards in your example, demonstrate the truth of my opinion . . .[16]

Smith spent some weeks with the Buccleuchs at Dalkeith from September and was obviously pleased with the couple he was to help introduce to this new role. He told David Hume: '. . . I flatter myself [they] will both be very agreable to the People of this country, I am not sure that I have ever seen a more agreeable woman than the Duchess. I am sorry that you are not here because I am sure you would be perfectly in love with her.'[17] It was perhaps a pity that the more extrovert Hume was not there for the celebrations, at which Smith does not seem to have been a great success. Alexander Carlyle, the parish minister, was not impressed:

. . . they assembled by cards about fifty ladies and gentlemen of their friends and the neighbourhood . . . The fare was sumptuous, but the company was formal and dull. Adam Smith, their only familiar at table, was but ill qualified to promote the jollity of a birthday, and their Graces were quite inexperienced . . . Had it not been for Alexander McMillan, W.S., and myself, the meeting would have been very dull, and might have dissolved without even drinking the health of the day . . . Smith remained with them for two months, and then returned to Kirkcaldy to his mother and his studies. I have often thought since, that if they had brought down a man of more address than he was, how much sooner their first appearance might have been; their own good sense and discernment enabled them sooner to draw round them as familiars a better set of people of their own choosing, than could have been picked out for them by the assistance of an aide-de-camp.[18]

But the Kirkcaldy years would hardly lack a social dimension; Smith had, after all, returned to the place of his birth and to a house-hold which included his mother and cousin, Janet Douglas. Nor did he neglect his friends, writing as he did to David Hume on 7 June 1767:

The Principal design of this Letter is to Recommend to your partic-ular Attention the Count de Sarsfield, the best and the most agreable friend I had in France. Introduce him, if you find it proper, to all the friends of your absent friend, to Oswald and to Elliott in Par-ticular. I cannot express to you how anxious I am that his stay in London should be rendered agreeable to him. You know him and must know what a plain, worthy honourable man he is. I have enclosed a letter for him which you may either send to him or rather, if the weighty affairs of state will permit it, deliver it to him yourself. The letter to Dr. Morton you may send by the Penny Post.[19]

Writing on 13 September, Smith enclosed yet another letter to Sarsfield and went on:

There is a very amiable, modest, brave worthy young Gentleman who lives in the same house with you. His name is David Skeene. He and I are Sisters' sons; but my regard for him is much more founded upon his personal qualities than upon the relation in which he stands to me. He acted lately in a very gallant manner in America of which he never acquainted me himself and of which I came to the knowledge only within these few days. If you can be of any service to him you could not possibly do a more obliging thing to me.[20]

Smith also kept abreast of current affairs through Hume's continuing contacts in high places. And Smith expressed indignation – in common with all his friends – at the outcome of the Douglas Cause when the House of Lords reversed the judgement of the Court of Session of 1767, rejecting the claims of the 7th Duke of Hamilton and sustaining those of Archibald Douglas. Archibald Douglas had claimed the estates of the 1st Duke of Douglas on the ground that he was the surviving son of the Duke's sister, Lady Jane Douglas, though allegedly born when she was 51. Smith had taken evidence for the case in France, and his interest in the final decision was keen. He was much incensed at the mob, including Boswell, who attacked the house of the Lord President, Robert Dundas of Arniston, when the result of the appeal became known. Hailes had been on the same side as the Lord President in the Court of Session majority of eight to seven, so Smith could safely write:

I cannot conclude this letter, though already too long, without expressing to your Lordship my concern and still more, my indignation at what has lately passed both at London and at Edinburgh. I have often thought that the supreme court of the United Kingdom very much resembled a jury. The Law Lords generally take upon them to sum up the Evidence, and to explain the Law to the other peers; who generally follow their opinion implicitly. Of the two Law

Lords, who upon this occasion, instructed them, the one has always run after the Applause of the Mob; the other, by far the most intelligent, has always shewn the greatest dread of popular odium; which, however, [he] has not been able to avoid. His inclinations [also] have always been suspected to favour one of the [par]ties. He has upon this occasion, I suspect, followed rather his fears and his inclinations than his judgment. I could say a great deal more upon this subject to your Lordship, but I am afraid I have already said too much. I would rather, for my own part, have the solid reputation of your most respectable President, though exposed to the insults of a brutal mob, than all the vain and flimsy applause that has ever yet been bestowed upon either or both the other two.[21]

Hailes replied:

if matters go on in the present course the Business of a judge will be very easy, he need not consult the law, nor his Conscience, he will find an infallible Rule in the Enemys of Glass windows, has any man an antipathy of Glass windows then he is in the right.

Seriously this is an unhappy Crisis, *incidimus in ea tempora*, that a Judge must study Causes under the protection of skrewed bayonets; this was my case for two nights; and I assure you, that next to Window-breakers they were the most disagreeable attendants that I ever met with. Judges must not only be free, but they must feel themselves free and the whole nation must have the Conviction of their being free — hitherto I imagined that I was answerable for my Conduct to the laws of my Country and to my God, and that I was subject to no other Tribunal — *now* there is a sovereign Tribunal at every Bonfire.[22]

Yet it is plain that Smith's letter to Hume of 7 June 1767 set the tone of his long stay in Kirkcaldy:

My Business here is Study in which I have been very deeply engaged for about a Month past. My Amusements are long, solitary walks by the Sea side. You may judge how I spend my time. I feel myself, however, extremely happy, comfortable, and contented. I never was, perhaps, more so in all my life.[23]

There was obviously much to be done to transform a lecture course on economic theory and policy which comprised only part of a more extensive course on jurisprudence into an extensive, highly finished treatise. Again it is clear that while Smith had already formulated his basic position with regard to the division of labour, the theory of price, and the doctrine of natural liberty, he had still to integrate the distinction between factors of production (land, labour and capital) and forms of return (rent, wages and profit) with the theory of price as developed in the *Lectures*, and to assimilate the physiocratic model of the economy into his general analytical structure. It is also known that, during this period, Smith read and absorbed the arguments of Sir James Steuart's *Principles of Political Economy* (1767) which had been brought out by his own publishers, writing as he did to William Pulteney on 3 September 1772 that:

> In the Book which I am now preparing for the Press I have treated fully and distinctly of every part of the subject which you have recommended to me; and I intended to have sent you some extracts from it; but upon looking them over, I find that they are too much interwoven with other parts of the work to be easily separated from it. I have the same opinion of Sir James Stewarts Book that you have. Without once mentioning it, I flatter myself, that every false principle in it, will meet with a clear and distinct confutation in mine.[24]

An extensive correspondence with Lord Hailes which occurred between January and May 1769 also suggests that he was working on the long Digression on Silver.[25] In January 1769 Smith told Hailes that he would very much appreciate being able to consult his papers on the prices of provisions in the past. Two months later he wrote again to tell Hailes that for reasons of security he would send a servant to collect these papers with a view to copying them. There is real urgency in these exchanges, suggesting hard endeavour on a difficult subject, although the correspondence is probably of even more importance for the light which it sheds on Smith's difficulties and on his methods of working. On 15 January he wrote that 'My own Papers are in a very great disorder and I wait for some further information which I expect from different quarters before I attempt to give them the last Arrangement', and later in the same letter, '. . . tho' in my present situation I have properly speaking nothing to do, my own schemes of Study leave me very little leisure, which go forward too like the web of Penelope, so that I scarce see any Probability of their ending'.[26] Together these comments indicate that after eighteen months' work on the *Wealth of*

Nations Smith was not progressing rapidly towards a conclusion. The Hailes correspondence also shows why. When it started Smith listed a number of secondary sources which he had already consulted, and all of which were to be used extensively in the *Wealth of Nations*; Hailes responded by providing a series of references to prices in Scotland from 1243 to 1561.[27] Smith was clearly not happy about some of these and others recorded elsewhere:

> ... all the estimated prices of grain among our ancestors seem to have been extremely Loose and inaccurate: and that the same nominal sum was frequently considered as the Average price both of grain and of other things during a course of years in which considerable alterations had been made upon the intrinsick value of the Coin.[28]

The correspondence continued throughout the first half of 1769 with Smith commenting extensively on prices and also on the reading of Scotch Acts,[29] Hailes's examination of the *Regiam Majestatem* and a variety of legal papers. In particular, discrepancies in the reports of prices kept intruding. With some feeling Smith commented:

> The real cause of those discrepancies seems to have been that either the Authors of those compilements, or perhaps the counts in the particulare Province had in some cases simply followed some antient valuation, and in other had accommodated that antient valuation to the changes that had afterwards been made in the Standard of the coin; and this pretty much as accidental circumstances had directed.[30]

Smith's brain was tortured as he acquired more material and the greater the evidence which came to light, the greater the intellectual dismay and distress it produced in the mind of someone seeking to explain complex social phenomena on the basis of a small number of basic principles. His material had become so extensive, and the innovatory system which he was to impose upon it such an intellectual challenge, that speedy completion was difficult. But in addition, Smith had personal attributes which inhibited progress. The first was his desire for perfection, for the intellectual satisfaction which he maintained was an essential element in any systematic exposition. The second, probably related to the first, was an apparent inability to dispose of material or to reject it when, though important, it may not have been immediately relevant to the problem in hand.

There is every indication that Smith went to Kirkcaldy in 1767 fully expecting that the work would be finished fairly soon. There is no reason to doubt James Boswell's comment on 29 July of the same year that Smith's 'Jurisprudence will be out in a year and a half' or to suppose that the reference was to any other work than the *Wealth of Nations*.[31] But as Smith remarked to Shelburne in January 1768 'Since I came to this country I have employed myself pretty much in the manner that I proposed. I have not, however, made all the Progress that I expected; I have resolved, therefor, to prolong my stay here till November next, perhaps, till after the Christmas holidays next winter'.[32] More than a year after writing the letter to Shelburne, Hume returned to Edinburgh, 'settled here', as he told Sir Gilbert Elliot, 'without casting the least Thought of Regreat to London, or even to Paris', still in his old house in James's Court, but looking forward to his move to more spacious quarters in the New Town where he would be able to 'display my great Talent for Cookery, the Science to which I intend to addict the remaining Years of my Life'.[33] As soon as he arrived, he wrote a challenge to Smith on 20 August 1769:

> I am glad to have come within sight of you, and to have a View of Kirkcaldy from my Windows; But as I wish also to be within speaking terms of you, I wish we coud concert measures for that purpose. I am mortally sick at Sea, and regard with horror, and a kind of hydrophobia the great Gulph that lies between us. I am also tir'd of travelling, as much as you ought naturally to be, of staying at home; I therefore propose to you to come hither, and pass some days with me in this Solitude. I want to know what you have been doing, and propose to exact a rigorous Account of the method, in which you have employed yourself during your Retreat. I am positive you are in the wrong in many of your Speculations, especially where you have the Misfortune to differ from me. All these are Reasons for our Meeting, and I wish you woud make me some reasonable Proposal for the Purpose. There is no Habitation on the Island of Inch-keith; otherwise I shoud challenge you to meet me on that Spot, and neither [of] us ever to leave the Place, till we were fully agreed on all points of Controversy.[34]

By February 1770 Hume had obviously heard that the book was nearing completion and wrote to his friend to enquire:

> What is the Meaning of this, Dear Smith, which we hear, that you are not to be here above a day or two, in your Passage to London? How can you so much as entertain a thought of publishing a Book, full of Reason, Sense, and Learning, to these wicked, abandon'd Madmen?[35]

Over two years later Hume wrote again, on 28 January 1772:

> I shoud certainly, before this time, have challenged the Performance
> of your Promise, of being with me about Christmas, had it not been
> for the Misfortunes of my Family. Last Month, my Sister fell danger-
> ously ill of a Fever; and though the Fever be now gone, she is still
> so weak and low, and recovers so slowly, that I was afraid it woud be
> but a melancholy House to invite you to. However, I expect, that
> time will re-instate her in her former Health, in which case, I shall
> look for your Company. I shall not take any Excuse from your own
> State of Health, which I suppose only a Subterfuges invented by
> Indolence and Love of Solitude. Indeed, my Dear Smith, if you
> continue to hearken to Complaints of this Nature, you will cut
> Yourself out entirely from human Society, to the great Loss of both
> Parties.[36]

The reference to illness is an important one, since we know that Smith
had complained of discomfort in a letter addressed to John Davidson,
dated Autumn 1771:

> I intended about a week ago to make a long visit to my friends on
> your side of the water. I had got wind in my stomach which I
> suspected a little dissipation might be necessary to dispel. By taking
> three or four very laborious walks I have entirely rid of it: so that I
> shall not [leave] my retreat for above a day these six months [to
> come].[37]

There is a story, possibly apocryphal, which dates from this period
to the effect that at least on one long walk Smith marched some fifteen
miles from Kirkcaldy to Dunfermline in his dressing-gown before
being awoken from his reverie by the sound of the church bells calling
the people to church![38] While this report, if true, suggests some strain,
it is at least certain that Smith informed William Pulteney in 1772 of
'interruptions occasioned partly by bad health arising from want of
amusement and from thinking too much upon one thing'.[39] But he also
referred to 'Public calamities' in which friends, including the Duke of
Buccleuch, were involved and to the fact that his 'attention has been
a good deal occupied about the most proper method of extricating
them.' The crisis had been unfolding over the summer and indeed, as
early as June, Hume wrote that:

> We are here in a very melancholy Situation; Continual Bankruptcies,

universal Loss of Credit, and endless Suspicions . . . The Case is little better in London. It is thought, that Sir George Colebroke must soon stop; and even the Bank of England is not entirely free from suspicion. Those of Newcastle, Norwich and Bristol are said to be stopp'd: The Thistle Bank has been reported to be in the same Condition: The Carron Company is reeling, which is one of the greatest Calamities of the whole; as they give Employment to near 10,000 People. Do these Events any-wise affect your Theory? Or will it occasion the Revisal of any Chapters?[40]

But the specific difficulty to which Smith referred in his letter to Pulteney was the collapse of the Ayr Bank in which the Duke of Buccleuch was a major shareholder. Smith seems to have had some success in this matter, for in October Hume wrote 'As soon as I came to Town, I ask'd the Question you proposed; and was told by Sir William Forbes, that tho' they did not commonly take the Air Notes, yet he woud upon your Account: You may therefore send them over by the first Opportunity.'[41] But by November 23 Hume had obviously received a plan from Smith which indicated that completion of his work was imminent, and responded:

I shou'd agree to your Reasoning, if I could trust your Resolution. Come hither for some weeks about Christmas: dissipate yourself a little; return to Kirkcaldy; finish your Work before Autumn; go to London; print it; return and settle in this Town; which suits your studious, independent turn even better than London: Execute this plan faithfully; and I forgive you.[42]

But on 10 April 1773 he could still write: 'I expect to see you soon. Have you been busy, and whether in pulling down or building up?'[43]. Within a week Smith was in Edinburgh on his way to London, at last, and on 16 April 1773, gave Hume, as his literary editor, instructions on how to dispose of his papers in the event of his sudden death.[44]

Notes

1. *The Letters and Journals of Lady Mary Coke*, ed. J.A. Home (1889-96), (reprinted 1970) i, 224.
2. Ibid, i, 211.
3. See below, p. 140.
4. *Corr.*, letter 101, Adam Smith to Lord Shelburne, 12 February 1767.
5. Ibid.

6. Ibid.
7. W.R. Scott, 'Adam Smith at Downing Street, 1766-7', *Economic History History Review*, 6 (October 1935), 82.
8. Ibid.
9. *Letters and Journals of Lady Mary Coke*, ed. J.A. Home, i, 166.
10. Ibid, i, 178.
11. Ibid, i, 192.
12. Ibid, i, 141.
13. *Corr.*, letter 102, Adam Smith to Thomas Cadell, 25 March 1767.
14. *Corr.*, letter 87, David Hume to Adam Smith, 5 September 1765.
15. *Corr.*, letter 88, Adam Smith to David Hume, September 1765.
16. Charles Townshend to the Duke of Buccleuch, 10 June [?] 1764. SRO. GD 224/296/4 in RH4/98/Reel 1.
17. *Corr.*, letter 109, Adam Smith to David Hume, 13 September 1767.
18. A. Carlyle, *Autobiography*, ed. J.H. Burton (1910) 512-3.
19. *Corr.*, letter 103, Adam Smith to David Hume, 7 June 1767.
20. *Corr.*, letter 109, Adam Smith to Count de Sarsfield, 13 September 1767.
21. *Corr.*, letter 116, Adam Smith to Lord Hailes, 5 March 1769.
22. *Corr.*, letter 117, Lord Hailes to Adam Smith, 6 March 1769.
23. *Corr.*, letter 103, Adam Smith to David Hume, 7 June 1767.
24. *Corr.*, letter 132, Adam Smith to William Pulteney, 3 September 1772.
25. *Corr.*, letters 115-120.
26. *Corr.*, letter 115, Adam Smith to Lord Hailes, 15 January 1769.
27. *Corr.*, letter 117, Lord Hailes to Adam Smith, 6 March 1769.
28. *Corr.*, letter 118, Adam Smith to Lord Hailes, 12 March 1769.
29. *Corr.*, letter 115, Adam Smith to Lord Hailes, 15 January 1769.
30. *Corr.*, letter 119, Adam Smith to Lord Hailes, 16 May 1769.
31. James Boswell to W.J. Temple, 29 July 1767 in *Boswell in Search of a Wife, 1766-1769*, eds. F. Brady and F.A. Pottle (London, 1957).
32. *Corr.*, letter 113, Adam Smith to Lord Shelburne, 27 January 1768.
33. *The Letters of David Hume*, ed. J.Y.T. Greig (Oxford, 1932) ii, 208.
34. *Corr.*, letter 121, David Hume to Adam Smith, 20 August 1769.
35. *Corr.*, letter 123, David Hume to Adam Smith, 6 February 1770.
36. *Corr.*, letter 129, David Hume to Adam Smith, 28 January 1772.
37. *Corr.*, letter 128, Adam Smith to John Davidson, Autumn 1771.
38. J. Rae, *Life of Adam Smith* (London, 1895), 259-60.
39. *Corr.*, letter 132, Adam Smith to William Pulteney, 3 September 1772.
40. *Corr.*, letter 131, 27 June 1772.
41. *Corr.*, letter 133, October 1772.
42. *Corr.*, letter 134, David Hume to Adam Smith, 23 November 1772.
43. *Corr.*, letter 136, David Hume to Adam Smith, 10 April 1772.
44. *Corr.*, letter 137, Adam Smith to David Hume, 16 April 1773.

13 LONDON, 1773-1776

While the need to arrange for the publication of the *Wealth of Nations* indicated the necessity of a visit to London, the timing of the move was determined by other business, most notably the attempts which were made to have Smith placed in other posts. Smith's friends were sufficiently influential, and he himself had such a reputation, that it is hardly surprising that tempting offers were made. William Pulteney tried to have him considered by the East India Company in September 1772, probably for an appointment to a commission of three which the Company proposed sending to India to examine its affairs. Adam Ferguson was anxious to obtain such an appointment, visiting London to push his claim but, as Hume told Smith, he 'return'd, fat and fair; and in good humour, notwithstanding his Disappointment, which I am glad of'.[1] Smith did not acknowledge Pulteney's action quickly[2] and did not visit London till the affair was concluded. He was probably not very enthusiastic, his only interest in the proposition being, as he told Pulteney, that 'There is no labour of any kind which you can impose upon me which I will not readily undertake.'[3]

Other proposals were more attractive. The Buccleuch tutorship had obviously been a success and Smith seems to have been more attracted to posts of that nature. Two of the tutors of the young Duke of Hamilton were old friends, William Mure of Caldwell and Andrew Stuart, which goes some way to explaining Smith's partisan support of their side in the Douglas Cause. They proposed that Smith should repeat his tour abroad, this time with the Duke of Hamilton. Years later, in 1780, Smith recalled that it was this proposal that took him to London in 1773 but that the Duke of Buccleuch 'was so good as to disuade [me] from accepting it',[4] perhaps because he held out prospects of the even better appointment which was to come Smith's way. Other reasons may have told against Smith. The tutor who eventually accompanied Hamilton was John Moore, Hamilton's family doctor, an important factor given the poor state of the Duke's health.

If Smith was not to become a tutor yet again, he was at least consulted by others on who might be, as when the 2nd Earl Stanhope consulted him about a tutor for the 5th Earl of Chesterfield. Smith suggested Adam Ferguson, who, though not appointed, showed that he was dissatisfied with his prospects in Edinburgh and saw the tutorship as a way to the long-term financial security which Smith enjoyed.[5]

Smith left Kirkcaldy in the spring of 1773 to begin a stay in London which was continuous for almost three years, until after the publication of the *Wealth of Nations*. From April 1776 to January 1777 he was out of London visiting Scotland, living both in Kirkcaldy and Edinburgh, chiefly for personal reasons. Otherwise the period from May 1773 to October 1777 is the London period of his life, when wider contacts flourished and multiplied.

Smith's notoriously bad correspondence led to the survival of only three letters from him during the period, one of which, addressed to David Hume, sets the tone of so much of Smith's correspondence:

> I should be ashamed to write to you, if I had not long ago conquered all modesty of that sort. Taking it for granted, therefore, that you hate apologies as much as I do, I meant both making them and receiving them, I shall not pretend to make any for my having so long neglected to write to you. I hope I need not tell you that my long silence did not arise from any want of the most affectionate and most grateful remembrance of you.[6]

If Smith's correspondence does not tell much about his activities, the main features can be deduced from other sources, most notably James Boswell. Initially Boswell was an admirer of Smith. As Pottle points out: 'Boswell spoke of Smith more highly than of any other teacher he had ever had, piling up adjectives like "beautiful", "clear", "accurate", and "elegant"',[7] and was probably much more impressed by the lectures in Smith's advanced class of rhetoric than any others. For his part, Smith told Boswell that he possessed 'a happy facility of manners', probably in a letter written after Boswell ran away from Glasgow to London on 1 March 1760. At any rate Boswell wrote to Andrew Erskine on 8 December 1761: 'It is a very strange thing that I James Boswell, Esquire, although possest of a "happy facility of manners" — to use the very words of Mr. Professor Smith, which upon honour were addresst to the above-mentioned Gentleman — If it was absolutely necessary, I could yet produce the Letter in which they are to be found . . .'[8] The pride in the attribution recurs in the Journal of 22 December 1765.[9] The compliment of 'the facility of manners' was recalled most often, but other comments were also remembered. In 1764 Boswell recalled that Smith had written to him some time ago to the effect that: 'Your great fault is acting upon system.' As Boswell rightly commented, 'What a curious reproof to a young man from a grave philosopher!', a comment particularly apposite to Smith, whose studies valiantly tried to provide intellectual systems out of apparently chaotic material. But still, as Boswell said with respect to this comment: 'It is, however, a just one, and but too well founded with respect to me.'[10] Even in the early days Boswell summed Smith up well as 'a learned, accurate, absent man'[11] and in the years before meeting Johnson, and for some time afterwards, the favourable view remained.

A change in attitude is evident in the mid-1770s when both Boswell and Smith were in London, and when the influence of Johnson had taken over. Yet although he would probably have resented being cast in the role, Boswell remains a first-rate source of information on Smith in London in that he provided a link between two worlds in which Smith moved when there: the world based on his old links with the expatriate Scots, from which Boswell wanted to escape, and the wider literary and intellectual circles, into which Boswell wished to insinuate himself.

The world of expatriate Scots was one which Smith had known since his first visit to London in 1761 on University business, and it was one to which he had easy access through his publishers alone. Smith once advised Hume that he should 'not live obscurely at Miss Elliots with six or seven scotchmen as before',[12] advice which Hume ignored.[13] Smith's own lodgings were as obscure and as nationally biased as the Elliot boarding house, staying as he did in Suffolk Street with John Home.[14] But the social centre of the expatriate Scots, to which Smith's mail was sent in his London visits, was the British Coffee House in Cockspur Street, kept by a sister of Bishop John Douglas of Carlisle and latterly of Salisbury, who came from Pittenweem and was at Balliol with Smith. Here Smith met all the Scottish contingent, and others, as he did at weekly dinners arranged by Alexander Wedderburn. Hume was therefore entitled to ask for news of what was happening, as in 1774 when he asked for an account of Benjamin Franklin's conduct when he had been examined before the Privy Council: 'I hear that Wedderburn's Treatment of him before the Council was most cruel, without being in the least blameable. What a Pity!'[15] But the queries apparently went unanswered. As expected, Smith did not pass the political and social gossip of the capital to Hume in the way Hume did when their roles were reversed.

The Scottish circle merged into a wider one. Recognition of Smith's reputation came on 27 May 1773 when he was formally admitted to the Royal Society, to which he had been elected in 1767. He was also elected to The Literary Club, better known without the adjective. This

Club had been founded in 1764 by Sir Joshua Reynolds and was chiefly renowned for the opportunities it gave to Johnson to display his prowess. Smith was elected the Club's twenty-fourth member, immediately after Edward Gibbon and shortly before the first meeting he attended on 1 December 1775.[16] Reynolds, one of the four members present that first night, was also a member of Wedderburn's dining club which met in the British Coffee House, and he may well have been the nominator.

The membership was distinguished by any standards and, thanks particularly to Boswell's documentation of Johnson, it is possible to use Smith's limited association with him as a means of throwing some light on his character. The two met relatively infrequently other than at the dinners of The Club, of which Smith attended only 16 during his stay in London in the mid-1770s. A story of an altercation between them, attributed to Sir Walter Scott, has been disproved but altercation there was. It took place at the house of William Strahan, a very probable port of call for Smith, and has been variously dated, though probably taking place during Smith's first visit to London on University business, and therefore some 18 months before Boswell first met Johnson on 16 May 1763. Two later references suggest the early dating. First, on 29 April 1768 William Robertson recalled that after the altercation Strahan had remonstrated with Johnson, fearing that he might act similarly to Robertson who was expected soon but, as Robertson remembered the meeting, he was 'gentle and good-humoured, and courteous with me the whole evening', leading him to attribute his good reception to the hostile one given to Smith.[17] Robertson and Johnson had therefore met by April 1768 at the latest, so the altercation between Smith and Johnson must have taken place previously. The second reference indicates an even earlier dating. On 14 July 1763 Boswell recollected how Smith in his lectures at Glasgow had praised rhyme over blank verse, to which Johnson replied 'Sir, I was once in company with Smith, and we did not take to each other; but had I known that he loved rhyme as much as you tell me he does, I should have HUGGED him.'[18] The only earlier occasion Smith was in London was in 1761, which may then be taken as the date of the original disagreements.

No precise cause can be offered, but there are a number of possibilities which might have ensured an argument even as early as 1761. The reasons suggested by W.R. Scott are not very convincing. Smith's review of the *Dictionary* can hardly be described as 'very critical';[19] Boswell's attribution to Smith of critical remarks on *The Rambler* on 21 September

1761, allowing the author 'nothing but Heaviness, weakness, and affected Pedantry'[20] are attributed to Kames and Blair as well as to Smith and were not given in Smith's lectures; while the allegation that in his lectures he 'nearly' spoke: 'Of all writers ancient and modern, he that keeps the greatest distance from common sense is Dr. Samuel Johnson' would seem to have been published first in an obituary notice in *The Times* of 6 August 1790.[21] If none of these explanations of the possible altercation are acceptable, other sources of contention are. Some are general differences, highlighted in the way in which Boswell became increasingly critical of Smith as his friendship with Johnson ripened, but there was one specific issue, which may have been more likely to emerge when Smith came from Glasgow in 1761. On 29 October 1773 when Boswell and Johnson were returning from their tour to the Hebrides they visited Glasgow, still at the time a beautiful city. Boswell recorded: 'He told me, that one day in London, when Dr. Adam Smith was boasting of it, he turned to him and said "Pray, sir, have you ever seen Brentford?"' to which even Boswell was driven to remark 'This was surely a strong instance of his impatience, and spirit of contradiction.'[22]

But perhaps personal differences were as important as any. The description of Smith's manners given by Alexander Carlyle — as at the Duke of Buccleuch's birthday party — does not indicate someone who would immediately establish warm relations with Johnson. Writing on 17 March 1776, Boswell commented:

> He [Bennet Langton] lamented The Club's being overwhelmed with unsuitable members. Dr Johnson had said to me yesterday that Adam Smith was a most disagreeable fellow after he had drank some wine, which, he said, 'bubbled in his mouth' . . . Langton . . . told me that he could perceive Beauclerk had lost his relish for Adam Smith's conversation, about which we had disputed last year.[23]

A month later, it was the same: 'Johnson said Adam Smith was as dull a dog as he had ever met with' and to cap that, Boswell followed in the next sentence, 'I said it was strange to me to find my old professor in London, a professed infidel with a bag-wig.'[24]

Yet, even from Johnson, the criticism was not all one-sided. A few days after the publication of the *Wealth of Nations* Boswell reported to Johnson that

> Sir John Pringle had the night before given his opinion that Smith,

who had never been in trade, could not be expected to write well on that subject, any more than I upon physic, I started [sic] this to Dr. Johnson. He thought that a man who had never traded himself might write well upon trade, and he said there was nothing that more required to be illustrated by philosophy.[25]

In the same way Smith saw both bad and good in Johnson. The bad was quite simple: Johnson was mad – or so he told Boswell when the latter called on him on 2 April 1775. 'Smith said that he imputed Johnson's roughness to a certain degree of insanity which he thought he had',[26] which was also the reason he advanced around 1780 in his explanation, published posthumously in *The Bee* of 1791, of Johnson's kneeling and repeating the Lord's Prayer without more ado in a company and doing so five or six times. 'It is not hypocrisy, but madness.'[27] And, in an episode which even he does not record fully or unambiguously, Boswell related to Goldsmith a statement by Smith where he referred to Johnson and Goldsmith as 'blockheads'[28] while at the same time believing that 'Johnson knew more books than any man alive'.[29]

But two events in particular occurred, during this period, both of which brought Smith into touch with a third circle of contacts, and may also be associated with contemporary developments in the argument of the *Wealth of Nations*.

The first problem resulted from an agitation in medical circles arising from the fact that the Universities of Aberdeen and St Andrews were in the habit of conferring medical degrees on persons who had neither attended classes nor passed an examination. The issue came to a head in 1771 when the recipient of such a degree was required to take the Diploma of the London College of Physicians and actually failed. As a result, the Edinburgh College drew up a memorial addressed to the Government, calling on the Universities to refrain from granting medical degrees (except honorary ones) without satisfactory evidence of residence and competence. Accordingly, Smith wrote an extremely long letter to Cullen in September 1774; a letter which so completely mirrors views later stated in the *Wealth of Nations* as to suggest that the section on education was being written at this time. Two points in particular may be taken from this document as illustrative of Smith's response:

You propose, I observe, that no person should be admitted to examination for his degrees unless he brought a certificate of his having studied at least two years in some University. Would not such a regulation be oppressive upon all private teachers, such as the Hunters, Hewson, Fordyce, etc? The scholars of such teachers surely merit whatever honour or advantage a degree can confer, much more than the greater part of those who have spent many years in some Universities, where the different branches of medical knowledge are either not taught at all, or are taught so superficially that they had as well not be taught at all. When a man had learnt his lesson very well, it surely can be of little importance where or from whom he has learnt it.

The monopoly of medical education which this regulation would establish in favour of Universities would, I apprehend, be hurtful to the lasting prosperity of such bodies-corporate. Monopolists very seldom make good work, and a lecture which a certain number of students must attend, whether they profit by it or no, is certainly not very likely to be a good one.

He went on:

There never was, and I will venture to say there never will be, a University from which a degree could give any tolerable security, that the person upon whom it had been conferred, was fit to practise physic. The strictest Universities confer degrees only upon students of a certain standing. Their real motive for requiring this standing is that the student may spend more money among them and that they may make more profit by him . . .

A degree can pretend to give security for nothing but the science of the graduate; and even for that it can give but a very slender security. For his good sense and discretion, qualities not discoverable by an academical examination, it can give no security at all. But without these, the presumption which commonly attends science must render it, in the practice of physic, ten times more dangerous than the grossest ignorance when accompanied, as it sometimes is, with some degree of modesty and diffidence.

If a degree, in short, always has been, and, in spite of all the regulations which can be made, always must be, a mere piece of quackery, it is certainly for the advantage of the public that it should be understood to be so.

Smith concluded:

After all, this trade in degrees I acknowledge to be a most disgraceful trade to those who exercise it; and I am extremely sorry that it should be exercised by such respectable bodies as any of our Scotch Universities. But as it serves as a corrective to what would otherwise soon grow up to be an intolerable nuisance, the exclusive and corporation spirit of all thriving professions and of all great Universities, I deny that it is hurtful to the public. . .

Adieu, my dear Doctor; after having delayed to write to you I am afraid I shall *get my lug* [ear] *in my lufe* [hand], as we say, for what I have written.[30]

Almost two years after this letter was written Hume enquired, with mounting anxiety:

By all Accounts your Book has been printed long ago; yet it has never yet been so much as advertised. What is the Reason? If you wait until the Fate of America be decided, you may wait long.

By all accounts you intend to settle with us this spring; Yet we hear no more of it. What is the Reason? Your Chamber in my House is always unoccupyed: I am always at home; I expect you to land here.

I have been, am, and shall be probably in an indifferent State of Health. I weighed myself t'other day, and find I have fallen five compleat stones. If you delay much longer, I shall probably disappear altogether.

The Duke of Buccleugh tells me, that you are very zealous in American Affairs. My Notion is that the Matter is not so important as is commonly imagind. If I be mistaken, I shall probably correct my Error when I see you or read you. Our Navigation and general Commerce may suffer more than our Manufactures. Should London fall as much in its Size as I have done, it will be the better. It is nothing but a Hulk of bad and unclean Humours.[31]

The American question was the second of the issues which attracted Smith's attention at this time. It was indeed the question of the hour, presenting economic, political and military dangers of considerable dimensions so that it is hardly surprising that Smith should have taken an interest in them. It is certainly true that the *Wealth of Nations* contains a long analysis of British colonial policy and an examination of the contradictions which it presented — and only reasonable to suppose that this material not only dates from the London period, but also helps to explain the delay in publication of which Hume complained.

A comparative analysis of the prosperity of colonies led Smith to provide a favourable interpretation of the progress of the American colonies. Their general importance was testified by his bold assertion that : 'The discovery of America, and that of a passage to the East Indies by the Cape of Good Hope, are the two greatest and most important events recorded in the history of mankind.'[32] He explained in more detail that the two great causes of the prosperity of all new colonies were 'plenty of good land, and liberty to manage their own affairs in their own way.'[33] The English colonies were 'abundantly provided' with the former, and although others were equal or superior to them in this respect, their political institutions were uniquely favourable.[34] Smith thus felt able to assert that 'there are no colonies of which the progress has been more rapid than that of the English in North America'.[35]

In describing the objectives of British policy towards the colonies, Smith concentrated mainly on its economic aspects and duly reported on the extensive range of restrictions which Britain had imposed on trade and manufactures, domestic as well as American. The regulating acts of navigation required that trade between the colonies and Great Britain had to be carried on in British ships, and that certain classes of commodities were to be confined initially to the market of the mother country: especially those which were either the peculiar produce of America or which were not produced in Britain. Smith also took notice of another feature of British policy, namely that the production of the more 'advanced or more refined manufactures' was discouraged in the colonies.[36] Thus woollen manufactures were forbidden, and although the colonists were encouraged to export pig-iron, they were prevented from erecting mills which might have led ultimately to the development of manufactures competitive with those of Great Britain.

In the case of Great Britain, the relationship with the colonies as defined by the regulating acts, was perceived by Smith to have created a self-supporting economic unit which gave her access to strategic materials, and thus contributed to national defence through the encouragement given to the mercantile marine.[37]

Smith also argued that the legislative arrangements governing trade with the mother country had contributed most materially to colonial development. In this connection he drew attention to the fact that 'the most perfect freedom of trade is permitted between the British colonies of America and the West Indies', thus providing a 'great internal market' for their produce.[38] He even argued that the restrictions imposed on the introduction of *manufactures* had benefited the colonies:

Unjust, however, as such prohibitions may be, they have not hitherto been very hurtful to the colonies. Land is still so cheap, and consequently, labour so dear among them, that they can import from the mother country, almost all the more refined or more advanced manufactures cheaper than they could make them for themselves. Though they had not, therefore, been prohibited from establishing such manufactures, yet in their present state of improvement, a regard to their own interest would, probably, have prevented them from doing so.[39]

Taken as a whole, Smith's argument seems designed to suggest that for a time at least the colonial relationship had both contributed to, and proved compatible with, a relatively high rate of growth in both the colonies and the mother country. Yet at the same time he evidently believed that there were contradictions inherent in the colonial relationship which must begin to manifest themselves over time. For example, while Smith took pains to emphasise the great stimulus given to the growth of the colonies, he also pointed out that the high and rapid rate of growth which they had attained must ultimately come in conflict with the restrictions imposed on colonial trade and manufactures; restrictions which could be regarded as the 'principal badge of their dependency'[40] and as a 'manifest violation of one of the most sacred rights of mankind':

In their present state of improvement, those prohibitions, perhaps, without cramping their industry, or restraining it from any employment to which it would have gone of its own accord, are only impertinent badges of slavery ... In a more advanced state they might be really oppressive and insupportable.[41]

As far as Great Britain was concerned Smith contended that although the colony trade was 'upon the whole beneficial, and greatly beneficial'[42] still the rate of growth was necessarily less than it would have been in the absence of the regulating acts, due to the fact that the pattern of British trade had been altered in such a way that her manufactures

instead of being suited, as before the act of navigation, to the neighbouring market of Europe, or to the more distant one of the countries which lie round the Mediterranean sea, have, the greater part of them, been accommodated to the still more distant one of the colonies.[43]

He went on:

> Her commerce, instead of running in a great number of small channels, has been taught to run principally in one great channel. But the whole system of her industry and commerce has thereby been rendered less secure; the whole state of her body politick less healthful, than it otherwise would have been. In her present condition, Great Britain resembles one of those unwholesome bodies in which some of the vital parts are overgrown, and which, upon that account, are liable to many dangerous disorders scarce incident to those in which all the parts are more properly proportioned.[44]

But Smith's account of the problem currently facing Great Britain is largely dominated by that of fiscal need. In Smith's opinion Britain's needs seemed to be growing more rapidly than her resources, and he noted in this connection that by January 1775 the national debt had reached the then astronomical figure of £130m (absorbing £4.5m in interest charges), much of which was due to the acquisition of the colonial territories. Smith therefore concluded that Great Britain must either tax the colonies or give them up, and by this means either solve the fiscal problem or abandon it by accommodating 'her future views and designs to the real mediocrity of her circumstances'.[45]

Smith quite plainly believed that Britain both could and should tax the colonies:

> It is not contrary to justice that both Ireland and America should contribute towards the discharge of the publick debt of Great Britain. That debt has been contracted in support of the government established by the Revolution, a government to which the protestants of Ireland owe, not only the whole authority which they at present enjoy in their own country, but every security which they possess for their liberty, their property, and their religion; a government to which several of the colonies of America owe their present charters, and consequently their present constitution, and to which all the colonies of America owe the liberty, security, and property which they have ever since enjoyed. That publick debt has been contracted in the defence, not of Great Britain alone, but of all the different provinces of the empire; the immense debt contracted in the late war in particular, and a great part of that contracted in the war before, were both properly contracted in defence of America.[46]

He added that such a change of policy should be accompanied by freedom of trade between all parts of the empire[47] and, most dramatically, that it would require a form of union which would give the colonies representation in the British Parliament and in effect create a single state:

> This, however, could scarce, perhaps, be done consistently with the principles of the British constitution, without admitting into the British parliament, or if you will into the states-general of the British Empire, a fair and equal representation of all those different provinces, that of each province bearing the same proportion to the produce of its taxes, as the representation of Great Britain might bear to the produce of the taxes levied upon Great Britain.[48]

Politically, Smith believed that this solution would have the advantage of avoiding dismemberment of the Empire while representing a logical development of British political experience:

> there is not the least probability that the British constitution would be hurt by the union of Great Britain with her colonies. That constitution, on the contrary, would be completed by it, and seems to be imperfect without it. The assembly which deliberates and decides concerning the affairs of every part of the empire, in order to be properly informed, ought certainly to have representatives from every part of it.[49]

The advantages of such a scheme to America would appear to have been overwhelming, since in Smith's judgement her rapid progress 'in wealth, population and improvement' had been such that:

> in the course of little more than a century, perhaps, the produce of American might exceed that of British taxation. The seat of the empire would then naturally remove itself to that part of the empire which contributed most to the general defence and support of the whole.[50]

After the loss of Saratoga, Smith was asked to advise the government on the state of the conflict with the Colonies, and this he did in the form of a memorandum addressed to Alexander Wedderburn, Solicitor-General in Lord North's administration.[51] In the memorandum Smith went over ground already covered in the *Wealth of Nations* passing in review the available options. One of these was the kind of union considered above; a solution which had been put forward in the 1750s by Benjamin Franklin and narrowly defeated at a meeting of the First Continental Congress as recently as 1774. But by 1776, and even more clearly two years later, Smith recognised that union commanded little support on either side of the Atlantic, causing him to complain that the plan which 'would certainly tend most to the prosperity, to the splendour, and to the duration of the empire, if you except here and there a solitary philosopher like myself, seems scarce to have a single advocate'.[52] A second solution was the popular one of military victory but this too was seen to be unrealistic, partly on account of the fact that while a professional standing army was likely to be superior to a militia, this need not be the case where the latter was long in the field:

> Should the war in America drag out through another campaign, the American militia may become in every respect a match for that standing army, of which the valour appeared, in the last war, at least not inferior to that of the hardiest veterans of France and Spain.[53]

Besides, as Smith noted in his memorandum, military victory would require a military government which would inevitably confront 'factious, mutinous and discontented subjects in time of peace; at all times, upon the slightest disobligation, disposed to rebel'.[54] Yet a third possibility was that Britain should simply give up her pretensions to dominion and by this generous act create a special relationship with her former colonies:

> By thus parting good friends, the natural affection of the colonies to the mother country, which, perhaps, our late dissensions have well nigh extinguished, would quickly revive. It might dispose them not only to respect, for whole centuries together, that treaty of commerce which they had concluded with us at parting, but to favour us in war as well as in trade, and, instead of turbulent and factious subjects, to become our most faithful, affectionate, and generous allies.[55]

But by 1778 this opportunity too seemed to have been lost:

> tho this termination of the war might be really advantageous, it would not, in the eyes of Europe appear honourable to Great Britain: and when her empire was so much curtailed, her power and

dignity would be supposed to be proportionably diminished. What is of still greater importance, it could scarce fail to discredit the government in the eyes of our own people ... [it] ... would have everything to fear from their rage and indignation at the public disgrace and calamity, for such they would suppose it to be, of thus dismembering the empire.[56]

And yet both military defeat and voluntary withdrawal were both consistent with a fine piece of Machiavellian policy:

If, with the complete emancipation of America, we should restore Canada to France and the two Floridas to Spain; we should render our colonies the natural enemies of those two monarchies and consequently the natural allies of Great Britain.[57]

But for Smith the most likely solution was the one which actually presented itself when peace was made in 1783 — the loss of the thirteen colonies and the retention of Canada — the most expensive, and the least satisfactory, of all the possibilities.

Smith's advice must have seemed bleak indeed to the government, since it seems clear that he regarded the unfolding relationship with America as the consequence of the kind of misguided policy, and misunderstanding which seemed to confirm an earlier assessment. As Smith wrote to Strahan on 3 June 1776:

The American Campaign has begun awkwardly. I hope, I cannot say that I expect, it will end better. England, tho' in the present times it breeds men of great professional abilities in all different ways, great Lawyers, great watch makers and Clockmakers, etc. etc., seems to breed neither Statesmen nor Generals.[58]

Yet Smith took a long view of these matters; he foresaw a special relationship based on a similarity of language and culture and did not fear the short run problems of economic dislocation. Indeed he was able to comfort Sir John Sinclair of Ulbster who had complained in reference to America that 'If we go on at this rate, the nation *must be ruined*', with the words, 'be assured, my young friend, that there is a great deal of *ruin* in a nation'.[59]

It is equally clear that Smith's views on the 'contest with America' exerted little influence on government policy, save in one important case. When parliamentary union with Ireland was concluded in 1800, the younger Pitt, well schooled in the *Wealth of Nations*, saw it through, aided by the attraction of free trade to Ireland, and in spite of the attempts of Wedderburn (Lord Loughborough) to raise the spectre of Catholic emancipation. Smith had hoped for something even more advantageous:

> By the union with England, the middling and inferior ranks of people in Scotland gained a compleat deliverance from the power of an aristocracy which had always before oppressed them. By an union with Great Britain the greater part of the people of all ranks in Ireland would gain an equally compleat deliverance from a much more oppressive aristocracy; an aristocracy not founded, like that of Scotland, in the natural and respectable distinctions of birth and fortune; but in the most odious of all distinctions, those of religious and political prejudices; distinctions which, more than any other, animate both the insolence of the oppressors and the hatred and indignation of the oppressed, and which commonly render the inhabitants of the same country more hostile to one another than those of different countries ever are. Without a union with Great Britain, the inhabitants of Ireland are not likely for many ages to consider themselves as one people.[60]

Notes

1. *The Letters of David Hume*, ed. J.Y.T. Greig (Oxford, 1932), ii, 266.
2. *Corr.*, letter 132, Adam Smith to William Pulteney, 3 September 1772.
3. Ibid.
4. *Corr.*, letter 208, Adam Smith to Andreas Holt, 26 October 1780.
5. *Corr.*, letters 138 and 139, Adam Ferguson to Adam Smith, 2 September 1773 and 23 January 1774.
6. *Corr.*, letter 146, Adam Smith to David Hume, 9 May 1775.
7. F.A. Pottle, *James Boswell: The Earlier Years, 1740-1769* (London, 1966), 42.
8. *The Correspondence of James Boswell with Certain Members of the Club* ed. C.N. Fifer, 3, 3.
9. *Boswell on the Grand Tour: Italy, Corsica and France, 1756-66*, eds. F. Brady and F.A. Pottle (London, 1955), 256 and in *Boswell: The Ominous Years*, eds. C. Ryskamp and F.A. Pottle (London, 1963), 119.
10. *Boswell in Holland, 1763-64*, ed. F.A. Pottle (London, 1952), 299-300.
11. *Boswell's London Journal, 1762-1763*, ed. F.A. Pottle (London, 1950), 248.
12. *Corr.*, letter 88, Adam Smith to David Hume, September 1765.
13. Hume, *Letters*, ii, 63-4.
14. *Corr.*, letter 232, Adam Smith to William Strahan, 20 November 1783.
15. *Corr.*, letter 140, David Hume to Adam Smith, 13 February 1774.
16. M.E.G. Duff, *The Club 1764-1905* (London, 1905), 133; *The Corres-*

pondence of James Boswell with Certain Members of the Club 3, xc-xcii.

17. James Boswell, *Life of Johnson* ed. R.W. Chapman, corrected by J.D. Fleeman (London, 1976), 978.

18 Ibid., 303.

19. W.R. Scott, *Adam Smith as Student and Professor* (Glasgow, 1937), 122.

20. *Private Papers of James Boswell from Malahide Castle in The Collection of Lt. Col. Ralph H. Isham*, i, ed. G. Scott (1928), 70.

21. Quoted in full in C.R. Fay, *Adam Smith and the Scotland of his Day* (Cambridge, 1956), 33.

22. James Boswell, *Journal of a Tour to the Hebrides*, ed. R.W. Chapman (1924), 411; Boswell, *Life of Johnson*, 1210.

23. *Boswell: The Ominous Years*, 264.

24. Ibid., 337.

25. Ibid., 257; also Boswell, *Life of Johnson*, 682.

26. *Boswell: The Ominous Years, 1774-76*, 115.

27. *The Bee or Literary Weekly Intelligencer*, 11 May 1791, 2-3.

28. *Boswell on the Grand Tour*, 313.

29. Boswell, *Life of Johnson*, 52.

30. *Corr.*, letter 143, Smith to Cullen 20 November 1774.

31. *Corr.*, letter 149, Hume to Smith, 8 February 1776.

32. *WN*, IV.vii.c.80.

33. Ibid., IV.vii.b.16.

34. Ibid., IV.vii.b.17.

35. Ibid., IV.vii.b.15.

36. Ibid., IV.vii.b.40.

37. Ibid., IV.ii.30.

38. Ibid., IV.vii.b.39.

39. Ibid., IV.vii.b.44.

40. Ibid., IV.vii.c.64.

41. Ibid., IV.vii.b.44.

42. Ibid., IV.vii.c.47.

43. Ibid., IV.vii.c.22.

44. Ibid., IV.vii.c.43.

45. Ibid., V.iii.92.

46. Ibid., V.iii.88.

47. Ibid., V.iii.72.

48. Ibid., V.iii.68.

49. Ibid., IV.vii.c.77.

50. Ibid., IV.vii.c.79.

51. The memorandum is unsigned but endorsed by Wedderburn, 'Smith's Thoughts on the State of the Contest with America, February, 1778'. The document is included in *Corr.*, Appendix B.

52. Ibid., 382.

53. *WN*, V.i.a.27.

54. *Memorandum*, 383.

55. *WN*, IV.vii.c.66.

56. *Memorandum*, 383.

57. Ibid., 382-3.

58. *Corr.*, letter 158, Adam Smith to William Strahan, 3 June 1776.

59. *The Correspondence of the Right Honourable Sir John Sinclair, Bart.* (London, 1831), i, 390-1.

60. *WN*, V.iii.89.

14 THE WEALTH OF NATIONS

The first edition of the *Wealth of Nations* was published on 9 March 1776 by Strahan and Cadell. It appeared in two volumes, at a cost of one pound and sixteen shillings. The second edition appeared in 1778 and the third six years later. The fourth edition is dated 1786, and the fifth and final version to be published in Smith's lifetime appeared in 1789, the year of the French Revolution.

The work has become one of the most influential to be published in the English language and has now been translated into Chinese, Czech, Dutch, Finnish, Italian, Portuguese, Russian, Serbo-Croat, Spanish, Swedish and Turkish. The first edition was sold out in six months, and was translated into Danish (1779-80), French (1778-9, 1788) and German (1776-8) before Smith died.

When the book appeared, many of its major themes would have been familiar to Smith's old students, his friends, and other contemporaries. The long analysis of the public debt in Book V, for example, drew attention to the dangerous influence of the moneyed interest, to the disincentive effects of the high levels of taxation needed to service it, and to the power which a developed government sector could exert in a constitutional sense. Smith also made effective use of the sociological analysis which he had developed in the context of the *Lectures on Jurisprudence*, most notably in the treatment of such necessary public services as defence and justice — areas of analysis where he returned to the problem not only of the costs of providing such services, but also to the links which exist between forms of economic organisation and the relationships between different social groups. In the same vein, Smith introduced his most complete analysis of the breakdown of feudalism and of the causes of the emergence of the modern system of commerce — the fourth stage of his lectures on history which embraced his account of the institutions of the exchange economy.[1] More striking still, perhaps, was Smith's concern with the problems faced by the modern citizen and the extent to which it was possible for him to fulfil the functions and obligations of his classical counterpart.[2] Here the most interesting feature is Smith's appreciation of the point that the division of labour, in his eyes the most important source of increased productivity, was also associated with important social costs. It was in fact his contention, that the individual who is confined to a small specialised function for a large part of the working day, was likely to become 'as stupid and ignorant as it is possible for a human creature to become', thus generating a sort of 'mental mutilation, deformity and wretchedness'. Smith believed that this development would erode martial spirit and adversely affect that capacity for moral judgement which had been considered in the *Theory of Moral Sentiments:*

> His dexterity at his own particular trade seems, in this manner, to be acquired at the expense of his intellectual, social, and martial virtues. But in every improved and civilised society this is the state into which the labouring poor, that is, the great body of the people, must necessarily fall, unless government takes some pains to prevent it.[3]

Such themes were not uncommon in writings published before 1776, especially in the circle of Smith's acquaintance, and yet the book made a great impact among the members of it. David Hume wrote joyously:

> Euge! Belle! Dear Mr Smith: I am much pleas'd with your Performance, and the Perusal of it has taken me from a State of great Anxiety. It was a Work of so much Expectation, by yourself, by your Friends, and by the Public, that I trembled for its Appearance; but am now much relieved.[4]

Hugh Blair commented:

> I Confess you have exceeded my expectations. One writer after another on these Subjects did nothing but puzzle me. I despaired of ever arriving at clear Ideas. You have given me full and Compleat Satisfaction and my Faith is fixed. I do think the Age is highly indebted to you, and I wish they may be duly Sensible of the Obligation. You have done great Service to the World by overturning all that interested Sophistry of Merchants, with which they had Confounded the whole Subject of Commerce. Your work ought to be, and I am perswaded will in some degree become, the Commercial Code of Nations. I did not read one Chapter of it without Acquiring much Light and instruction. I am Convinced that since Montesquieu's *Esprit des Loix*, Europe has not received any Publication which tends so much to Enlarge and Rectify the ideas of mankind.

Your arrangement is excellent. One chapter paves the way for another; and your System gradually erects itself. Nothing was ever better suited than your Style is to the Subject; clear and distinct to the last degree, full without being too much so, and as tercly as the Subject could admit. Dry as some of the Subjects are, It carried me along. I read the whole with avidity; and have pleasure in thinking that I shall with some short time give it a Second and more deliberate perusal.[5]

Joseph Black, though writing primarily to inform Smith of Hume's declining health began:

I have no doubt that the Views you have given of many parts of your Subject will be found by experience to be as just as they are new and interesting and although it be admired immediately by discerning and impartial Judges [,] It will require some time before others who are not so quick sighted and whose minds are warped by Prejudice or Interest can understand and relish such a comprehensive System composed with such just and liberal sentiments.[6]

William Robertson had high expectations of the work:

but it has gone far beyond what I expected. You have formed into a regular and consistent system one of the most intricate and important parts of political science, and if the English be capable of extending their ideas beyond the narrow and illiberal arrangements introduced by the mercantile supporters of Revolution principles . . . I should think your Book will occasion a total change in several important articles both in policy and finance.[7]

Adam Ferguson had:

been for sometime so busy reading you, and recommending and quoting you, to my students, that I have not had leisure to trouble you with letters. I suppose, however, that of all the opinions on which you have any curiosity, mine is among the least doubtful. You may believe, that on further acquaintance with your work my esteem is not a little increased. You are surely to reign alone on these subjects, to form the opinions, and I hope to govern at least the coming generations.[8]

These assessments are interesting precisely because they show how quickly some of Smith's friends grasped his purpose, which was to produce, in the first instance, an analytical system or what a notable critic, Governor Pownall, was to describe as 'an institute of the Principia *of those laws of motion*, by which the operations of the community are directed and regulated, and by which they should be examined'.[9] In making a similar point, Hume felt moved to remark that the book was unlikely to achieve popular appeal, since:

> the Reading of it necessarily requires so much Attention, and the Public is disposed to give so little, that I shall still doubt for some time of its being at first very popular: But it has Depth and Solidity and Acuteness, and it is so much illustrated by curious Facts, that it must at last take the public Attention.[10]

A week later Hume wrote to William Strahan, who had also published Edward Gibbon's *Decline and Fall*: 'Dr Smith's . . . is another excellent Work that has come from your Press this Winter; but I have ventured to tell him, that it requires too much thought to be as popular as Mr Gibbon's.'[11] Adam Ferguson sized up the situation well: 'You are not to expect the run of a novel, nor even of a true history; but you may venture to assure your booksellers of a steady and continual sale, as long as people wish for information on these subjects.'[12]

In the event the fears of Smith's friends were disproved, precisely because the book appealed differently to separate groups. Smith's friends admired the comprehensive and systematic explanation of economic life which it embodied, but were worried about those features which made it look, in the words of Hugh Blair, 'too much like a publication for the present moment'. But at the same time, it was this practical aspect which appealed to a wider readership. The *Wealth of Nations* was not only an intellectual achievement of the greatest magnitude, embracing as it does the explanation of complex social relations on the basis of a few principles, but also a work which provided practical prescriptions for the problems of the day.

The systematic or analytical aspect of Smith's contribution emerges in a number of different ways. To begin with, there are the links with other aspects of his thought, all of which remind the reader of the interrelations which exist between the different parts of the lectures given from the chair of moral philosophy. In the context of his largely economic analysis, Smith required to make some judgement as to the activities of men, and in fact relied mainly on the self-regarding propensities already detailed in the *Theory of Moral Sentiments*. He did not suggest that these propensities provided of themselves an adequate statement of man's psychology, but simply contended that within the economic sphere man is motivated by a desire for gain. As he put it in a famous passage, 'it is not from the benevolence of the butcher, the brewer, or the baker, that we expect our dinner, but from their regard to their own interest'.[13] Smith also recognised in examining economic phenomena, that he was concerned with only one aspect of the activities of man in society, and that the analysis must depend upon some prior judgement as to the nature of the social bond. The formal analysis of the latter problem is also contained in the *Theory of Moral Sentiments* in the sense that the individual must be restrained from hurting his fellows in respect of their persons and property: the basic minimum condition of justice. The analytical side of Smith's contribution is also related to his historical treatment of jurisprudence, or at least to that aspect of it which helped to explain the origins of the exchange economy and, therefore, some of its leading features.

Smith was concerned with a situation where there were three main forms of economic activity: agriculture, manufacture and trade, all of which were carried on through the use of three factors of production – land, labour and capital. Smith ascribed a great deal of importance to the distinction between factors of production, and to the particular forms of return which they generated for each of the socio-economic groups with which they were associated.

Smith defined wages as a form of return which accrued to those who must earn subsistence through the sale of their labour power, arguing that this particular type of monetary reward is payable by those (undertakers) who require the factor. Rent on the other hand, accrues to the owners (proprietors) of land and is paid by those who need it (the farmers) because the resource is both productive and scarce. Rent thus emerges as a surplus in the sense that it accrues to the owner of land independently of any effort made by him so that the proprietors appear to be the only group 'whose revenue costs them neither labour nor care, but comes to them, as it were, of its own accord'. On the other hand, profit is that type of return which accrues to undertakers (or capitalists to use the modern term) as the reward for the trouble taken, and the risks incurred, in combining the factors of production. As Smith put it:

As soon as stock has accumulated in the hands of particular persons, some of them will naturally employ it in setting to work industrious people, whom they will supply with materials and subsistence, in order to make a profit by the sale of their work, or by what their labour adds to the value of the materials.[14]

By stock Smith meant either fixed capital (such as that embodied in plant, 'useful machines') or circulating capital (devoted to the purchase of raw materials or labour).

Looked at in this way, all groups in society are in a sense interdependent. The proprietors depend on the undertakers engaged in agriculture for their income; wage-labour depends on the undertakers operating in all three sectors for employment; while the undertakers engaged in different types of activity depend upon each other and the two remaining groups in respect of the services which they provide, and the expenditures which they incur. The parallel with the physiocratic perspective is obvious, and so too is Smith's vision of the pattern of interdependencies which emerge. The point is made with particular clarity in Book II where Smith employs a kind of 'period' analysis in a way which may demonstrate his debt to physiocracy in general and to the work of Turgot in particular.

Suppose, following Smith, that we examine the performance of the economy during a particular year, from the standpoint of the beginning of the period in question. Under these circumstances it is reasonable to assume that there will be certain stocks of goods in existence, reflecting the level of output attained in the previous period, together with the quantities of (consumption and investment) goods purchased during it; stocks which may be divided into three main parts.

First, there is that part of total stock which is reserved for immediate consumption, and which is held by all consumers (capitalists, labour and proprietors). The characteristic feature of this part of the total stock is that it affords no revenue to its possessors since it consists in 'the stock of food, clothes, house-hold furniture, etc., which have been purchased by their proper consumers, but which are not yet entirely consumed'.[15]

Secondly, there is that part of the total stock which may be described as 'fixed capital' and which will again be distributed between the various groups in society. This part of the stock, Smith suggested, is composed of the 'useful machines' purchased in preceding periods and held by the capitalists engaged in manufacture; the quantity of useful buildings and of 'improved land' in the possession of the capitalist farmers and the proprietors, together with the 'aquired and useful abilities' of all the inhabitants.[16]

Thirdly, there is that part of the total stock which may be described as 'circulating capital' and which again has several components, these being:

(a) The quantity of money necessary to carry on the process of circulation. In this connection Smith observed that:

> The sole use of money is to circulate consumeable goods. By means of it, provisions, materials, and finished work, are bought and sold, and distributed to their proper consumers. The quantity of money therefore, which can be annually employed in any country must be determined by the value of the consumable goods which can be annually circulated within it.[17]

(b) The stock of provisions and other agricultural products which are available for sale during the current period, but which are still in the hands of either the farmers or merchants.

(c) The stock of raw materials and work in process, which is held by merchants, undertakers, or those capitalists engaged in the agricultural sector (including mining, etc.).

(d) The stock of manufactured goods (consumption and investment) created during the previous period, but which remain in the hands of undertakers and merchants at the beginning of the present year.[18]

Perhaps the logic of the process can be best represented by artificially splitting up the activities involved. Suppose at the beginning of the time period in question, that the major capitalist groups possess the total net receipts earned from the sale of products in the previous period, and that the undertakers engaged in agriculture open by transmitting the total rent due to the proprietors of land, for the use of that factor. The income thus provided will enable the proprietors to make the necessary purchases of consumption (and investment) goods in the current period, thus contributing to reduce the stocks of such goods with which the undertakers and merchants began the period. Secondly, assume that the undertakers engaged in both sectors, together with the merchant groups transmit to wage-labour the content of the wages fund, thus providing this socio-economic class with an income which can be used in the current period. Thirdly, the undertakers in agriculture and manufactures make purchases of consumption and investment goods from each other through the medium of retail and wholesale merchants thus generating a series of expenditures linking the two sectors. Finally the process of circulation may be seen to be completed by the purchases made by individual undertakers within their own sectors. Once again these purchases will include consumption and investment goods, thus contributing still further to reduce the stocks of commodities which were available for sale when the period under examination began.

Given these points, the working of the system can be seen to involve a series of flows whereby income is exchanged for commodities in such a way as to generate a series of withdrawals from the 'circulating' capital of society. As Smith pointed out, the consumption goods thus withdrawn from the existing stock may be entirely used up within the current period, or used to increase the stock 'reserved for immediate consumption' or to replace the more durable goods (e.g. clothes) which had reached the end of their life in the course of the same period. Similarly, the undertakers as a result of their purchases, will add to their stocks of raw materials and/or their fixed capital, or replace the machines which had finally worn out in the current period. Looked at in this way, the 'circular flow' may be seen to involve a certain level of purchases which takes goods from the market but which is at the same time matched by a continuous process of replacement by virtue of the productive activity which is currently carried on.

While this vision of the economic process is important in its own right, Smith also used it to demonstrate the importance of a wide range of economic problems as well as the interconnections which exist between them. The first and most obvious problem in the context of the exchange economy is that of *price* and its determinants. In handling this problem, Smith assumed the existence of what he called 'ordinary' or 'average' rates of wages, profit, and rent; rates of return which may be said to prevail within any given society or neighbourhood during any given time period (such as a year). These rates of return determine the natural or supply price of any commodity, defined by Smith as that amount which is 'neither more nor less than what is sufficient to pay the rent of the land, the wages of the labourer, and the profits of the stock' according to their prevailing and natural rates.[19] By contrast, market price is now defined as that price which may prevail at any given point in time, being regulated by 'the proportion between the quantity which is actually brought to market, and the demand of those who are willing to pay the natural price of the commodity'.[20] The two prices are interrelated in that in a competitive situation any divergence between them will cause the rates of return accruing to factors to rise above or fall below their 'natural' rates, thus generating an inflow or outflow of resources to or from the employment affected — with consequent effects on the supply of the commodity. In short the natural price of commodities emerges as the equilibrium or 'central' price, 'to which the prices of all commodities are continually gravitating'.[21]

Following on from this argument, Smith's next task was to elucidate the forces which determine the level of the ordinary or average rates of return to factors, applying to this problem the same 'demand and supply' type of analysis just considered.

The process of wage determination was seen by Smith to involve a kind of bargain or contract:

> What are the common wages of labour depends every where upon the contract usually made between . . . two parties whose interests are by no means the same. The workmen desire to get as much, the masters to give as little as possible. The former are disposed to combine in order to raise, the latter in order to lower the wages of labour.[22]

While Smith recognised that the balance of advantage would often lie with the masters due to their legal privilege to combine, he also pointed out that demand and supply relationships would frequently cause individual employers 'to voluntarily break through the natural combination of masters not to raise wages'. Indeed the only rate which Smith felt able to define clearly was the subsistence wage:

> A man must always live by his work, and his wages must at least be sufficient to maintain him. They must even upon most occasions be somewhat more; otherwise it would be impossible for him to bring up a family, and the race of workmen could not last beyond the first generation.[23]

Profits, on the other hand, Smith argued, must be affected by the selling price of the commodity and the cost of production (including wages). Profits are likely to be particularly sensitive to changes in demand, together with the 'good or bad fortune' of both rivals and customers; facts which make it difficult to identify an 'ordinary' or 'average' rate of return. However, Smith suggested that the rate of interest would provide a reasonably accurate guide to the prevailing rates, basically on the ground that the rate paid for borrowed funds would be reflected in the profits expected: 'It may be laid down as a maxim, that wherever a great deal can be made by the use of money, a great deal will commonly be given for the use of it; and that wherever little can be made by it, less will commonly be given for it.'[24] At least as a broad generalisation Smith felt able to state that the rate of profit prevailing would be determined by the wage rate and the quantity of stock (capital), taken in conjunction with the outlets for profitable investment.

The final form of return, rent, is in many ways the least satisfactory aspect of Smith's argument, although he did offer a number of interesting insights, later to be taken up by David Ricardo. Rent for Smith was a 'monopoly' price at least in the sense that it is generally the highest which can be got 'in the actual circumstances of the land'.[25] He clearly perceived that rent payments would vary with the fertility of the soil and location — thus making it difficult to speak of a particular rate of rent in the same sense in which we refer to a particular rate of interest. But the analysis does seem to suggest that in any given time period rent payments will be related to the quantity of land in use, which must, in turn, be affected by the level of population. Further, Smith's argument indicates that during any given time period rent payments will be related, not only to the productivity of the soil, but also to the prevailing rates of wages and profit.

The treatment of price and distribution leads directly to another analytical step in Smith's system. It will be recalled that costs of production are incurred by those who create commodities, thus providing individuals with the income needed to purchase them. It follows that if the price of each commodity (in a position of equilibrium) comprehends payments made for rent, wages and profit, according to their natural rates, then 'it must be so for all commodities which compose the whole annual produce of the land and labour of every country, taken complexly'. Smith concluded: 'The whole price or exchangeable value of that annual produce, must resolve itself into the same three parts, and be parcelled out among the different inhabitants.'[26] In this way Smith drew attention to the distribution of total income between wages, profit and rent but also to the relationship between aggregate output and aggregate income. Or, as he put it, 'the gross revenue of all the inhabitants of a great country, comprehends the whole annual produce of their land and labour'.[27] This income, once generated would obviously be used in part to purchase consumption goods — including those services which do not directly contribute to physical output and which cannot therefore be said to contribute to generate that level of income associated with it. Smith suggested that the services of 'players, buffoons, opera singers, and musicians' fall within this class, and added that:

> The sovereign . . . with all the officers both of justice and war who serve under him − the whole army and navy, are unproductive labourers. They are the servants of the publick and are maintained by a part of the annual produce of the industry of other people.[28]

On the other hand, some part of aggregate income will be saved, notably by the entrepreneurial groups, with a view to purchasing items of both fixed and variable capital. The working of the circular flow can thus be visualised in rather different terms from those used at the outset; that is, in terms of an economic system where consumption and investment goods are annually produced, sold, and replaced, in a seemingly endless cycle, and where any changes in the direction of demand for commodities will, by virtue of the operation of the price mechanism, generate changes in the use of available resources.

This particular, and essentially modern, way of looking at the economic process leads on to yet another change of focus represented by Smith's preoccupation with economic growth. Remaining with the period analysis of the previous examples, Smith noted that:

> The annual produce of the land and labour of any nation can be increased in its value by no other means, but by increasing either the number of its productive labourers, or the productive powers of those labourers who had before been employed.[29]

Smith recognised that both sources of increased output would require an additional capital, devoted either to increasing the wages fund or to the purchase of fixed capital equipment which would 'facilitate and abridge labour'. In both cases an increase in the funds devoted to savings is required; a perception which is linked to three characteristic features of his argument. First, Smith suggested that net savings will always be possible during each (annual) period, and that such savings will be prompted by 'the desire of bettering our condition, a desire which though generally calm and dispassionate, comes with us from the womb, and never leaves us till we go into the grave'.[30] Secondly, he argued that savings once made will always be used effectively, thus stating a basic assumption which was to become one of the features of classical economics: 'What is annually saved is as regularly consumed as what is annually spent, and nearly in the same time too; but it is consumed by a different set of people.'[31] Finally Smith suggested that savings when so used must create successively higher levels of output, since:

> Parsimony, by increasing the fund which is destined for the maintenance of productive hands, tends to increase the number of those hands whose labour adds to the value of the subject upon which it is bestowed. It tends therefore to increase the exchangeable value of the annual produce of the land and labour of the country. It puts into motion an additional quantity of industry, which gives an additional value to the annual produce.[32]

The higher levels of output and income thus attained, make it possible to reach still greater levels of savings and investment in subsequent periods, thus generating further increases in output and income. Once started, the process of capital accumulation may be seen as a self-generating process, indicating that Smith's model of the flow should be seen, not as a circle of given size, but rather as a spiral of constantly expanding dimensions. A further point demands notice, in this connection, namely Smith's perception that the rate of growth will depend on the proportion of income devoted to savings, and on the extent to which the different outlets for productive activity (agriculture, manufacture, trade) put in motion greater or lesser quantities of 'industry' for a given injection of capital. It was Smith's contention that investment in agriculture would be productive of greater levels of surplus than manufacture, and that manufacture would make a more significant contribution to growth than trade.

Although Smith's treatment of distribution was developed in Book I, thus anticipating to some extent the treatment of capital accumulation, it is the latter discussion which helps to explain many of the earlier judgements. If for example subsistence wages were paid during a given annual period and net savings took place, then the consequence would be an increase in demand for labour and the payment of wage rates in excess of the minimum level. Where sustained over a period of time, high market wages would tend to cause an increase in the level of population, thus enhancing the demand for food and the utilisation of land. It was thus Smith's view that wages would always *tend* towards the subsistence level as population increased over time. He also considered that profit levels would tend to decline in the long run, partly in consequence of the gradual increase in stock, and partly because of increasing difficulty in finding 'a profitable method of employing any new capital'.[33] Smith was quite clear in respect of rent however, arguing that rent payments would increase over time, partly in consequence of increased use of the available stock of land, and partly because 'those improvements in the productive powers of labour, which tend directly to reduce the real price of manufactures, tend indirectly to raise the real rent of land'.[34]

It is one thing to talk of tendencies and another of trends — and here Smith pointed out that economies could be stationary (such as China), declining (he cites amongst others the case of Bengal) or advancing. In the last case the examples cited were America and Great Britain. If the latter had a slower growth rate than America, Smith was able to point out that real wages had risen in the eighteenth century while profit rates had been sufficient to sustain the rapid rate of growth required. Obviously such judgements are the reflections of the economic circumstances prevailing, although Smith was quick to point out that one very important reason for them was institutional:

> though the profusion of government must, undoubtedly, have retarded the natural progress of England towards opulence and improvement, it has not been able to stop it. The annual produce of its land and labour is, undoubtedly, much greater at present than it was either at the restoration or at the revolution. The capital, therefore, annually employed in cultivating this land, and in maintaining this labour, must likewise be much greater. In the midst of all the exactions of government, this capital has been silently and gradually accumulated by the private frugality and good conduct of individuals, by their universal, continual, and uninterrupted effort to better their own condition. It is this effort, protected by law and allowed by liberty to exert itself in the manner that is most advantageous, which has maintained the progress of England towards opulence and improvement in almost all former times, and which, it is to be hoped, will do so in all future times.[35]

The account given above is possibly sufficient to show that Smith's system was a considerable intellectual achievement, and to reveal that the system takes two forms. First, there is an account of the economy as a system, and, secondly, the provision of an analytical system which shows the links between those different problems which a review of the economy reveals. But, as the last quotation also implies, the system in both senses draws attention to a number of policy recommendations;

recommendations which were more readily grasped than the intellectual work which underpins them, and which help to explain the contemporary popularity of the book.

One of the most striking features of the economic system, in Smith's eyes, was that individuals in pursuing their own interest unwittingly contribute to ends which they did not originally intend to promote — whether reference is made to the working of the allocative mechanism or the process of economic growth. In a policy sense Smith thus recommended that governments should take steps to eliminate legislative arrangements which impeded individual activity, such as the laws of succession and entail, on the ground that they were no longer relevant. In a similar vein, he called for the repeal of those regulations which established the privileges of corporations and regulated the system of apprenticeship: 'The statute of apprenticeship obstructs the free circulation of labour from one employment to another, even in the same place. The exclusive privileges of corporations obstruct it from one place to another, even in the same employment.'[36] Smith also commented on the problems presented by the Poor Laws and the Laws of Settlement and summarised his appeal to government in these terms:

> break down the exclusive privileges of corporations, and repeal the statute of apprenticeship, both which are real encroachments upon natural liberty, and add to these the repeal of the law of settlements, so that a poor workman, when thrown out of employment either in one trade or in one place, may seek for it in another trade or in another place, without the fear . . . of a prosecution.[37]

Smith also objected to positions of privilege, such as monopoly powers, on the ground that they were impolitic and unjust; unjust in that a monopoly position was one of privilege and advantage, and therefore: 'contrary to that justice and equality of treatment which the sovereign owes to all the different orders of his subjects';[38] impolitic in that the prices at which goods so controlled are sold are 'upon every occasion the highest that can be got' so that : 'The monopolists, by keeping the market constantly understocked, by never fully supplying the effectual demand, sell their commodities much above the natural price, and raise their emoluments, whether they consist in wages or profit, greatly above their natural rate.'[39] He added that monopoly is 'a great enemy to good management' and that it had the additional defect of restricting the flow of capital to the trades affected because of the legal barriers to entry which were involved.[40]

Finally, Smith's objection to monopoly in general may also be distinguished from his criticism of one expression of it; namely, the mercantile *system* which he described as the 'modern system' of policy, best understood 'in our own country and in our own times'.[41] Here Smith considered regulations which defined the trade relations between one country and another and which often reflected the state of animosity between them. In this context Smith examined a policy which sought to produce a net inflow of gold by means of such 'engines' as bounties on exportation, drawbacks, and controls over imports. But his main emphasis fell on one of the chief features of the system from a British point of view, the old colonial relationship with North America which was currently breaking up. Smith objected to any policy of control and restraint, because it artificially restricted the extent of the market and, therefore, the possibilities for further extension of the division of labour and economic growth. In particular Smith insisted that this pattern of infringement of liberty was liable to:

> that general objection which may be made to all the different expedients of the mercantile system; the objection of forcing . . . part of the industry of the country into a channel less advantageous than that in which it would run of its own accord.[42]

The belief that regulation will always distort the use of resources by breaking the 'natural balance of industry' dates back to Smith's days as a lecturer in Glasgow and represents his main criticism both of monopoly in general and its manifestation in mercantile policy as a whole. The general position is usefully summarised in the statement that:

> No regulation of commerce can increase the quantity of industry in any society beyond what its capital can maintain. It can only divert a part of it into a direction into which it might not otherwise have gone: and it is by no means certain that this artificial direction is likely to be more advantageous to the society than that into which it would have gone of its own accord.[43]

While many of Smith's specific objections to current policy did not distinguish between legislation and its actual implementation, none the less his recommendations amount to an impressive programme of reform designed to implement the 'obvious and simple' system of natural liberty. Yet it is the direction of change, as distinct from its complete success which was seen by him to be the most important. He was after all eminently realistic, and indeed criticised Quesnay for seeming to have implied that the economy 'would thrive and prosper only under a certain precise regimen of perfect liberty and perfect justice'. As Smith saw, 'If a nation could not prosper without the enjoyment of perfect liberty and perfect justice, there is not in the world a nation which could ever have prospered.'[44]

But even with existing restraints Smith's tone was optimistic, clearly believing that the drive to better our condition was capable of overcoming 'a hundred impertinent obstructions with which the folly of human laws too often encumbers its operations; though the effect of these obstructions is always more or less to encroach upon its freedom, or diminish its security'.[45]

At the same time Smith recognised that the type of economy in question was not without its problems, and drew attention to the need to regulate activities which might affect the general interest in a variety of ways. Hence for example he recommended regulation of the rate of interest, in such a way as to ensure that 'sober people are universally preferred, as borrowers, to prodigals and projectors', together with control over the small note issue.[46] Again in the name of the public interest he supported taxes on the retail sale of liquor to discourage the multiplication of alehouses, and differential taxes on beer and spirits in order to discourage the consumption of the latter. To take another example, Smith advocated higher taxes on those who demanded rent in kind, as a means of discouraging a practice which was injurious to the tenant.[47] Cases of this kind can be multiplied but are of greater importance because they illustrate two principles. First, Smith was prepared to interfere with activities which reflected imperfect knowledge on the part of the individual, while, secondly, he was prepared to control activities, such as the small note issue, where imperfect knowledge was not necessarily the problem. As he remarked by way of answer to those who objected to a proposal of the latter kind, 'The obligation of building party walls, in order to prevent the communication of fire, is a violation of natural liberty, exactly of the same kind with the regulations of the banking trade which are here proposed.'[48] Indeed Smith went further in stating a principle of potentially wide application: 'those exertions of the natural liberty of . . . individuals, which might endanger the security of the whole society, are, and ought to be, restrained by the laws of all governments; of the most free, as well as of the most despotical'.[49] He also added that the state should ensure the provision of public services, ranging from education to canals, harbours, bridges and roads — services which are: 'of such a nature, that the profit could never repay the expence to any individual, or small number of individuals, and which it therefore cannot be expected that any individual or small number of individuals should erect or maintain'.[50] Once more this criteria could be used to justify a very wide range of activities in that it supports intervention in cases of market failure.

Yet two points deserve notice by way of qualification. First it is evident that while Smith might defend the provision of a wide range of services, he always insisted that they should be organised in a way which recognised the facts of human nature, believing as he did in the value of incentive and in the proposition that 'Public services are never better performed than where their reward comes only in consequence of their being performed, and is proportioned to the diligence employed in performing them.'[51]

Secondly, it is appropriate to recall that the optimistic tone found in Smith's assessment of economic growth was qualified by his recognition of the 'oppressive inequality' of the modern state; of the influence exerted on governments by the 'clamourous importunity' of partial and especially mercantile interests,[52] and by that recognition of the social costs of the division of labour which dates back to his days as a lecturer in Glasgow. The mocking tone with which he sometimes treated the pursuit of wealth in the *Theory of Moral Sentiments* ('place, that great object which divides the wives of aldermen')[53] is matched only by his sympathy for the isolation of the individual who, finding himself in a large city or manufactory, finds himself also to be 'sunk in obscurity and darkness'.[54]

Notes

1. See especially, Book III.
2. For comment, D. Winch, *Adam Smith's Politics* (Cambridge, 1978).
3. *WN*, V.i.f.50.
4. *Corr.*, letter 150, David Hume to Adam Smith, 1 April 1776.
5. *Corr.*, letter 151, Hugh Blair to Adam Smith, 3 April 1776.
6. *Corr.*, letter 152, Joseph Black to Adam Smith, April 1776.
7. *Corr.*, letter 153, William Robertson to Adam Smith, 8 April 1776.
8. *Corr.*, letter 154, Adam Ferguson to Adam Smith, 18 April 1776.
9. *Corr.*, 354, *A letter from Governor Pownall to Adam Smith*.
10. *Corr.*, letter 150.
11. *The Letters of David Hume*, ed. J.Y.T. Greig (Oxford, 1932), ii, 314.
12. *Corr.*, letter 154.
13. *WN*, I.ii.2.

14. Ibid., I.vi.5.
15. Ibid., II.i.12.
16. Ibid., II.i.13–17.
17. Ibid., II.iii.23.
18. Ibid., II.i.19–22.
19. Ibid., I.vii.4.
20. Ibid., I.vii.8.
21. Ibid., I.vii.15.
22. Ibid., I.viii.11.
23. Ibid., I.viii.15. It should be emphasised that Smith believed wages would be above subsistence in progressive states (*WN*, I.viii.22f). He also anticipated the modern view that high rates of return encourage productivity (*WN*, I.viii.43, 44).
24. Ibid., I.ix.4.
25. Ibid., I.xi.a.1.
26. Ibid., II.ii.2.
27. Ibid., II.ii.5.
28. Ibid., II.iii.2.
29. Ibid., II.iii.32.
30. Ibid., II.iii.28.
31. Ibid., II.iii.18.
32. Ibid., II.iii.17.
33. See for example, ibid., I.ix.2, and I.ix.10.
34. Ibid., I.xi.p.4.
35. Ibid., II.iii.36.
36. Ibid., I.x.c.42.
37. Ibid., IV.ii.42.
38. Ibid., IV.viii.30.
39. Ibid., I.vii.26.
40. Ibid., I.xi.b.5., I.vii.26.
41. Ibid., IV.2.
42. Ibid., IV.v.a.24.
43. Ibid., IV.ii.3.
44. Ibid., IV.ix.28.
45. Ibid., IV.v.b.43.
46. Ibid., II.iv.15. Jeremy Bentham objected to the policy of regulation on the ground that it was inconsistent with Smith's general position. See his *Defence of Usury* (1787). The 'letters' are printed in *Corr.*, 386–404.
47. See in particular, Jacob Viner, 'Adam Smith and Laisser-Faire', in *Adam Smith 1776–1926, Lectures to Commemorate the Sesquicentennial of the Publication of the Wealth of Nations* (Chicago, 1928).
48. *WN*, II.ii.94.
49. Ibid.
50. Ibid., V.i.c.i.
51. Ibid., V.i.b.20.
52. See, for example, *WN*, I.xi.p.10, and IV.ii.43.
53. *TMS*, I.iii.2.8.
54. *WN*, V.i.g.12.

15 THE DEATH OF HUME

In the eighteen months from the publication of the *Wealth of Nations* in March 1776 until Smith returned to settle in Scotland finally in the autumn of 1777, he spent the period from April to December 1776 in Scotland for personal reasons. The age of his mother and the health of Hume brought him north. The latter was the more compelling, since by the spring of 1776 Hume was failing rapidly. In February he told Smith that he had lost five stones[1] in weight and two months later Adam Ferguson reported to John Home, the dramatist, that '. . . David, I am afraid, loses ground. He is chearful, and in good spirits as usual, but I confess that my hopes, from the effects of the turn of the season towards spring have, very much abated . . .'[2] Smith set out for Scotland at the end of April in the company of John Home, but — unknown to him — Hume set out in the reverse direction at much the same time to consult Sir John Pringle in London about his health. They met at Morpeth.[3] Smith went on to Kirkcaldy where, he reported to Strahan:

> From this obscure and remote part of the country there is nothing to write you about except, the worst of all subjects, ones self. And even upon that subject I have nothing to say except that I am in perfect health and that I found my mother as much so as it is possible for anybody to be who is past eighty.[4]

The next six or seven months were spent in Kirkcaldy except for occasional visits to Edinburgh and as far as Dalkeith. While in Kirkcaldy he had serious reports from Strahan about the deteriorating state of Hume's health. Sir John Pringle sent him first to Bath but an initially favourable response to the waters was soon gone and he was sent to Buxton. From Kirkcaldy Smith wrote an unusually long letter showing little faith in any medication:

> I am very sorry to Learn by Mr Strahan that the Bath Waters have not agreed with you for some time, so well as they appeared to do at first. You have found one Medicine which has agreed with you; travelling and change of air. I would continue, if I was you, during the continuance of the fine Season the constant application of that medicine without troubling myself with any other, and would

spend the summer in Sauntering thro all the different corners of England without halting above two or three nights in any one place. If before the month of October you do not find yourself thoroughly re'established, you may then think of changing this cold climate for a better, and of visiting the venerable remains of antient and modern arts that are to be seen about Rome and the Kingdom of Naples. A mineral water is as much a drug as any that comes out of the Apothecaries Shop. It produces the same violent effects upon the Body. It occasions a real disease, tho' a transitory one, over and above that which nature occasions. If the new disease is not so hostile to the old one as to contribute to expell it, it necessarily weakens the Power which nature might otherwise have to expell it. Change of air and moderate exercise occasion no new disease: they only moderate the hurtful effects of any lingering disease which may be lurking in the constitution; and thereby preserve the body in as good order as it is capable of being during the continuance of that morbid state. They do not weaken, but invigorate, the power of Nature to expel the disease. I reckon it probable that the Bath Waters had never agreed with you, but that the good effects of your journey not being spent when you began to use them, you continued for some time to recover, not by means of them, but in spite of them. Is it probable that the Buxton waters will do you more good? The Prescription supposed most likely to do good is always given first. If it fails, which it does nine times in ten, the second is surely likely to fail ninety nine time a hundred. The journey to Buxton, however, may be of great service to you; but I would be sparing in the use of the water.[5]

Smith went to Edinburgh on 18 June and was there when Hume arrived back on 3 July,

by no means in the state in which I could have wished to have seen him. His spirits, however, continue perfectly good; and his complexion, I think, is clearer than when I saw him at Morpeth; But his strength, I am afraid, is a good deal wasted so that he cannot now bear the jolting of a Post chaise upon our rough roads.[6]

By mid-August Smith was back in Kirkcaldy, but with Hume still much in his mind as is obvious in a letter to Alexander Wedderburn on 14 August :

I have nothing to tell you that will be very agreable. Poor David Hume is dying very fast, but with great chearfulness and good humour and with more real resignation to the necessary course of things, than any Whining Christian ever dyed with pretended resignation to the will of God. On thursday last he showed me a letter from his old friend Collonel Edmondstone bidding him an eternal adieu. I alledged that as his spirits were so very good there was still some chance that his disease might take a favourable turn. He answered 'Smith, your hopes are groundless; an habitual diarrhaea, which has now continued for several years, is a dangerous disease to a man of any age. At my age it is a mortal one. When I rise in the morning I find myself weaker than when I went to bed at night, and when I go to bed at night weaker than when I rose in the morning, so that in a few days I trust the business will be over'. I said, that at any rate he had the comfort of thinking that he left all his friends in prosperity particularly his brothers family whose circumstances would be greatly improved by his means. He replied, their circumstances were good independent of me and gave me some account of them: but, continued he, I so far agree with you, that when I was lately reading the dialogues of Lucian in which he represents one Ghost as pleading for a short delay till he should marry a young daughter, another till he should finish a house he had begun, a third till he had provided a portion for two or three young Children, I began to think of what Excuse I could alledge to Charon in order to procure a short delay, and as I have now done everything that I ever intended to do, I acknowledge that for some time no tolerable one occurred to me; at last I thought I might say, Good Charon, I have been endeavouring to open the eyes of people; have a little patience only till I have the pleasure of seeing the churches shut up, and the Clergy sent about their business; but Charon would reply, O you loitering rogue; that wont happen these two hundred years; do you fancy I will give you a lease for so long a time? Get into the boat this instant. Since we must lose our friend the most agreable thing that can happen is that he dyes [as] a man of sense ought to do. I left Edinburgh for a few days till he should recall me. He is so weak, that even my company fatigues him, especially as his spirits are so good that he cannot help talking incessantly when anybody is with him. When alone he diverts himself with correcting his own works, and with all [the] ordinary amusements.[7]

Less than a week later, Joseph Black reported that Hume:

sits up, goes down Stairs once a day and amuses himself with reading, but hardly sees any Body. He finds that the conversation of even his most intimate friends fatigues and oppresses him for the most part. And it is happy that he does not need it for he is quite free from Anxiety, impatience or low Spirits and passes his time very well with the assistance of amuseing Books. He says he wrote to you lately and expects an answer.[8]

Hume had written to Smith on the 15th of the month, but the letter took over a week to reach him. Smith replied:

My Dearest Friend, I have this moment received your Letter of the 15th inst. You had, in order to save me the sum of one Penny sterling, sent it by the carrier instead of the Post; and (if you have not mistaken the date) it has lain at his quarters these eight days and was, I presume, very likely to lie there for ever.

But Smith added: 'I hope I need not repeat to you that I am ready to wait on you whenever you wish to see me. Whenever you do so, I hope you will not scruple to call on me.'[9] Hume replied in the hand of his nephew, 'I cannot submit to your coming over here on my account as it is possible for me to see you so small a Part of the day.' In a postscript he acknowledged that 'It was a strange blunder to send your Letter by the Carrier '[10] – and with this exchange a long and affectionate correspondence closed. On Monday 26 August, Black wrote:

Yesterday about 4 o'clock afternoon Mr. Hume expired ... He continued to the last perfectly sensible and free from much pain or feelings of distress. He never dropped the smallest expression of impatience but when he had occasion to speak to the people about him always did it with affection and tenderness. I thought it improper to write to bring you over, especially as I heard that he had dictated a letter to you on Thursday or Wednesday desiring you not to come. When he became very weak it cost him an effort to speak and he died in such a happy composure of mind that nothing could have made it better.[11]

Hume was buried in the new cemetary on the Calton Crags and later covered by a round tower designed by Robert Adam – which Smith is alleged to have described as 'the greatest piece of vanity I ever saw in my friend Hume'.[12]

Hume's long illness obviously caused Smith a good deal of anxiety; an anxiety which was compounded by the problem of his *Dialogues concerning Natural Religion*. Hume had written the work in the 1750s but had been persuaded, notably by Sir Gilbert Elliott, that it would be impolitic to publish.[13] Hume accepted the advice but still hankered after publication, complaining to Elliott: 'Is it not hard & tyrannical in you, more tyrannical than any Act of the Stuarts, not to allow me to publish my Dialogues? Pray, do you not think that a proper Dedication may atone for what is exceptionable in them?'[14] Hume planned to bequeath this delicate problem to Smith, in a will dated 4 January 1776. Smith was given full discretion over all papers except that he was required to publish the *Dialogues*, but not material which he suspected might be more than five years old. Though Hume's will concluded 'I can trust to that intimate and sincere friendship, which has ever subsisted between us, for the faithful execution of this part of my will'[15] he bequeathed Smith the sum of £200 to be paid after the publication of the *Dialogues*. Smith could well have done without both bequests. He still feared the outcry which had led Elliot and others to dissuade Hume from publication in the 1750s, and throughout his life so shrank from outright confrontation with religious orthodoxy that he carefully phrased and planned his own work to avoid it. He now feared that even posthumous publication would blow the embers of controversy into a blaze which would envelop him and at the same time do little for Hume's reputation. Hume had little or no contact with Smith between the completion of the will and the meeting at Morpeth, which was probably the occasion of the first discussion of Hume's testamentary command to publish the *Dialogues*. On 3 May, just after reaching London, he sent Smith a formal letter with a covering note stating that it was sent 'conformably to your Desire. I think, however, your Scruples groundless . . .'[16] 'Both on account of the Nature of the Work and of your Situation', the formal letter left 'entirely to your Discretion at what time you will publish that Piece, or whether you will publish it at all'. It also provided further, and apparently innocent information which, as events transpired, was to cause Smith as much trouble as anything. A few days before leaving Edinburgh Hume had written 'a very inoffensive Piece, called *My Own Life* . . . There can be no Objection, that this small piece should be sent to Messrs. Strahan and Cadell and the Proprietors of my other Works to be prefixed to any future Edition of them.'[17]

Smith's attitude must have worried the dying Hume, who became very anxious to ensure publication of the *Dialogues*. On 8 June he told

Strahan that when he returned to Edinburgh, he intended printing an edition of 500, of which he would give away 100 in presents and make the rest over to Strahan.[18] His deteriorating health ruled out that option and on 7 August he added a codicil to his will leaving all his manuscripts to Strahan, requiring him to publish the *Dialogues* within two years, and giving him discretion over the publication of two essays, 'Of Suicide' and 'Of the Immortality of the Soul'.[19] Then, to make doubly sure that his objective would be realised, and to ensure that there was no possible excuse for not publishing the work, he made provision that, if Strahan should not publish within two and a half years, the property in the *Dialogues* should pass to his nephew, David Hume, 'whose Duty, in publishing them as the last request of his Uncle, must be approved by all the World'.[20] But Smith was not excluded from the arrangements, though no longer with any personal responsibility for publishing. Though a copy of the *Dialogues* was to be sent to both Strahan and his nephew, Hume proposed ordering a third copy to be consigned to Smith, 'It will bind you to nothing, but will serve as a Security.' Hume went further and proposed that the property in them should be left to Smith if they had not been published five years after Hume's death.[21] Smith responded at once, accepting custody of the third copy of the *Dialogues* — 'if I should happen to die before they are published, I shall take care that my copy shall be as carefully preserved as if I was to live a hundred years', but hedging any acceptance of ultimate responsibility for publishing them, an ultimate responsibility which he suggested was unnecessary: 'There is no probability of his [Strahan] delaying it, and if anything could make him delay it, it would be a clause of this kind, which would give him an honourable pretence for doing so.' Perhaps to make amends for such apparent lack of co-operation, Smith asked leave to add a few lines to the account of his own life which Hume had prepared, in particular with the objective of

> giving some account, in my own name, of your behaviour in this illness, if, contrary to my own hopes, it should prove your last . . . You have in a declining state of health, under an exhausting disease, for more than two years together, now looked at the approach, or what you at least believed to be the approach of Death with a steady chearfulness such as very few men have been able to maintain for a few hours, tho' otherwise in the most perfect Health.[22]

Hume's last letter granted Smith's request.[23]

Smith's apprehensions over the publication of the *Dialogues* emerged immediately after Hume's death. He wrote to Strahan explaining clearly Hume's wish that the *Dialogues* be published. Smith's view was unchanged: The *Dialogues*

> tho' finely written I could have wished had remained in Manuscript to be communicated only to a few people. When you read the work you will see my reasons without my giving you the trouble of reading them in a letter. But he has ordered it otherwise . . . I once had persuaded him to leave it entirely to my discretion either to publish them at what time I thought proper or not to publish them at all. Had he continued of this mind the manuscript should have been most carefully preserved and upon my decease restored to his family; but it never should have been published in my lifetime. When you have read it you will, perhaps, think it not unreasonable to consult some prudent friend about what you ought to do.

The extent of Smith's apprehension was even more evident in a further comment he added to the letter. 'I propose to add to his life a very well authenticated account of his behaviour during his last Illness. I must, however, beg that his life and those dialogues may not be published together; as I am resolved, for many reasons, to have no concern in the publication of those dialogues.'[24] Smith suggested that the account of his life be published with the next edition of his works, which Smith had promised Hume he would authenticate according to his last corrections.

Smith quickly wrote his account of Hume, which he cast in the form of a letter to Strahan, sending it for approval first to Hume's brother, who made a few minor corrections, and to Joseph Black, who consulted John Home and some other friends. When he sent the account to Strahan, he was obviously still apprehensive about the *Dialogues*. Strahan had agreed that it should be printed separately.

> I even flatter myself that this arrangement will contribute, not only to my quiet, but to your interest. The clamour against the dialogues, if published first, might hurt for some time the sale of the new edition of his works and when the clamour has a little subsided, the dialogues might hereafter occasion a quicker sale of another edition.[25]

The account of Hume's life was short and when Strahan received it he pointed out that Hume's own account together with Smith's addition were so brief that they would not constitute a volume of even the smallest size, so he suggested the addition of some of his letters on political subjects:

> you may perhaps add greatly to the Collection from your own Cabinet and those of Mr John Home, Dr Robertson, and others of your mutual Friends, which you may pick up before you return hither. But if you wholly disapprove of this Scheme, say nothing of it, here let it drop, for without your Concurrence I will not publish *a single Word* of his.[26]

Smith's reply was unqualified:

> Mr Humes constant injunction was to burn all his Papers, except the Dialogues and the account of his own life . . . Many things would be published not fit to see the light to the great mortification of those who wish well to his memory . . . I should, therefore, be sorry to see any beginning given to the publication of his letters.[27]

Strahan must have had some lingering apprehension over the *Dialogues* which were not published until 1779, presumably by Hume's nephew, but the *Life* and Smith's letter were published in 1777. If Smith thought his piece was inoffensive, he was mistaken. He was soon the object of criticism, some of it vitriolic. James Boswell recalled visiting Hume in July 1776 when he was 'just a-dying'. 'It surprised me to find him talking of difficult matters with a tranquility of mind and a clearness of head which few men possess at any time. Two particulars I remember: Smith's *Wealth of Nations*, which he commended much, and Monboddo's *Origin of Language*, which he treated contemptuously.'[28] Less than a week later, on 9 July 1777, he wrote to Johnson:

> Without doubt you have read what is called *The Life* of David Hume, written by himself, with the letter from Dr. Adam Smith subjoined to it. Is not this an age of daring effrontery? My friend Mr. Anderson, Professor of Natural Philosophy at Glasgow, at whose house you and I supped, and to whose care Mr. Windham, of Norfolk, was entrusted at that University, paid me a visit lately; and after we had talked with indignation and contempt of the poisonous productions with which this age is infested, he said there was now an excellent opportunity for Dr. Johnson to step forth. I agreed with him that you

might knock Hume's and Smith's heads together, and make vain and ostentatious infidelity exceedingly ridiculous. Would it not be worth your while to crush such noxious weeds in the moral garden?[29]

George Horne, who was then President of Magdalen College, Oxford, and ended his days as Bishop of Norwich, did publish such an attack[30] which led Smith to recollect ruefully in 1780 that

A single, and as I thought a very harmless Sheet of paper, which I happened to Write concerning the death of our late friend Mr Hume, brought upon me ten times more abuse than the very violent attack I had made upon the whole commercial system of Great Britain.[31]

One other matter from Hume's will remained to trouble Smith and that was the legacy of £200, which Smith alleged was meant to accompany the obligation to publish the *Dialogues*, which had later been taken off his shoulders. Hume's brother argued otherwise, although the final outcome of this friendly exchange is unclear.[32]

Smith must have gone to Edinburgh immediately after Hume's death. At the end of August he was at Dalkeith House where he stayed for a week before returning to Kirkcaldy. He evidently planned to be in London at the beginning of November,[33] although he did not actually arrive in the city until the following January.[34] At one stage, Smith seems to have considered settling permanently in London. The possibility was mentioned in correspondence between Smith and his publisher Strahan about Smith's mother, whom Strahan knew well. In June he was 'very glad to hear ... that your worthy Parent is as well as can be expected' and asked to be remembered to her 'with great Respect';[35] in September he hoped that 'your Mother's Health will not prevent you from returning hither at the time you propose';[36] in November, 'My Wife and Daughter join kindest Compliments to your amiable Parent, who I hope is still able to enjoy your Company, which must be her greatest Comfort';[37] in June 1776 he wondered if 'she will be able to accompany you to London about the End of the Summer.';[38] in September, 'You know I once mentioned to you how happy I thought it would make you both if you could bring her along with you to spend the Remainder of her Days in this Place, but perhaps it will not be easy to remove her so far at this time of her Life.'[39] Unless Smith's thoughts were moving towards settlement in London the discussion about taking his mother there — faint and uncertain though it was — would have been irrelevant. His mother's age and the difficulty of moving may have led him to surrender such ideas, or the stay in Scotland in 1776 may have persuaded him that there were positive attractions in returning and settling there, because during his stay in London from January to October 1777 he seems to have taken steps to make provision for an appointment in Scotland.

A more immediate problem during his stay in London in 1777 was negotiations with Strahan over various plans for publication. Smith had offered to help Strahan in the publication of Hume's works, even when he was carefully dissociating himself from the publication of the *Dialogues*, but the second edition of the *Wealth of Nations* was also a live issue. In October 1776 he asked Strahan for information on sales and the balance between them,[40] and in the following month suggested the second edition should appear in four volumes octavo, printed at Strahan's expense, with the profits divided between them.[41] Strahan accepted this proposal as 'very fair' and 'very agreeable' to Cadell and himself.[42]

The second edition was not published until early in 1778, by which time Smith was back in Kirkcaldy, still having to deal at a distance with corrections to the forthcoming edition. When he left London is uncertain but he was in Kirkcaldy in October 1777, perhaps having encountered a highwayman on the way north, according to a rather enigmatic comment in a letter to him from Wedderburn, who refers to

the Account of your mercy to the highwaymen, in which I suspect there was a little mixture of Prudence; Nor am I convinced that the ardour of your Mans Courage would have misdirected his Pistol, and if he had shot I shou'd have been in more pain for your danger than the Highwayman's.[43]

When he returned to Kirkcaldy Smith settled down to his 'old retirement' to work on a book on the imitative arts, but probably the good offices of the Duke of Buccleuch then opened up another and more profitable way in which he was to spend the last decade of his life.[44] In October 1777 Smith became a candidate for a vacant post as Commissioner of Customs and asked Strahan to let him know the outcome as soon as he could.[45] Sir Grey Cooper wrote Smith on 7 November with favourable news. He referred to an earlier recommendation of someone for appointment and contrasted it with the one he had received from Smith himself:

I remember well the zeal, the assiduity, and the warmth of heart with which you recommended him, and I reflect with satisfaction that it was in my power to give success to that application; you now sollicit a place at the Board of Customs at Edinburgh for another Person, but in this case, instead of a warm and eager application, I find nothing But Phlegm, Composure and Indifference; It is however fortunate that the person whom you so faintly support, does not want yours or any other great mans recommendation; and tho you seem to have no very high opinion of him, His merit is so well known to Lord North and to all the world, That (Alas what a Bathos!) He will very soon, if I am not much mistaken be appointed a Commissioner of the Customs in Scotland.[46]

The news broke in London in November, though by December Smith had still not heard officially and, lest the delay was because of the need to pay appropriate fees, he authorised Strahan to pay any on his behalf.[47] Though Smith's letters to Strahan, and to Strahan's nephew John Spottiswoode, who transacted the payment of fees at the Treasury on behalf of Smith, indicate that he was on edge over the appointment, the latter admitted when all was over that the matter had been concluded expeditiously by the standards of the time. He received the Commission on 2 February 1778 — 'four days after my name had appeared in the Gazette; I am assured that there is scarce an example of any such commissions coming to Edinburgh in less than four weeks after publication'.[48] Smith was a fully fledged Commissioner of Customs, worth £600 a year, £500 as Commissioner of Customs and £100 as Commissioner of the Salt Duties. He still retained the Duke of Buccleuch's pension of £300 a year, which Buccleuch refused to allow him to surrender.[49] Smith could rightly say that his 'present situation is therefore as fully affluent as I could wish it to be'.[50] He had three times the salary of a University professor and £200 more than that of a judge in the court of session. Yet Smith's appointment was ironic, as Gibbon pointed out when he wrote to congratulate him:

Among the strange reports, which are every day circulated in this wide town, I heard one to-day so very extraordinary, that I know not how to give credit to it. I was informed that a place of Commissioner of the Customs in Scotland had been given to a Philosopher who for his own glory and for the benefit of mankind had enlightened the world by the most profound and systematic treatise on the great objects of trade and revenue which had ever been published in any age or in any Country. But as I was told at the same time that this Philosopher was my particular friend, I found myself very forcible inclined to believe, what I most sincerely wished and desired.[51]

Notes

1. *Corr.*, letter 149, David Hume to Adam Smith, 8 February 1776.
2. John Home, *Works*, ed. H. Mackenzie (Edinburgh, 1822), i, 167.
3. Ibid., i, 168.
4. *Corr.*, letter 158, Adam Smith to William Strahan, 3 June 1776.
5. *Corr.*, letter 161, Adam Smith to David Hume, 16 June 1776.
6. *Corr.*, letter 162, Adam Smith to William Strahan, 6 July 1776.
7. *Corr.*, letter 163, Adam Smith to Alexander Wedderburn, 14 August 1776.
8. *Corr.*, letter 167, Joseph Black to Adam Smith, 22 August 1776.
9. *Corr.*, letter 166, Adam Smith to David Hume, 22 August 1776.
10. *Corr.*, letter 168, David Hume to Adam Smith, 23 August 1776.
11. *Corr.*, letter 169, Joseph Black to Adam Smith, 26 August 1776.
12. J. Rae, *Life of Adam Smith* (London, 1895), 302.
13. E.C. Mossner, *The Life of David Hume* (Oxford, 1954), 320.
14. *The Letters of David Hume*, ed. J.Y.T. Greig (Oxford, 1932), i, 380.
15. Quoted in *Corr.*, 195–6, n.1.
16. *Corr.*, letter 156, David Hume to Adam Smith, 3 May 1776.
17. *Corr.*, letter 157, David Hume to Adam Smith, 3 May 1776.
18. Hume, *Letters*, ii, 323.
19. Mossner, *Life of Hume*, 592.
20. Ibid., 593.
21. *Corr.*, letter 165, David Hume to Adam Smith, 15 August 1776.
22. *Corr.*, letter 166, David Hume to Adam Smith, 22 August 1776.
23. *Corr.*, letter 168, David Hume to Adam Smith, 23 August 1776.
24. *Corr.*, letter 172, Adam Smith to William Strahan, 5 September 1776.
25. *Corr.*, letter 177B, Adam Smith to William Strahan, October 1776.
26. *Corr.*, letter 180, William Strahan to Adam Smith, 26 November 1776.
27. *Corr.*, letter 181, Adam Smith to William Strahan, 2 December 1776.
28. *Boswell in Extremis*, ed. C.M. Weiss (New York, 1970), 12-14.
29. Boswell, *Life of Johnson*, 810.
30. (George Horne), *A Letter to Adam Smith, LL.D. on the Life, Death, and Philosophy of his Friend David Hume Esq.* by one of the People Called Christians (Oxford, 1777).
31. *Corr.*, letter 208, Adam Smith to Andreas Holt, 26 October 1780.
32. *Corr.*, letters 170, 171, 175, 176 between Adam Smith and John Home, 31 August, 2 September, 7 and 14 October 1776.
33. *Corr.*, letter 172, Adam Smith to William Strahan, 5 September 1776.
34. *Corr.*, letter 182, Adam Smith to Governor Pownall.
35. *Corr.*, letter 160, William Strahan to Adam Smith, 10 June 1776.
36. *Corr.*, letter 173, William Strahan to Adam Smith, 16 September 1776.
37. *Corr.*, letter 180, William Strahan to Adam Smith, 26 November 1776.
38. *Corr.*, letter 160, William Strahan to Adam Smith, 10 June 1776.
39. *Corr.*, letter 173, William Strahan to Adam Smith, 16 September 1776.
40. *Corr.*, letter 177B, Adam Smith to William Strahan, October 1776.
41. *Corr.*, letter 179, Adam Smith to William Strahan, 13 November 1776.

42. *Corr.*, letter 180, William Strahan to Adam Smith, 26 November 1776.
43. *Corr.*, letter 185, Alexander Wedderburn to Adam Smith, 30 October 1777.
44. *Corr.*, letter 208, Adam Smith to Andreas Holt, 26 October 1780.
45. *Corr.*, letter 184, Adam Smith to William Strahan, 27 October 1777.
46. *Corr.*, letter 186, Sir Grey Cooper to Adam Smith, 7 November 1777.
47. *Corr.*, letter 188, Adam Smith to William Strahan, 20 December 1777.
48. *Corr.*, letter 193, Adam Smith to William Strahan, 5 February 1778.
49. *Corr.*, letter 208, Adam Smith to Andreas Holt, 26 October 1780.
50. Ibid.
51. *Corr.*, letter 187, Edward Gibbon to Adam Smith, 26 November 1777.

16 COMMISSIONER OF CUSTOMS

After Smith was appointed a Commissioner of Customs he adopted a more settled way of life, one more reminiscent of the years in Kirkcaldy between 1767 and 1773. As in these years, his family was at the centre of his life. He soon installed his mother and his cousin, Janet Douglas, in Panmure House in the Canongate, which remained his home until his death. During this period he introduced into the household young David Douglas, born in 1769, the son of Janet Douglas's brother. He became Smith's heir and was to assume the judicial title of Lord Reston on his appointment as a Senator of the College of Justice. Smith's major employment at this time was as Commissioner of Customs and Salt Duties. He attended his first meeting of the Board and took the appropriate oath[1] as a Commissioner in Scotland on 3 February 1778, the day after receiving his commission. The Board was a demanding activity for anyone who attended as regularly as Smith did, and it absorbed a large part of his time as he grew older, as his own comments bear out. In 1780 he was able to provide yet another of his many excuses for being a poor correspondent:

> I am ashamed of having delayed so long to answer your very obliging letter; but I am occupied four days in every Week at the Custom House; during which it is impossible to sit down seriously to any other business; during the other three days too, I am liable to be frequently interrupted by the extraordinary duties of my office, as well as by my own private affairs, and the common duties of society.[2]

Years later, in 1787, when acknowledging his appointment as Rector at Glasgow, he indicated to the Principal that Christmas would be a suitable time for his installation:

> We have commonly at the board of Customs a vacation of five or six days at that time. But I am so regular an attendant that I think myself entitled to take the play for a week at any time. It will be no inconveniency to me, therefor, to wait upon you at whatever time you please.[3]

Normally the Board met on Monday, Tuesday, Wednesday and

199

Thursday, only rarely on other days and then usually only to deal with some item of special business. Brief holidays marked Christmas, Easter and Whitsun, to which were added occasional days off to mark royal anniversaries — including the usual birthdays and accessions, as well as the 'martyrdom' of King Charles and the Gunpowder Plot — New Year's Day, Handsel Monday, the various fasts and days of preparation for the sacrament, and Leith Races. The Board was therefore more or less in continuous session and it was unusual for no business to be transacted at its meetings, even if much of it was routine.

The work fell heavily on those few commissioners, such as Smith, who did not avoid the burdensome work by absenting themselves. The procedure was for a commissioner to take the chair at all meetings in one week, whether the normal four or a lesser number. If the chairman of the week was not present at all the meetings of the week, another member took his place. On many occasions Smith acted as such a substitute chairman, but he had rarely to call on aid from others to take his place.

Details of Smith's record of attendance show the extent of the commitment which the Board required of him and whether he was in Edinburgh at certain times. The number of meetings he attended each year were: 1778 — 169; 1779 — 186; 1780 — 183; 1781 — 185; 1782 — 133; 1783 — 180; 1784 — 169; 1785 — 185; 1786 — 180; 1787 — 77; 1788 — 85; 1789 — 111; 1790 — 45. Smith never missed a meeting of the Board from 3 February 1778 until 19 March 1782. When he first absented himself from attendance on 19 March it was because he had been granted leave of absence for four months 'to attend to his private Affairs'.[4] He resumed attendance on 11 July 1782 and from then until 1787 missed only 24 meetings, six being when his mother died. Two distractions account for the periods of absence. They were the desire to advance his own private study, and ill-health. These distractions also occasioned visits to London in both 1782 and 1787, the only two occasions in which Smith seems to have been there after he settled in Edinburgh in 1778.

In his four months leave of absence in 1782, when Smith was living as usual at 27 Suffolk Street, Charing Cross, the mixture of motives behind the visit can be discerned. Ill-health was not the prime motive in the early visit as it was in the latter, though it may not have been entirely absent. At any rate in the autumn of 1781 Smith turned down an invitation to attend an election dinner given by James Hunter Blair: 'I had all yesterday a very disagreeable pain in my stomach, and in addition I have got this day a pain in my side, I am afraid an Election dinner is not the proper remedy for these complaints.'[5] And, when he was in London, Henry Mackenzie wrote to him from Edinburgh on 7 June, hoping that 'your former Indisposition has been long quite removed, and that you have escaped the Influenza, which has raged in London and now begins to rage here'.[6] Whatever the state of Smith's health, the main reason for the visit of 1782 was to forward his own work, but he was not allowed to escape entirely from the work of the Board of Customs. In April 1782 his fellow-commissioners on the Board in Edinburgh were told that the Treasury, on the suggestion of the Lord Advocate, had asked Smith to consider a proposal from the Convention of Royal Burghs for a precise table of fees from all ports in Scotland, but that, since he had no relevant papers with him those which he needed were to be sent to him. He had obviously gone to London not prepared to undertake business for the Board although willing to carry it out when required.

Though it is virtually certain that Smith's attendance at the Board of Customs precluded any more visits to London before 1787, the prospect of others seems to have been in his mind. In November 1783 he told William Strahan that he would live with John Home, the dramatist, 'if [he] will receive me . . . in whatever part of the town he may happen to be settled', but that if that were not possible Home or Strahan should 'look out for a good lodging for me on the first floor somewhere in Suffolk Street, the price not to exceed two guineas a week', because he proposed leaving for London on 6 January 1784.[7] Two reasons may have been behind this projected visit of the winter of 1783/4. The first was affairs of state. Late in 1783 Smith was corresponding with George Dempster and William Eden. The former had invited Smith to give his views on ways of preventing smuggling to a House of Commons committee which had just been appointed, always provided that there was no dissolution. The second was Smith's own publishing arrangements. In October 1783 he told Cadell 'I intended to have asked a four months leave of absence . . . in order to have attended to the reprinting of my Book. But a Welch Newphew of mine tells me that unless I advance him two hundred pounds he must sell his commission in the army. This robs me of the money with which I intended to defray the expence of my expedition.'[8] Cadell must have offered funds, because they were declined with thanks as Smith's own resources were adequate to finance a trip from 6 January 1784.[9] Smith did not travel south on that day; instead he was in the chair at a meeting of the Board of Customs in Edinburgh. Certainly the four months' leave which was once anticipated did not materialise. Smith probably remained in Edinburgh, stirring from the capital only briefly in April, when he accompanied Edmund Burke to his installation as Rector at the University of Glasgow on the 10th. Thereafter Smith and Burke went on a short sight-seeing tour which, by including Loch Lomond and Carron ironworks, encompassed both the old and the new Scotland.

The second major period of absence from meetings of the Board after 3 January until 30 July 1787, saw Smith's last visit to London, dominated this time by ill-health. One indication of the difference between the two visits lies in the pattern of attendance at The Club: seven times in 1782 but only once in 1787, and that on 12 June, after he had been in London for some time. But, if ill-health took him south he no longer needed to rely on lodging with John Home or nearby at not more than two guineas a week. Henry Dundas wrote to him in March:

> I am glad you have got Vacation. Mr Pitt, Mr Greenville and your humble Servant are clearly of opinion you cannot spend it so well as here. The Weather is fine, My Villa at Wimbledon a most comfortable healthy Place. You shall have a comfortable room and as the Business is much relaxed we shall have time to discuss all your Books with you every Evening. Mr Greenville who is an unconsciously sensible man is concert in this Request.[10]

Smith's illness was diagnosed as an inflammation of the bladder and very bad piles. John Hunter operated for the latter and it was reported to Jeremy Bentham that 'the other complaint is since much mended. The physicians say he may do some time longer.[11] Ill or not, Smith was still closeted with the great in the affairs of state. Boswell, visiting him on 27 May and feeling 'a little awkward', found Lord Loughborough with him.[12] By 12 June he was sufficiently recovered to attend his only dinner of this visit at The Club.[13] On 14 July Bentham was told:

> He is much with the ministry; and the clerks at the public offices have orders to furnish him with all papers, and to employ additional hands, if necessary, to copy for him. I am vexed that Pitt should have done so right a thing as to consult Smith; but if any of his schemes are effectuated, I shall be comforted.[14]

How much Smith was consulted was a matter of dispute and in view of the state of his health and the duration of the entire visit was only three to four months the consultations must have been limited. But in this last visit to London Smith was established and recognised both as a major scholar and as a valued commentator on public affairs. It was on this visit to London, and in Dundas's house that Pitt, Addington, Wilberforce and Grenville are all alleged to have stood until Smith was seated because, as Pitt is supposed to have said, they were all his scholars.[15]

Smith's attendance at the Board of Customs was resumed on 3 July 1787 but was much more irregular than in earlier years. In the three years of life which remained to him he had three substantial periods of absence, though none was complete as each was marked by an occasional attendance. Smith did not attend meetings from 11 February 1788 to 11 August 1788 with five exceptions; from 16 December 1788 to 19 March 1789, also with five exceptions; and from 21 April 1789 to 1 July 1789, with three exceptions. The most obvious explanation of the different pattern of attendance from that of earlier years might seem to be ill-health, which continued to dog him after the visit to London in the first half of 1787, and that may be considered to be confirmed by the occasional attendances with which the long periods of absence were interspersed, perhaps indicative of someone struggling hard to attend whenever possible.

But by the late 1770s Smith was also anxious to advance his own work, particularly major revisions of the *Theory of Moral Sentiments*. In a letter to Cadell, dated on 15 March 1788, he told him that he had taken four months' leave to enable him to press on with the revision of the *Theory of Moral Sentiments*,[16] After the end of the next period of absence, he wrote to Cadell again, on 31 March 1789, reporting that he was

labouring very hard in preparing the proposed new edition of the Theory of Moral Sentiments. I have even hurt my health and have been obliged to return, within these few days, to my usual attendance at the Custom house (from which the indulgence of my Colleagues had excused me) I may say principally for the sake of relaxation, and a much easier Business.[17]

Since Smith stated in the same letter that he would not finish his work on the *Theory of Moral Sentiments* till after midsummer, it is probable that the third of the periods of absence after 1787 was also taken up with the substantial revision of the *Theory* of which the sixth edition was published in May 1790.

Whether in London or not Smith was closely linked with many of the major figures involved in the complicated political changes of the last decade of his life. Direct evidence of his thinking on current affairs is not readily available. Nowhere does he provide a continuous commentary. From the advice he gave on specific aspects of public policy when asked and from his other writings it is possible to form a fairly comprehensive view of his attitude towards such major issues as colonial policy and the quarrel with America. His views on the day-to-day cut and thrust of political life are much less easily determined. Indeed, his comments on some of the changes in the administration can be taken to reveal someone with an intimate knowledge of political life, but not always fully aware of its implications, perhaps even to indicate someone who was politically naïve. Two characteristics offer the possibility of a reasonably consistent interpretation of his views. These were, first, his desire to avoid dissension in the body politic, especially when he was satisfied that its constitutional provision ensured appropriate control of royal power, and secondly, his simple but firm loyalty to his friends, even when they were on different sides in a political argument. The influence of both factors coloured his views on the political activities of Burke and Shelburne and provide an explanation of apparent ambivalence on the issues of the day. Smith's links with Shelburne stretched back to his days at Glasgow when he had been tutor to his younger brother and of the friendship and high regard in which Smith held Burke there can be no doubt. The regard existed even before they had met. In 1759, on the publication of the *Theory of Moral Sentiments*, Burke wrote a fulsome letter of congratulation and placed on Hume the responsibility of introducing them when Smith was next in London, and in 1784 Smith conducted Burke to his installation as Rector at Glasgow. The strengths of these friendships and the desire to avoid dissension emerge in Smith's responses to the political coalitions of the 1790s. Rockingham succeeded North in 1782 in an attempt to reach a settlement with the American colonists. So long as both Burke and Shelburne were in the Rockingham administration, both of Smith's friends held office, and the inclusion of both Fox and Shelburne in the administration provided a coalition of the type which Smith seems to have favoured temperamentally. Rockingham's death on 1 July 1782 produced an interesting response from Smith. He was about to leave London for Edinburgh, but, bad correspondent and all as he was, he managed to write Burke twice within a week. In the first, on the day of Rockingham's death:

I cannot avoid writing you a few lines to tell you how deeply I feel your affliction. I hope and trust that you will exert your usual firmness and that your friends and you will immediately plight unalterable faith to one another, and with unanimous consent chuse a leader whose virtues may command the same confidence with that which you all had in the worthy man whom it has pleased God to take from you.[18]

and in the second, five days later:

I cannot go into the Post Chaise without writing these few lines to you to tell you how much I approve and admire every part of your conduct, tho' I feel, perhaps, more than you do, for some of the effects of it . . .

It must afflict every good citizen that any circumstance should occur which could make men of their probity, prudence and moderation judge it proper in these times to withdraw from the service of their country.[19]

It is possible from the tenor of these letters that Smith had hopes that Burke and his friends would support Shelburne. The hope may have reflected Smith's desire to see the old administration continuing, even if under a new leader, but in this case the leader was also a friend of Smith, of even longer standing than Burke. On the other hand Smith's opinion of Shelburne as a person is much less clear than his opinion of Burke. The links were close, not only in the Glasgow days, but when Smith returned from his continental tour and advised Shelburne on a number of matters. A year later Smith acknowledged Shelburne's kindness not only to himself but later to Count de Sarsfield.[20] In 1786, he still had close contact because he wrote to the Abbé Morellet of 'our most valuable friend, the Marquis of Lansdown' (as Shelburne had become on 6 December 1784).[21] But much earlier, in 1763, David Hume, who in his days in office had been a major purveyor of political gossip to Smith, provided a possibly significant qualification to this regard, when he wrote: 'I see you are much displeased with that Nobleman [Shelburne] but he always speaks of you with regard.'[22]

Whatever Smith's views on the Shelburne administration – whether he wished to see it succeed as the best way of perpetuating the high hopes which he entertained of the Rockingham administration, or because of his own personal links with Shelburne – it came to an end early in 1783. In April of that year the Fox/North Coalition came to power and it met with Smith's warmest approval. Deep down he probably shared the widespread distrust of Shelburne, but the main reason for his approval of the new administration was that it represented a coalition.

> It would give me the greatest pleasure to believe that the present Administration rests on a solid Basis. It comprehends the worthiest and ablest men in the nation, the heads of the two great Aristocracies, whose disunion has weakened the . . . Government so much as at last to occasion the dismemberment of the empire. Their coalition, instead of being unpopular, was most devoutly to be wished for . . . I trust that the usual folly and impertinence of next winters opposition will more effectually reconcile the King to his ministers, than . . . any address of theirs has yet been able to do.[23]

In addition the change had one personal repercussion which greatly pleased Smith. It brought Burke back into office as Paymaster General. Smith's pleasure was neatly expressed:

> I never should have changed my opinion concerning the propriety of your conduct last summer, whatever might have been the event of it; and, I dare to say, you would still less have changed your own. It gives me, however, great satisfaction to see, that what was so agreeable to the highest principles of honour may in the end prove not inconsistent with interest.[24]

The end of the North/Fox Coalition, after the defeat by the Lords of Fox's East India Bill, shows where Smith's political interests lay. On 15 December 1783 he wrote to William Eden:

> I heartily congratulate you upon the triumphant manner in which the East India Bill has been carried through the Lower House. I have no doubt of its passing through the Upper House in the same manner. The decisive judgement and resolution with which Mr Fox has introduced and supported that Bill does him the highest honour.[25]

Smith's prediction proved false, but the fall of the North/Fox Coalition led to the rise of Pitt to power.

With the accession of Pitt to head the administration in December 1783, Smith was directly linked to someone who approved of his views and who admired him, but Smith had an even more direct link through Henry Dundas, 'the Gentleman who may be considered as our present Minister for Scotland',[26] as he described him in 1786. Smith's links with Dundas were varied. As with so many others in Scotland, he sought Dundas's assistance on a wide range of matters of patronage. He recommended to Dundas's 'protection' his kinsman Robert Douglas, Lieutenant in the 58th regiment of foot;[27] possible appointments at Chelsea Hospital for John Hunter — 'nothing is too good for our friend John';[28] the promotion of the Deputy Collector of Customs at Greenock to the post of Collector;[29] the continuation of the tack of the revenues of the Archbishopric of Glasgow to the University; a pension for the widow of the lecturer in chemistry at Glasgow; and a pension for the daughters of Richard Gardiner.[30] And through the Duke of Buccleuch he seems to have made application to Dundas for appointments at the Board of Customs[31] and for provision for William Cullen's daughters.[32] It is hardly surprising that Smith was therefore involved in the other side of Scottish politics of the eighteenth century: the provision of the political influence for which the patronage was often the appropriate return. Shortly after Dundas became Lord Advocate in 1775 Smith wrote to him a letter, so typical of the involved Scottish politics of the day, on the political position in his native Fife, where his family still had landed interests.[33] Dundas was therefore a direct link to Pitt, but much of the admiration was for Pitt, as when he wrote to Dundas of the way in which Pitt had denied full powers to the Prince of Wales during the regency crisis of 1788-9 when George III was temporarily insane:

I need not, I flatter myselfe, inform you at this time, what pleasure, the late happy, (and to my own melancholy and evil boding mind, I acknowledge, unexpected) event, has given to your friends, here and, I will venture to say, to all the real friends of the country. The firmness, propriety and prudence of every part of your young friends conduct must, as long as it is remembered, place him very high in the estimation of every wise and thinking man in the Kingdom.[34]

Though he was not actively involved in the political scene, Smith was obviously fully apprised of events and formulated his views on them. His limited correspondence reveals little except loyalty to his friends, notably to someone such as Burke whom he greatly respected, and above all a desire to see some compromise of the various factions in office, a compromise which often meant some limitation on royal power. The difficulty in dealing with Smith's political views in a consistent fashion is that they were affected by his private friendships. His general position was of the Whigs who originally followed Rockingham and his admiration for Burke a leading principle, so that he commended Burke or Burkean principles in political action, especially if the action also seemed to be commanding wide support. So he supported the Rockingham administration and the North/Fox Coalition, especially the East India Bill of Fox. When these failed he did not go into the political wilderness, partly because it was another of his friends who moved into office in the persons of Shelburne and later Pitt. In all the changes in political fortune Smith had direct personal links with the administration.

It is not surprising that in his latter years requests for aid continued from many of these influential friends. William Eden sought Smith's views on various aspects of trade policy. Only a handful of letters of their correspondence survives, which in itself makes an evaluation of various questions and answers difficult. The evaluation is more difficult because references in the letters show that much of the discussion on matters of policy took place personally when Smith was on his visits to London in the 1780s. But there is enough to show that the views passed on by Smith accorded with those expressed in the *Wealth of Nations*, though perhaps they were views which, if implemented, may have made him redundant as a Commissioner of Customs. On the key issue of trade with Ireland Smith's opinion was clear, both in his correspondence and in the *Wealth of Nations*. Dundas triggered off a query from Eden following the acceptance of free trade with Ireland by the Irish Parliament in October 1779. He explained his position to Smith, probably knowing it would be likely to receive his endorsement: 'There is trade enough in the world for the Industry both of Britain and Ireland.'[35] Dundas was not worried about any consequential damage from free trade for Ireland to a few places in Britain, but only over the possibility that Ireland might be able to undercut British producers in foreign markets 'from the want of Taxes and the Cheapness of labour'. The danger could be overcome by union which Dundas thought 'the best' if it could be accomplished, and, if not − probably with his Scottish experience in mind − 'the Irish Parliament must be managed by the proper distribution of the Loaves and fishes'. Smith responded almost identically to both Dundas and the 5th Earl of Carlisle, the President of the Board of Trade. Since he was uncertain of the proposal of the Irish Parliament, Smith could only speculate on four possible forms of free trade. Every case met with his approval, even when some of Britain's own interests might have suffered, but that Smith was not an academic recluse, giving advice without recognising the difficulties of its implementation is evident in the concluding part of his letter to Dundas:

> Whatever the Irish mean to demand in this way, in the present situation of our affairs, I should think it madness not to grant it. Whatever they may demand our manufacturers, unless the leading and principal men among them are properly dealt with beforehand, will probably oppose it. That they may be so dealt with, I know from experience, and that it may be done at little expense and with no great trouble. I could even point out some persons, who, I think, are fit and likely to deal with them successfully for this purpose. I shall not say more upon this till I see you; which I shall do the first moment I can get out of this town.[36]

To both his correspondents Smith stated the reasons why he did not fear competition from Ireland. To Dundas the explanation was brief: 'Ireland has neither coal nor Wood.'[37] To Carlisle the explanation was more extensive and very perceptive:

> Ireland has little Coal; the Coallieries about Lough Neagh being of little consequence to the greater part of the Country. It is ill provided with Wood; two articles essentially necessary to the progress of Great Manufactures. It wants order, police, and a regular administration of justice both to protect and to restrain the inferior ranks of people, articles more essential to the progress of Industry than both coal and wood put together, and which Ireland must continue to want as long as it continues to be divided between two hostile nations, the oppressors and the oppressed, the protestants and the Papists.[38]

Smith was still of the view expressed in favour of Union in the *Wealth of Nations*, 'Without a union with Great Britain, the inhabitants of Ireland are not likely for many ages to consider themselves as one people.'[39]

The remainder of the correspondence with Eden is more fragmentary and deals with wider issues, generally on matters on which Smith, as a Commissioner of Customs was likely to have views. The issues referred to Smith for advice varied: how the public revenue could be increased without levying additional burdens;[40] what attitudes should be adopted to the commercial policy of the 'revolted subjects' in America;[41] an account of Scottish revenues and expenditure[42] all showing that Smith was someone whose views on public property were sought. The responses are predictable in light of the writings but have their lighter side as well:

> Prohibitions do not prevent the importation of prohibited goods. They are bought everywhere, in the fair way of trade, by people who are not in the least aware that they are buying them. About a week after I was made a Commissioner of the Customs, upon looking over the list of prohibited goods, (which is hung up in every Customhouse and which is well worth your considering) and upon examining my own wearing apparel, I found, to my great astonishment, that I had scarce a stock, a cravat, a pair of ruffles, or a pocket handkerchief which was not prohibited to be worn or used in Great Britain. I wished to set an example and burnt them all. I will not advise you to examine either your own or Mrs Edens apparel or household furniture, least you be brought into a scrape of the same kind.[43]

Smith's reputation might have been expected to lead to even more frequent resort to his opinions than the surviving evidence would indicate. His disinclination to correspond, even when he was living in comparative isolation, may explain the lack of surviving evidence rather than any reluctance to give aid when asked. Whatever the explanation, the surviving examples of Smith having been consulted are few, but they cover various topics. If some are on matters of high policy, others are less so and some are trivial.

An interesting example of what may be considered to fall in an intermediate category was when Smith was consulted by George Chalmers, who was seeking various statistical series which he doubtless planned to use in one of the various editions of his work on *An Estimate of the Comparative Strength of Great Britain*. He seems to have asked, in a letter of which no copy has survived, for information on the census of Scotland compiled by Alexander Webster on behalf of the fund for the maintenance of the widows and orphans of ministers. Smith's approach to Webster's work started from the sceptical principle which he had enunciated in the *Wealth of Nations*: 'I have no great faith in political arithmetick'.[44] a principle which he reiterated to Chalmers, but in which he classified Webster as 'the most skilful . . . of all the men I have ever known'.[45] Smith explained the principles on which the census had been compiled and felt able to classify it as 'a very accurate account' of the population of Scotland in 1755, the only snag being that Webster had told him shortly before his death that the numbers were too low and should have been increased from 1.25 to 1.5 million, a story − Smith concluded −which 'does not contribute to mend my opinion of it [political arithmetic]'.[46] Later Smith withdrew the imputation, as not the result 'of any serious or deliberate consideration or enquiry. It was, indeed, at a very jolly table, and in the midst of much mirth and jollity, of which the worthy Doctor, among many other useful and amiable qualities, was a very great lover and promoter.'[47] Smith had tracked down a more considered judgement of Webster in 1779, that his figures were reliable in 1755 and were probably as reliable in 1779 in the aggregate, because though 'the numbers in the great trading and manufacturing towns and Villages were considerably increased, yet the Highlands and islands were much depopulated, and even the Low Country, by enlargement of farms, in some degree'.

In his later years Smith's advice was sought by others less elevated in the affairs of state, but still providing him with problems to tackle, though of a very different kind. Such was Charles MacKinnon of MacKinnon, who sent Smith a treatise on fortifications which he wished to have published, and also sent him £5 to that end. MacKinnon's objective was to try to ensure that no one plagiarised his works, an occurrence which he obviously feared. Smith did not share his fears, nor MacKinnon's high opinion of his proposals, but did offer to retain the study and so to be able to vouch for MacKinnon's originality if anyone brought out his ideas later − and to return the £5.[48]

Notes

1. Minutes of the Board of Customs, SRO. CE 1/15. p. 289.
2. *Corr.*, letter 208, Adam Smith to Andreas Holt, 26 October 1780.
3. *Corr.*, letter 274, Adam Smith to Archibald Davidson, 16 November 1787.
4. Minutes of the Board of Customs, SRO. CE 1/17. p. 291.
5. *Corr.*, letter 214, Adam Smith to James Hunter Blair, 29 October 1781.
6. *Corr.*, letter 215, Henry Mackenzie to Adam Smith, 7 June 1782.
7. *Corr.*, letter 232, Adam Smith to William Strahan, 20 November 1783.
8. *Corr.*, letter 231, Adam Smith to William Strahan, 6 October 1783.
9. *Corr.*, letter 232, Adam Smith to William Strahan, 20 November 1783.
10. *Corr.*, letter 267, Henry Dundas to Adam Smith, 21 March 1787.
11. J.R. Christie (ed.), *The Correspondence of Jeremy Bentham* (London, 1971) 3,557.
12. *Private Papers of James Boswell from Malahide Castle in the Collection*

of Lt. Col. Ralph H. Isham, vol. 17 (1934), 32.
13. Ibid., 37.
14. Christie, *The Correspondence of Jeremy Bentham*, 557.
15. W.R. Scott, *Adam Smith as Student and Professor* (Glasgow, 1937), 302.
16. *Corr.*, letter 276, Adam Smith to Thomas Cadell, 15 March 1788.
17. *Corr.*, letter 287, Adam Smith to Thomas Cadell, 31 March 1789.
18. *Corr.*, letter 216, Adam Smith to Edmund Burke, 1 July 1782.
19. *Corr.*, letter 217, Adam Smith to Edmund Burke, 6 July 1782.
20. *Corr.*, letter 113, Adam Smith to Lord Shelburne, 27 January 1768.
21. *Corr.*, letter 259, Adam Smith to Abbé Morellet, 1 May 1786.
22. *Corr.*, letter 75, David Hume to Adam Smith, 13 September 1763.
23. *Corr.*, letter 231, Adam Smith to William Strahan, 6 October 1783.
24. *Corr.*, letter 226, Adam Smith to Edmund Burke, 15 April 1783.
25. *Corr.*, letter 233, Adam Smith to William Eden, 15 December 1783.
26, *Corr.*, letter 259, Adam Smith to Abbé Morellet, 1 May 1786.
27. *Corr.*, letter 272, Adam Smith to Henry Dundas, 18 July 1787.
28. Ibid.
29. *Corr.*, letter 280, Adam Smith to Henry Dundas, 1 September 1788.
30. *Corr.*, letter 286, Adam Smith to Henry Dundas, 25 March 1789.
31. *Corr.*, letter 210, Duke of Buccleuch to Adam Smith, 26 November 1780.
32. *Corr.*, letter 293, Duke of Buccleuch to Adam Smith, 24 February 1780.
33. *Corr.*, letter 148, Adam Smith to Henry Dundas, 13 December 1775.
34. *Corr.*, letter 286, Adam Smith to Henry Dundas, 25 March 1789.
35. *Corr.*, letter 200, Henry Dundas to Adam Smith, 30 October 1779.
36. *Corr.*, letter 201, Adam Smith to Henry Dundas, 1 November 1779.
37. Ibid.
38. *Corr.*, letter 202, Adam Smith to Lord Carlisle, 8 November 1779.
39. *WN*, V.iii.89.
40. *Corr.*, letter 203, Adam Smith to William Eden, 3 January 1780.
41. *Corr.*, letter 233, Adam Smith to William Eden, 15 December 1783.
42. *Corr.*, letter 235, Adam Smith to William Eden, 1783.
43. *Corr.*, letter 203, Adam Smith to William Eden, 3 January 1780.
44. *WN*, IV.v.b.30.
45. *Corr.*, letter 249, Adam Smith to George Chalmers, 10 November 1785.
46. Ibid.
47. *Corr.*, letter 252, Adam Smith to George Chalmers, 3 January 1786.
48. *Corr.*, letter 219, Adam Smith to Charles McKinnon [sic], 21 August 1782.

17 LAST DAYS

The last decade of Smith's life was marked not only by the obligations of a Commissioner of Customs, but also by activities of a more personal nature. Smith read a good deal, and his library of several thousand volumes contained many works by classical authors, political and commercial studies, historical works and accounts of travel, the authorities with which Smith replaced more traditional sources. But his library was not simply a collection of the sources which he used directly in his professional work. It also contained a wide range of literary works, of which he was a keen reader and critic. Though much more effort has been made to trace the details of the library since the first attempt by James Bonar, his very rough classification is still valid and is as good an indication as any of the variety of interests which it covered. Bonar divided the library into fifths; literature and art; Latin and Greek classics; law, politics and biography; political economy and history; science and philosophy. In view of Smith's interest in the classics and in the works of continental writers, especially French, it is hardly surprising that only about one-third was English.

The details of the headings of Smith's library are important in any discussion of the development of his thought and the nature and extent of its originality, but of more general interest is the obvious bias towards classical and literary studies. It is not surprising therefore that many of the visitors to him in Edinburgh in his later years found him immersed once again in the classics.

If Smith showed little interest, as far as can be found, in some aspects of contemporary literature, he shared the enthusiasm of others for Gaelic poetry and literature as portrayed by James Macpherson's alleged translations in his various works of the 1760s, particularly his alleged translation of Ossian in 1765. Hume records that Smith even listened to a piper of the Argyllshire Militia repeating 'all those poems which Mr. Macpherson has translated, and many more of equal beauty'.[1] Since presumably Smith had no idea what the piper was saying, his judgement of the beauty of the language may be accepted as, also, may his gullibility over Macpherson's claim. He provides some endorsement to Johnson's jibe at the whole affair: 'A Scotchman must be a very sturdy moralist, who does not love *Scotland* better than truth.'[2] Johnson was a sturdy moralist; the others were carried away with what was a passing literary fashion, very different from the native literary tradition which Burns represented, and which was far removed from the literary endeavours which strove to remove scotticisms from all speech and writing.

But there were other, more specific activities. Though Smith spent many years revising the *Wealth of Nations*, he did not seem worried about his earliest editions nor felt that they needed radical revision. While the second edition has many changes, Smith was entitled to claim that he had 'made no material alteration' and that 'none' of the 'good number of corrections ... affect even in the slightest degree, the general principles, or Plan of the System'.[3] He did not claim 'this second edition though a good deal more correct than the first, is entirely exempted from all errors' and even admitted 'I have myself discovered several inaccuracies.' Though he mentioned specifically the extreme and penetrating criticism of Thomas Pownall, MP and sometime Governor of Massachusetts, whom Smith met in London in 1777, the author of a pamphlet on the militia, and James Anderson as critics — apart from 'the inumerable squibs thrown out upon me in the newspapers', Smith seemed reasonably satisfied. 'I have however, upon the whole been much less abused than I had reason to expect; so that in this respect I think myself rather lucky than otherwise.'[4]

Though Smith seemed satisfied in 1780, the third edition was still some time away, and the changes were to be by way of additions strengthening and confirming, rather than changing, his argument. At the end of 1782 he apologised to Cadell for:

> my Idleness since I came to Scotland. The truth is, I bought at London a good many, partly new books, and partly either new editions of old books, or editions that were new to me; and the amusement I found in reading and diverting myself with them debauched me from my proper business; the preparing of a new edition of the Wealth of nations. I am now, however, heartily engaged at my proper work and I hope in two or three months to send you up the second Edition corrected in many places, with three or four very considerable additions.[5]

In May 1783 he told Strahan 'I have for these several months been labouring as hard as the continual interruption which my employment necessarily occasions, will allow me.'[6] In October:

> The alterations and additions which I propose to make to my new

Edition of the Wealth of Nations are now either finished compleatly (or soon will be) . . . I still . . . wait for the Accounts which our good friend Sir Grey Cooper was so kind as to promise me soon after the late political revolution.[7]

The following month the accounts promised by Sir Grey Cooper were still not to hand and he wrote Strahan asking him to try to obtain them[8] but by then the revision was far advanced. One favourable aspect of the work in the Customs House lay in the insight it gave him into the work of the mercantile system which he so vigorously attacked in the *Wealth of Nations* and so in a peculiar, and almost perverse way enabled him to introduce stronger and perhaps even better informed criticism of the system which he was privileged to see from the inside. The effect was most obvious in the third edition of the *Wealth of Nations*, which was to become the definitive edition as far as Smith was concerned. 'The Edition will probably see me out and I should therfor chuse to leave it behind me as perfect as I can make it.'[9] He also thought the changes so important that he gave instructions that they were 'to be printed separately and to be sold for a shilling, or half a Crown, to the purchasers of the old Edition'.[10] The general drift of the insertions, and of their tone, is evident in a letter of Smith to Strahan:

> Some new arguments against the corn bounty; against the Herring buss bounty; a new concluding Chapter upon the mercantile System; A short History and, I presume, a full exposition of the Absurdity and hurtfulness of almost all our chartered trading companies.[11]

The additions read strangely given the office of their author. One example of the paradox will suffice. In a completely new chapter, a conclusion to Book IV, which attacked the mercantilist system, he wrote:

> It is unnecessary, I imagine, to observe, how contrary such regulations are to the boasted liberty of the subject, of which we affect to be so very jealous; but which, in this case, is so plainly sacrificed to the futile interests of our merchants and manufacturers.[12]

The same attack on drawbacks, bounties and trading companies appeared in the additions of 1784. His years in the Customs House had not led Smith to change his views of the iniquity of the network of customs duties and regulations which he was upholding. If he was not convinced of the desirability of the mercantile system, he does not seem to have been troubled by an inconsistency in his own position as an upholder of it. The insight into its operation helped him to provide a clearer account and to use official material in doing so, as in his account of the herring bounty, particularly in Scotland, and in his account of the trading companies.[13]

The third edition of the *Wealth of Nations* was only just published when Smith embarked on the major revision of the *Theory of Moral Sentiments*. Cadell wrote to him in March 1785 that a fourth edition of the *Wealth of Nations* was called for and, when he replied, Smith added that 'If a new edition of the theory is wanted I have a few alterations to make of no great consequence which I shall send to you.'[14] The revision of the *Theory of Moral Sentiments* was not to be accomplished so quickly and both the fourth and fifth editions of the *Wealth of Nations* were to precede it, though they had only minor changes. So, once again, the anticipated minor revision became a major work. In 1788 a determined effort was made. He explained how matters stood, and the difficulties of making progress, to Cadell in March 1788:

> My subject is the *theory of moral Sentiments* to all parts of which I am making many additions and corrections. The chief and the most important additions will be to the third part, that concerning *the sense of Duty* and to the last part concerning *the History of moral Philosophy*. As I consider my tenure of this life as extremely precarious, and am very uncertain whether I shall live to finish several other works which I have projected and in which I have made some progress, the best thing, I think, I can do is to leave those I have already published in the best and most perfect state behind me. I am a slow, a very slow workman, who do and undo everything I write at least a dozen of times before I can be tolerably pleased with it; and tho' I have now, I think, brought my work within compass, yet it will be the month of June before I shall be able to send it to you. I have told you already, and I need not tell you again, that I mean to make you a present of all my Additions. I must beg, therefore, that no new edition of that book may be published before that time.[15]

Almost exactly a year later he reported only slow progress:

> Ever since I wrote to you last I have been labouring very hard in

preparing the proposed new edition of the Theory of Moral Sentiments. I have even hurt my health and have been obliged to return,
within these few days, to my usual attendance at the Customs House
(from which the indulgence of my Colleagues had excused me) I
may say principally for the sake of relaxation and a much easier
Business. Besides the Additions and improvements I mentioned to
you; I have inserted, immediately after the fifth part, a compleat
new sixth part containing a practical system of Morality, under the
title of the Character of Virtue. The Book now will consist of seven
Parts and will make two pretty large 8vo Volumes. After all my
labours, however, I am afraid it will be Midsummer before I can
get the whole Manuscript in such proper order as to send it to you. I
am very much ashamed of this delay; but the subject has grown
upon me. I would fain flatter myself that your Profit from the
additions will fully compensate the loss you may have suffered by
the delay.[16]

The additions went to the printer on December 1789 and the edition
was published shortly before Smith died in 1790.

But there were difficulties in making progress, partly resulting from
poor health and from the fact that Smith was always a slow worker.
The demands of office too took their toll. In October 1780, probably
not very seriously, he told William Strahan that 'I had almost forgot I
was the Author of the enquiry concerning the Wealth of Nations'.[17]
In the same month he provided evidence that he had not forgotten that
he was, when he wrote to Andreas Holt, Commissioner of the Danish
Board of Trade and Economy. He recorded his response to a number of
his critics, but the letter had a significant conclusion, which began with
a reference to

my present Office; which though it requires a good deal of attendance is both easy and honourable, and for my Way of living
sufficiently beneficial . . .My present situation is therefore fully as
affluent as I could wish it to be. The only thing I regret in it is the
interruptions to my literary pursuits, which the duties of my office
necessarily occasion. Several Works which I have projected are likely
to go on much more slowly than they otherwise would have done.[18]

In 1785 Smith explained his plans more fully, but with a qualification
which was to prove valid:

I have likewise two other great works upon the anvil; the one is a sort of Philosophical History of all the different branches of Literature, of Philosophy, Poetry and Eloquence; the other is a sort of theory and History of Law and Government. The materials of both are in a great measure collected, and some Part of both is put in tollerable good order. But the indolence of old age, tho' I struggle violently against it, I feel coming fast upon me, and whether I shall ever be able to finish either is extremely uncertain.[19]

Although Smith's ambitions were not fulfilled, the promise of further contributions was repeated in the 'advertisement' to the final edition of the *Theory of Moral Sentiments*, where Smith remarked that:

In the last paragraph of the first Edition of the present work, I said, that I should in another discourse endeavour to give an account of the general principles of law and government, and of the different revolutions which they had undergone in the different ages and periods of society; not only in what concerns justice, but in what concerns police, revenue, and arms, and whatever else is the object of law. In the Enquiry concerning the *Nature and Causes of the Wealth of Nations*, I have partly executed this promise; at least, so far as concerns police, revenue, and arms. What remains, the theory of jurisprudence, which I have long projected, I have hitherto been hindered from executing, by the same occupations which had till now prevented me from revising the present work. Though my very advanced age leaves me, I acknowledge, very little expectation of being able to execute this great work to my own satisfaction; yet, as I have not altogether abandoned the design, and as I wish to continue under the obligation of doing what I can, I have allowed the paragraph to remain as it was published more than thirty years ago, when I entertained no doubt of being able to execute every-thing which it announced.

But life also had its more social side, and Smith's family, which meant so much to him in his later years, was supplemented by a wide circle of friends. Hardly surprising in a city where, according to Samuel Rogers 'the inhabitants (at least the most eminent of them) devoted their whole time to the entertainment of strangers',[20] Smith fell into a pattern of entertaining widely. Rogers's recollections of his visits to Smith in the year before his death provide a useful and unique illustration of both the frequency and readiness with which he received guests in these later years and the wide range of conversation which led Smith to recall earlier experiences and contacts. Rogers went to supper on Sunday evening 19 July 1789 and, among other recollections, heard Smith speak on Turgot and Voltaire. The Sunday evening suppers may have been the most common times of companionship and discussion, and Rogers had a similar experience at dinner the following day. More interesting still, is his account of calling on Smith shortly after he arrived in Edinburgh, and breakfasting on strawberries:

> Fruit, he said was his favourite diet at this season. Strawberries were a northern fruit. In the Orkneys and in Sweden they were to perfection. Said that Edinburgh deserved little notice; that the old town had given Scotland a bad name; that he was anxious to move into the new town, and had set his heart on St. George's Square; that Edinburgh was entirely supported by the three Courts – the Exchequer, the Excise, and the Justiciary Courts; that Loch Lomond was the finest lake in Great Britain – the islands were very beautiful, and formed a very striking contrast to the shores; that the soil of Scotland was excellent, but that its harvests, from the severity of the climate, were too often overtaken by winter; that the Scotch on the borders were to this day in extreme poverty; and that when he first left Scotland, he was on horseback, and was struck with the transition as he approached Carlisle; that our late refusal of corn to France must excite indignation and contempt – the quantity required was so trifling that it would not support Edinburgh for a day. Said that in Paris as well as in Edinburgh, the houses were piled one upon another. Spoke contemptuously of Sir John Sinclair, but said that he never knew a man who was in earnest and who did not do something at last. Said he did not know Mrs. Piozzi, and believed her to be spoiled by keeping company with odd people.[21]

One other caller left an account of an unusual entertainment Smith provided for him. Faujas de St. Fond, who also recorded Smith's views on Voltaire, found that he 'loaded me with polite attentions, and sought to procure for me every information and amusement that could interest me . . .' One such amusement was a bagpipe competition, to which Smith conducted the visitor, probably less for his delight than because Smith wanted to observe his response to 'a kind of music of which is it impossible you can have formed any idea'. Smith asked St. Fond to give the competition his whole attention and to report his impression. The report was hardly favourable. The first piper, he wrote, 'in his costume of Roman soldier', was 'blowing the noisiest and most discordant sounds from an instrument which lacerates the ear'.

> ... the whole was so uncouth and extraordinary; the impression which this wild music made upon me contrasted so strongly with that which it made on the inhabitants of the country, that I am convinced we should look upon this strange composition not as essentially belonging to music but to history.[22]

Beyond his own immediate family circle and his entertaining at Panmure House Smith's social life in Edinburgh soon settled into a pattern which had been formed in some of his earlier days there. Hume was, of course, dead when Smith returned in 1778, but a wide circle of friends remained. The two most intimate, who became his literary executors, were Joseph Black and James Hutton. Together they founded and dominated the Oyster Club, a dining club, which met initially in a second-rate inn in the Grassmarket, but the venue was changed to maintain secrecy when it was sought out by numerous candidates for admission who 'became clamorous and troublesome'.[23] One of the recollections, taken from the obituary on Hutton, delivered to the Royal Society of Edinburgh, will suffice:

> As all the three [founders] possessed great talents, enlarged views and extensive information, without any of the stateliness and formality which men of letters think it sometimes necessary to affect, as they were all three easily amused; were equally prepared to speak and to listen; and as the sincerity of their friendship had never been darkened by the least shade of envy; it would be hard to find an example, where everything favourable to good society was more perfectly united, and every thing adverse more entirely excluded.[24]

The Royal Society of Edinburgh was formed in Smith's later years in the city, in 1782, though its roots go back through the Philosophical Society of Edinburgh to the Medical Society founded in 1731. When an independent proposal to discuss philosophical issues had appeared in 1737, Colin Maclaurin grafted it into the Medical Society and the Philosophical Society came into being, but it languished following the Jacobite Rebellion and Maclaurin's death in 1746. Revival came, possibly in 1751, more probably in 1752 with Hume actively involved in its affairs. Smith became a member in the same year. The Philosophical Society, which excluded theology, morals and politics, fell into another period of stagnation from which it was revived in the presidency of Lord Kames from 1777. In 1780 another organisation in the intellectual life of Edinburgh appeared and indirectly precipitated the transformation of the Philosophical Society into the Royal Society of Edinburgh. This was the Society of Antiquaries, the brainchild of Smith's pupil at Glasgow, the Earl of Buchan. In 1782 the Society petitioned for a Royal Charter and met with opposition from the Edinburgh literati whose relations with Buchan were not amicable. Cullen, as secretary, petitioned against the granting of the charter on behalf of the Philosophical Society but, when the opposition went on to propound its own scheme for a Royal Society of Edinburgh based on European models, the Antiquaries pointed out quite fairly in reply that this 'magnificent project of a Royal Society was never heard of till the Antiquarian Society had subsisted for near two years'.[25] In the end both bodies were chartered on the same day, 29 March 1783. All members of the Philosophical Society were admitted to the Royal Society, which followed the practice of the earlier body and maintained two sections, literary and physical. After 1798 the former faded away.

As a member of the Philosophical Society Smith immediately entered the Royal Society. He was not a member of the Society of Antiquaries and in 1786 showed his lack of interest in his response to a paper on vitrified forts sent him by A.F. Tytler, later Lord Woodhouselee: 'This is a subject of which I am totally ignorant.'[26] Even in the affairs of the Royal Society he took little part, and showed more interest, at least to the extent of obtaining the transactions of its London equivalent. He was aging; he had other preoccupations, and the Royal Society quickly became absorbed in matters which, like vitrified forts, were not his special interest. But in 1787 he was one of three judges appointed by the Society which had been asked through Smith by Count J.N. de Windeschgraetz to act with two other learned literary societies, to determine the most successful legal terminology for every type of deed, which would be so clear that it would eliminate lawsuits yet not impede natural liberty. Smith was sceptical if a solution was possible, so it is perhaps hardly surprising that in January 1788 he reported that neither he nor his two fellow judges from the Royal Society of Edinburgh thought any of the three dissertations submitted provided a solution. Perhaps Smith's links with the Royal Society are not inaccurately summed up by an account of a meeting in the following year, 1789, by Samuel Rogers. 'Only seven persons there. Dr. Anderson read an essay on Debtors and the revision of the laws that respect them, written by himself, very long and dull. Mr. Commissioner Smith fell asleep . . .'[27]

But this pleasant, clubbable life was marred first by the death of Smith's mother for whom he felt a deep and abiding affection, of which we get some inkling from a letter written to William Strahan, where he spoke of delay in correcting the proofs of the *Wealth of Nations*:

> I had just then come from performing the last duty to my poor old Mother; and tho' the death of a person in the ninetieth year of her age was no doubt an event most agreable to the course of nature; and, therefore, to be forseen and prepared for; yet I must say to you, what I have said to other people, that the final separation from a person who certainly loved me more than any other person ever did or ever will love me; and whom I certainly loved and respected more than I ever shall either love or respect any other person, I cannot help feeling, even at this hour, as a very heavy stroke upon me. Even in this state of mind, however, it gives me very great concern to hear that there is any failure in your health and spirits. The good weather, I hope, will soon reestablish both in their ordinary vigour. My friends grow very thin in the world, and I do not find that my new ones are likely to supply their place.[28]

An old servant of Smith's Robert Reid, had obviously perceived the closeness of the relationship, for he wrote the following year on Margaret Smith's death:

> It was at Breakfast with Sir Charles (Douglas) that I first heard my late worthy Mistress Smith had paid the debt of Nature. The powers of language fail to express my feelings when I heard the melancholy news. Permit me to say that I sympathise with you on the loss of so virtuous and so loving a mother.[29]

The next break in the long-standing domestic relations came a few years later with the death of Janet Douglas in 1788. A sense of melancholy hangs over a letter of 14 September:

> Poor Miss Douglas has been confined to her bed now for some time. Without any hope of recovery she preserves her usual spirit and Chearfulness, directs the affairs of the family, which she expects to leave in a few days, with as much care and distinctness as ever; and tho' sorry to part with her friends, seems to die with satisfaction

and contentment, happy in the life she has spent, and very well pleased with the lot that has fallen to her, and without the slightest fear or anxiety about the change she expects so soon to undergo.[30]

Smith's own health, always a cause of concern, was also deteriorating. There is some evidence that he could be unusually concerned with his health. When in Oxford in 1744 he commended tar water to his mother as a remedy 'for almost all diseases' and told her 'It has perfectly cured me of an inveterate scurvy in the head.'[31] Subsequent evidence indicates that Smith was subject to bouts of illness, which were apparently frequently the accompaniment of intense work. As early as 1753 Hume heard of an illness from Leechman and attributed it to the fatigues of the new classes at Glasgow and advocated 'more Leizure and Rest'.[32] Years later, in 1775, James Boswell recalled, though Smith disputed it, that he had suffered from low spirits and that at Glasgow Smith had talked of 'a day in bed — a day in bed'.[33] In 1760 Cullen ordered Smith on a jaunt to England to help him survive the next winter,[34] and in 1772 Hume, perhaps scenting hypochondria, warned him 'if you continue to hearken to Complaints of this Nature, you will cut yourself off entirely from human Society'.[35] But the old complaints are much more numerous in Smith's correspondence after his return to Edinburgh in 1778. In 1781 he complained, 'I had all yesterday a very disagreeable pain in my stomach, and in addition I have got this day a pain in my side'.[36] In 1782 he told Sir John Sinclair that 'Sore eyes have made me delay writing to you so long.'[37] In 1784 he was 'much indisposed'.[38] In 1787:

I am in my grand Climateric; and the state of my health has been a good deal worse than usual. I am getting better and better, however, every day; and I begin to flatter myself that, with good pilotage, I shall be able to weather this dangerous promontory of Human life; after which, I hope to sail in smooth water for the remainder of my days.[39]

But within three years, Smith was again unwell. Probably with approaching death in mind, Smith instructed his literary executors, Black and Hutton, to fulfil their promise to burn sixteen folio volumes of manuscripts; we may surmise that the pieces which survived the conflagration, and which duly appeared in the *Essays on Philosophical Subjects*, were all specified by Smith. It is to Samuel Rogers, that we owe an account of his last evening's entertainment, derived in turn from

from Henry Mackenzie. 'He was very cheerful, but we persuaded him not to sup with us, and he said, about half-past nine, as he left the room: "I love your company, gentlemen, but I believe I must leave you – to go to another world".'[40] He died on 17 July 1790.

At his death, Smith's library was transmitted to David Douglas (Lord Reston) who left it in turn to his two daughters, the Mrs Cunningham and Bannerman – with the latter receiving the bulk of the books on economics. Mrs Bannerman retained the collection until her death in 1884. Ten years later her son gave it to New College Edinburgh – the largest single concentration of Smith's volumes. In 1878 Mrs Cunningham sold part of her collection, but passed the major portion to her son, Professor R.O. Cunningham, who in turn left some of the books to Queen's University, Belfast. In 1918 the remainder were sold in London to a Japanese Professor, Inazo Nitobe, who donated the books to the Faculty of Economics in the University of Tokyo.[41] There they still remain, having successfully survived the great earthquake of 1923 and the Second World War.

Notes

1. *The Letters of David Hume*, ed. J.Y.T. Greig (Oxford, 1932), i, 329.
2. S. Johnson, *Journey to the Western Islands of Scotland*, ed. R.W. Chapman, 1930), 108.
3. *Corr.*, letter 208, Adam Smith to Andreas Holt, 26 October 1780.
4. Ibid.
5. *Corr.*, letter 222, Adam Smith to Thomas Cadell, 7 December 1782.
6. *Corr.*, letter 227, Adam Smith to William Strahan, 22 May 1783.
7. *Corr.*, letter 231, Adam Smith to William Strahan, 6 October 1783.
8. *Corr.*, letter 232, Adam Smith to William Strahan, 20 November 1783.
9. *Corr.*, letter 227, Adam Smith to William Strahan, 22 May 1783.
10. *Corr.*, letter 222, Adam Smith to Thomas Cadell, 7 December 1782.
11. *Corr.*, letter 227, Adam Smith to William Strahan, 22 May 1783.
12. *WN*, IV. viii. 47.
13. *Corr.*, letter 227, Adam Smith to William Strahan, 22 May 1783.
14. *Corr.*, letter 244, Adam Smith to Thomas Cadell, 21 April 1785.
15. *Corr.*, letter 276, Adam Smith to Thomas Cadell, 15 March 1788.
16. *Corr.*, letter 287, Adam Smith to Thomas Cadell, 31 March 1789,
17. *Corr.*, letter 207, Adam Smith to William Strahan, 26 October 1780.
18. *Corr.*, letter 208, Adam Smith to Andreas Holt, 26 October 1780.
19. *Corr.*, letter 248, Adam Smith to le Duc de la Rochefoucauld, 1 November 1785.
20. P.W. Clayden, *Early Life of Samuel Rogers* (London, 1887), 90.
21. Ibid. 92-3.
22. B. Faujas de St. Fond, *A Journey through England and Scotland to the Hebrides in 1784*, ii, 245, 248, 250.
23. John Sinclair, *Memoirs of the life and works of the late Rt. Hon. Sir John Sinclair, Bt* (Edinburgh, 1837), i, 41-2.

24. Obituary of Hutton.

25. Quoted in D.D. McElroy, *Scotland's Age of Improvement* (Washington State University, 1969), 78.

26. *Corr.*, letter 254, Adam Smith to A.F. Tytler, 4 February 1786.

27. Clayden, *Early Life of Samuel Rogers*, 96.

28. *Corr.*, letter 237, Adam Smith to William Strahan, 10 June 1784.

29. *Corr.*, letter 246, Robert Reid to Adam Smith, 11 September 1785.

30. *Corr.*, letter 281, Adam Smith to Dr. James Monteath, 16 September 1788.

31. *Corr.*, letter 6, Adam Smith to his mother, 2 July 1744.

32. *Corr.*, letter 13, David Hume to Adam Smith, 26 May 1753.

33. *Boswell: the Ominous Years*, 115.

34. *Corr.*, letter 51, Adam Smith to Lord Shelburne, 15 July 1760.

35. *Corr.*, letter 129, David Hume to Adam Smith, 28 January 1772.

36. *Corr.*, letter 214, Adam Smith to James Hunter Blair, 29 October 1781.

37. *Corr.*, letter 221, Adam Smith to Sir John Sinclair, 14 October 1782.

38. *Corr.*, letter 238, Adam Smith to Maxwell Garthshore, 18 June 1784.

39. *Corr.*, letter 266, Adam Smith to Bishop John Douglas, 6 March 1787.

40. Clayden, *Early Life of Samuel Rogers*, 167.

41. The details are given in Bonar's Catalogue, but see also H. Mizuta's account (Cambridge, 1967) and the introduction to T. Yanaihara *Catalogue of Adam Smith's Library* (Tokyo, 1940).

INDEX

226